Television and Politics in Evolving European Democracies

Lynda Lee Kaid
Editor

Nova Science Publishers, Inc.
Commack, New York

9/00

TELEVISION AND POLITICS IN EVOLVING EUROPEAN DEMOCRACIES

Editorial Production:	Susan Boriotti
Office Manager:	Annette Hellinger
Graphics:	Frank Grucci and Jennifer Lucas
Information Editor:	Tatiana Shohov
Book Production:	Donna Dennis, Patrick Davin, Christine Mathosian, Tammy Sauter and Lynette Van Helden
Circulation:	Maryanne Schmidt
Marketing/Sales:	Cathy DeGregory

Library of Congress Cataloging-in-Publication Data

Television and politics in evolving European democracies / Lynda Lee Kaid, editor.
                  p.   cm.
    Includes bibliographical references and index.
    ISBN 1-56072-753-5
    1. Television in politics--Europe, Eastern. 2. Television in politics--Europe, Central. I. Kaid, Lynda Lee.
HE8700.76.E852 T44   1999
324.7'3'0947--dc21   99-054103

Copyright © 1999 by Nova Science Publishers, Inc.
    6080 Jericho Turnpike, Suite 207
    Commack, New York 11725
    Tele. 516-499-3103   Fax 516-499-3146
    e-mail: Novascience@earthlink.net
    e-mail: Novascil@aol.com
    Web Site: http://www.nexusworld.com/nova

Printed in the United States of America

CONTENTS

ACKNOWLEDGEMENTS

This project owes debts to many people and organizations without whose support it would not have been possible. The project is particularly grateful to the Council for European Studies (CES) at Columbia University. As a European Research Planning Group for CES, the project received both financial support and the continued assistance of Executive Director, Ioannis Sinanoglou.

The project also received financial support from the Political Communication Center at the University of Oklahoma. In addition, the project benefitted greatly from the coordination, planning, and organizational expertise of the Center's Administrative Coordinator, Marie Mathos.

In addition, many individual contributors received financial assistance for travel and research assistance from others at their individual institutions which are mentioned in each chapter. The editor also wishes to thank the Council for International Exchange of Scholars (CIES) and the Fulbright Commission for support of her own efforts related to the project.

Chapter 1

OVERVIEW OF TELEVISION AND POLITICS IN ESTABLISHED AND EVOLVING DEMOCRACIES

Lynda Lee Kaid

Throughout the world, television has become an important part of the way in which political candidates and parties present their messages to voters during election campaigns. This is particularly true in campaigns at the national level where voters have little personal contact with candidates and must rely on experiencing candidates through the media. As a result of this emphasis on television, Gurevitch and Blumler (1990) have argued that American style politics has become the model for other democracies. Because of the need to have more direct control over the style and image that are conveyed to voters, political advertising provides a unique opportunity for the candidate to control this interaction with the voter and to control the way he/she is presented through television (Kaid, 1981). In a recent book on political advertising in Western democracies, Kaid and Holtz-Bacha (1995) argued that this message-control aspect has made televised political advertising and its European counterpart, party-controlled broadcasts, an increasingly important element of candidate-voter communication in democratic systems.

In the United States it is well-established that television spots often dominate presidential campaign communication (Diamond & Bates, 1984; Jamieson, 1992; Kaid, 1981). Recent works on France (Charlot, 1975; Grosser, 1975; Kaid, Gerstlé, & Sanders, 1991), on Britain (Blumler & McQuail, 1969; Kaid & Tedesco, 1993; Semetko, Blumler, Gurevitch & Weaver, 1991), in Germany (Holtz-Bacha, 1990; Holtz-Bacha & Kaid, 1993; Wachtel, 1988), and in Italy (Mazzoleni & Roper, 1993) have suggested that television also plays a major role in campaigns in these countries. Research has also documented that television spots in several European countries are responsible for alterations in voter perceptions of candidate images and in voter recollections about issues and candidate characteristics (Kaid, Gerstlé, & Sanders, 1991; Kaid & Holtz-Bacha, 1993; Kaid & Holtz-Bacha, 1995; Mazzoleni & Roper, 1993).

New and developing democracies in Eastern and Central Europe have been quick to see the significance of televised political programming for the building of coalitions and party strength. In the 1993 Yugoslavian elections, a multitude of large and small parties produced and aired television ads in an attempt to influence the electorate (Nedeljkovich, 1994). In Bulgaria studies of the elections in the early 1990s indicated that a majority of the electorate believe party election programs are influential (Raycheva, 1994).

Since 1989 when many countries in Eastern and Central Europe cast off communist dominance in their political systems, the struggle to introduce democratic governmental principles has met with varying degrees of success. As individuals and political parties have sought to establish themselves and to solidify their power, they have been confronted with the need to find ways of communicating their political philosophies and issue agendas to an increasingly skeptical public. The media have played an important role in this process, providing the most direct way for parties and candidates to communicate with potential voters. As Sayre (1994) suggests, "Since 1989, countries emerging from communism and plagued with a citizenry skeptical of the written word...have turned to broadcast media for election communications" (p. 108). Sayre used Rokeach's value categories to analyze Hungarian political spots and found that "political commercials are useful for identifying prevailing values and can contribute to an understanding of a nation's culture" (p. 97) which further substantiated that: "Campaign communications can be an active agent in a country emerging from communism because...it is at the level of political advertising that democracy is spread" (p. 97).

BACKGROUND AND DEVELOPMENT OF GOVERNMENT AND MEDIA INTERACTIONS

The years since 1989/90 have not been easy ones for most of the Eastern and Central European countries. Throwing off the communist yoke, a task that seemed almost impossible to observers a decade ago, now seems like a simple task compared to the political and economic reform challenges faced in the aftermath. Forming new, and multiple, political parties was an early outgrowth of the new freedom, and a proliferation of new media outlets also followed (Jakubowicz, 1995a). However, most of the new political parties found it very difficult to form stable governments and to initiate viable market economies. The changes in the media systems and the uncertainties of government-media interaction raised even more questions for these new governments.

One of the most important current concerns has been the growing level of cynicism, hostility to democracy, and alienation expressed by citizens in these new democracies. As Szabó (1992) indicates about Hungary, "The political consequence of economic and social crises is a low level of political participation, especially in elections" (p. 43). Indeed, he suggests, "Low participation within the sphere of institutionalized politics on the one hand and nonconventional or even illegal and violent political protests on the other could endanger or at least destabilize the new democracies of Eastern Europe" (p. 44).

A January, 1991, survey in three countries documented the low level of political trust among the electorate. Miguel and Berland (1992) found that citizens in Hungary, Poland,

and Czechoslovakia expressed a great deal of frustration with government, largely due to economic uncertainties, and in none of the three countries did a majority feel that the government was "performing well." McIntosh and MacIver (1992) have pointed out that this cynicism was a result of disappointment with the slow pace of reform: "Instead of full-fledged democracy and economic prosperity, Central and East Europeans confronted political turmoil and economic uncertainty" (p. 376).

However, the increasing cynicism and frustration with political reform has made the role of the media even more important. Most scholars and political observers acknowledge that one of the underlying principles of democratic systems is that the media must "serve the public's 'right to know' and offer options for meaningful political choices and nourishment for effective participation in civic affairs" (Gurevitch & Blumler, 1991, p. 269). Thus, finding a way both to organize media for the benefit of the public's right to information flow and to use the media for the cementing of their own power and right to govern has represented an important goal for new democratic systems. Blumler (1987) makes this point even more clear by suggesting that "...at a time when the public's confidence in many social and political institutions has steeply declined, both parties and voters have become more dependent on media resources, the former for means of access to the electoral audience, ...the latter for impressions of what is at stake..." (p. 170).

Despite the importance of the media for voter-government interaction, however, many new reform governments in the post-communist era in Eastern European countries failed to appreciate the demands of creating workable new media systems. Simultaneously, the new political party structures realized immediately the importance of media access in creating party support and electoral success (Jakubowicz, 1995a). Even more importantly, these demands on the evolving government-media relationships have come at a time when there are massive changes in the development of media technology and information flow throughout all of Europe (Corcoran & Preston, 1995; Swanson & Mancini, 1996).

Despite the significance of the media, particularly television, in the struggle for power in newly evolving democracies of Eastern and Central Europe, very little research has been devoted to this aspect of European politics. The research and analyses in this volume address many questions related to the growing role of television in these democratic systems. Included are discussions of (1) how the media systems of Eastern and Central European countries have been reorganized or reconfigured as a result of government reforms, (2) how new political parties used television in elections since 1989/90, (3) what types of electoral communications have been carried on television during these elections, and (4) to what extent such electoral communications have been influenced by the media systems and formats of political communications from established Western democracies. Various chapters also consider what cultural and political system values have affected the impact of party uses of election media among the Eastern and Central European countries and how these new systems of political communication effected voters in the various countries discussed.

ISSUES RELATED TO TELEVISED ELECTORAL MESSAGES

As mentioned earlier, while the use of party and candidate-sponsored television messages has a long history in the United States and is now relatively common in most Western democracies (Kaid & Holtz-Bacha, 1995), evolving Eastern and Central European states have only recently confronted the issues inherent in such political media use. In the United States, for instance, candidates and parties have relatively unlimited access to paid commercial television time during electoral periods, and most Western European countries either provide free time for televised party messages during elections or allow a system that combines the allocation of free time and the right to buy additional time on private, commercial media outlets. However, as they were catapulted into quick elections in the early 1990s, Poland, Hungary, Bulgaria, Romania, and others had no experience with such systems and found themselves developing rules and producing television programs for voters with little prior knowledge of how such programs might affect voters or how they might make maximum use of the television medium for communicating their political agendas.

A few examples of how the use of party programs on television have developed and the challenges faced in these countries help to set the stage for the issues considered in this volume. For instance, Poland's early success in gaining recognition for its Solidarity movement led to opportunities for the party to use television for communicating its messages. From 1981 on the Solidarity movement "perceived democratic communication as an integral element of political democracy and an essential part of the process of democratic governance" (Jakubowicz, 1995b, p. 131). This position implied an affirmative obligation for the government to create ways for the various political points of view to have outlets for communicating their ideas to the electorate. It was agreed prior to the 1989 election that all parties and movements would be given time slots for broadcast during the election, with Solidarity getting 23% of these slots. A content analysis of these party programs between May 10 and June 18th for the 1989 elections revealed that many of the television presentations did not give the political affiliation/party of the candidates and that the personality of the candidate was the most important thing presented in the programs, although Solidarity candidates stressed personalities a bit less than others (Kedrzejewski, 1992). This trend suggests a similarity to findings in recent Western democracies that increasing use of television in elections has tended to diminish the emphasis on parties and enhance the emphasis on candidate personalities and images (Kaid & Holtz-Bacha, 1995; Semetko & Schoenbach, 1994).

Journalists have observed similar trends in the recent Russian parliamentary elections where voters were "deluged by 60-second, 30-second, and 10-second political television commercials" (Stanley, 1995b, p. 5) in which Zhirinovsky's ads stressed his sex appeal and Rubkin's left of center group used talking cows. A heavy influence of "American style" advertising was in the forefront, with one politician hiring rock star Hammer to do campaign spot music. The conclusion has been that "...all the major parties are producing slick television advertisements that concentrate on image more than substance" (Stanley, 1995a, p. A-8).

The above discussion also suggests a need to understand the different media system structures and the allocation of time for political advertising on television in the different countries involved. Jakubowicz (1992) has outlined some of these rules and regulations, although the exact rules change frequently from election to election as the countries stabilize their systems and enact new broadcasting regulations. Many countries now use the "equal time" system for allocating television time during elections, rather than a proportionate allocation system, and some do allow parties to purchase additional time on private or commercial stations. In Chapter 2, Tedesco, Chanslor, and Jones centralize data on these questions in order to provide listings of current regulations and television allocations for the countries discussed in this volume.

The following countries are covered in this volume: Bulgaria, Romania, Poland, Hungary, Turkey, Yugoslavia, Russia, the Czech Republic, Greece, and Eastern Germany. These countries were chosen because they have all undergone substantial changes in their media and electoral systems in the past decade, and each represented an opportunity to gather appropriate materials for study. Most are countries that have been facing the difficult transition from Communist domination to democracy. Others, such as Greece and Turkey, represent evolving democracies that have struggled with military coups and other threats to the maintenance of a stable political system.

THEORETICAL AND METHODOLOGICAL APPROACH

This volume approaches the research on political television in evolving democracies from a meta-theoretical perspective that embraces the notion that the interaction of media messages and audience message processing results in the formation of political reality. In other words, the content, style, and processes of media transmission of political messages (in this case, party election programming) intersects with voter attitudes, culture, and values to determine how voters perceive parties, their leaders, and their policy programs. This approach, also similar to that described by Nimmo and Combs (1990), was used by a cross-national study of the 1988 French and U.S. presidential election (Kaid, Gerstlé, & Sanders, 1991) and described as one of the fundamental ways of approaching cross-national research theory development by Swanson (1992).

The various chapters in the volume embrace a combination of historical and legal analysis, content analysis, experimental studies, and survey research. Historical and legal analysis were utilized to answer questions about reorganization and characteristics of the media and political system reforms affecting party broadcasts. This is the approach used by John Tedesco, Mike Chanslor, and Clifford Jones in their overview of various legal and political system characteristics in Chapter 2 and also by Elizabeth Hughes in her analysis of political television in the Czech Republic (Chapter 12) and Misha Nedeljkovich in his overview of Yugoslavia (Chapter 8).

Content analysis was used to analyze sets of political party programs from many of the countries involved. A systematic coding process was developed, adapting from those utilized by Kaid and Holtz-Bacha and described in their work on political advertising in

Western democracies (Kaid & Holtz-Bacha, 1995). This research approach used categories that analyze the "videostyle" (Kaid & Davidson, 1986) of the television programs, incorporating an analysis of the verbal, nonverbal, and television production techniques. Wojciech Cwalina, Andrzej Falkowski, and Bohdan Roznowski used this approach to analyze Polish campaign messages (Chapter 4), Baki Can used similar methods in Turkey (Chapter 10), as did Athanasion Samaras in Greece (Chapter 11). Jolán Róka applied another categorization system to assess Hungarian political techniques.

Experimental methods were used in a few countries to determine effects of the television programming directly on voters. This involved using groups of voters as subjects and incorporating a before-after design to measure the effects of exposure to political programs. These studies took place during election campaigns and followed procedures already applied successfully in the U.S. and in Western European democracies (Kaid, Gerstlé, & Sanders, 1981; Kaid & Holtz-Bacha, 1993; 1995). Cwalina, Falkowski, and Roznowski used this approach in Poland (Chapter 4), Holtz-Bacha reports such results for Eastern Germany (Chapter 3), and Miron, Marinesçu, and McKinnon analyze experimental and focus group results for Romania (Chapter 6).

Survey research methods are costly and not always reliable in many evolving democracies, but where they were possible, they yielded additional insight for some of the countries reported here. Miron, Marinesçu, and McKinnon (Romania, Chapter 6) and Lilia Raycheva (Bulgaria, Chapter 5) were able to provide survey research to supplement their analyses, and Sarah Oates had access to some survey data for Russia (Chapter 9).

The final chapter in the volume attempts to bring together and summarize the findings of the various chapters (Kaid, Chapter 13). This concluding chapter also compares the findings of some of the empirical work (experimental and content analyses) on several evolving democracies reported here with previous work on the United States and other Western democracies.

CONCLUSION

The various scholars who participated in this project and who worked on the various projects were members of a Research Planning Group, sponsored by the Council for European Studies at Columbia University and the Political Communication Center at the University of Oklahoma. The group met on several occasions to discuss the procedures and processes for the research involved. In addition to the individual chapters reported here, many participants continue their work in this area.

REFERENCES

Blumler, J. G. (1987). Election communication and the democratic political system. In D. L. Paletz (Ed.), *Political communication research* (pp. 167-175). Norwood, NJ: Ablex Publishing Co..

Blumler, J. G., & McQuail, D. (1969). *Television in politics*. London: Faber and Faber.

Charlot, M. (1975). The language of television campaigning. In H. R. Penniman (Ed.), *France at the polls: The presidential election of 1974* (pp. 227-253). Washington, D.C.: American Enterprise Institute.

Corcoran, F., & Preston, P., Eds. (1995). *Democracy and communication in the new Europe: Change and continuity in East and West*. Cresskill, NJ: Hampton Press.

Diamond, E., & Bates, S. (1984). *The spot*. Cambridge, MA: MIT Press.

Grosser, A. (1975). The role of the press, radio, and television in French political life. In H. R. Penniman (Ed.), *France at the polls: The presidential election of 1974* (pp. 207-226). Washington, D.C.: American Enterprise Institute.

Gurevitch, M., & Blumler, J. G. (1990). Comparative research: The extending frontier. In D. Swanson & D. Nimmo (Eds.). *New directions in political communication: A sourcebook*. Newbury Park, CA: Sage.

Gurevitch, M., & Blumler, J. G. (1991). Political communication systems and democratic values . In J. Lichtenberg (Ed.), *Democracy and the mass media* (pp. 269-89). Cambridge: Cambridge University Press.

Holtz-Bacha, C. (1990). Nur bei den Wasserwerken Effekte? Eine Studie zur parteipolitischen Spot-Werbung vor Europawahlen. *Medium, 20 (3)*, 50-53

Holtz-Bacha, C., & Kaid, L. L. (Eds.). (1993). *Die Massenmedien im Wahlkampf.* Opladen: Westdeutscher Verlag.

Jakubowicz, K. (1992). Electoral campaigns on radio and television: General principles. In A. Pragnell, & I. Gergely (Eds.), *The political content of broadcasting* (pp. 48-55). London: John Libbey & Co.

Jakubowicz, K. (1995a). Media as agents of change. In D. L. Paletz, K. Jakubowicz, & P. Novosel (Eds.), *Glasnost and after: Media and change in Central and Eastern Europe* (pp. 19-47). Cresskill, NJ: Hampton Press.

Jakubowicz, K. (1995b). Poland. In D. L. Paletz, K. Jakubowicz, & P. Novosel (Eds.), *Glasnost and after: Media and change in Central and Eastern Europe* (pp. 129-148). Cresskill, NJ: Hampton Press.

Jamieson, K. H. (1992). *The packaging of the presidency*, 2nd. ed. New York: Oxford University Press.

Kaid, L. L. (1981). Political advertising. In D. Nimmo & K. Sanders (Eds.), *Handbook of political communication* (pp. 249-271). Beverly Hills, CA: Sage Publications.

Kaid, L. L., & Davidson, D. (1986). Elements of videostyle: A preliminary examination of candidate presentation through televised advertising. In L. L. Kaid, D. Nimmo, & K. R. Sanders (Eds.), *New perspectives on political advertising* (pp. 184-209). Carbondale, IL: Southern Illinois University Press.

Kaid, L. L., Gerstlé, J., & Sanders, K. (Eds.). (1991). *Mediated politics in two cultures: Presidential campaigning in the United States and France.* New York: Praeger.

Kaid, L. L., & Holtz-Bacha, C. (1993). Audience reactions to televised political programs: An experimental study of the 1990 German national election. *European Journal of Communication, 8,* 77-99.

Kaid, L. L., & Holtz-Bacha, C.(Eds.). (1995). *Political advertising in Western democracies.* Thousand Oaks, CA: Sage Publications.

Kaid, L. L., & Tedesco, J. (1993, May). *A comparison of political television advertising in the 1992 British and American elections.* Paper presented at the International Communication Association Convention, Washington, D.C.

Kedrzejewski, S. (1992). [Political advertising in Poland]. In A. Pragnell, & I. Gergely (Eds.), *The political content of broadcasting* (pp. 74-91). London: John Libbey & Co.

McIntosh, M. E., & Mac Iver, M. A. (1992). Coping with freedom and uncertainty: Public opinion in Hungary, Poland, and Czechoslovakia 1989-1992. *International Journal of Public Opinion Research, 4(4),* 375-391.

Mazzoleni, G., & Roper, C. (1993). *The presentation of Italian parties and candidates through television advertising.* Paper presented at the International Communication Association Convention, Washington, D. C.

Miguel, M. M., & Berland, M. J. (1992). The future of democracy in Eastern Europe. In T. Vanhanen (Ed.), *Strategies of democratization* (pp. 77-87). Washington, D.C.: Crane Russak/Taylor & Francis.

Nedeljkovich, M. (1994). *New television in the third Yugoslavia: Coverage and equal access.* Paper presented at the Turbulent Europe: Conflict, Identity and Culture Conference of the British Film Institute, London.

Nimmo, D., & Combs, J. (1990). *Mediated political realities,* 2nd ed. New York: Longman.

Raycheva, L. (1994, March). *Mass media and Bulgaria.* Paper presented at the Sooner Communication Conference, University of Oklahoma, Norman, Oklahoma.

Sayre, S. (1994, March). Images of freedom and equality: A values analysis of Hungarian political commercials. *Journal of Advertising, 23(1),* 97-109.

Semetko, H. A., Blumler, J.G., Gurevitch, M., & Weaver, D.H. (1991). *The formation of campaign agendas: A comparative analysis of party and media roles in recent American and British elections.* Hillsdale, NJ: Lawrence Erlbaum.

Semetko, H.A., & Schoenbach, K. (1994, Fall). Red socks, hotheads, and Helmut vs. the "Troika": Party advertising in the German 1994 Bundestag election campaign. *Political Communication Report, 5(3),* 4,7.

Stanley, A. (1995a, November 16). Russians vie for votes, and anything goes. *New York Times,* A-1, A-8.

Stanley, A. (1995b, December 17). Russian democracy: A voter's-eye view. *New York Times,* sec. 4, p. 5.

Swanson, D. L. (1992). Managing theoretical diversity in cross-national studies of political communication. In J. G. Blumler, J. M. McLeod, & K. E. Rosengren (Eds.), *Comparatively speaking: Communicating culture across space and time* (pp. 19-34). Newbury Park, CA: Sage Publications.

Swanson, D. L., & Mancini, P. (Eds.). (1996). *Politics, media and modern democracy.* Westport, CT: Praeger.

Szabó, M. (1992). Was there a strategy? Hungary's path to democracy. In T. Vanhanen (Ed.), *Strategies of democratization* (pp. 37-54). Washington, D.C.: Crane Russak/Taylor & Francis.

Wachtel, M. (1988). *Die Darstellung von Vertrauenswürdigkeit in Wahlwerbespots: Eine argumentationsanalytische und semiotische Untersuchung zum Bundestagswahlkampf 1987.* Tübingen: Max Niemeyer.

Chapter 2

POLITICAL TELEVISION IN EVOLVING EUROPEAN DEMOCRACIES: POLITICAL, MEDIA, AND LEGAL SYSTEM ISSUES

John Tedesco, Clifford A. Jones, and Mike Chanslor

In *Political Advertising in Western Democracies*, Kaid and Holtz-Bacha (1995) present findings from a broad investigation of the content and effects of political advertising in established democratic countries. Their cross-national investigation of media and political structure in nine established democracies (United States, Israel, Denmark, Finland, France, Germany, Italy, the Netherlands, and United Kingdom) provides a solid framework for the comparison presented here (Holtz-Bacha & Kaid, 1995). In *Western Democracies*, identification of sponsorship, electoral systems, access, allocation, number and length, and restrictions on broadcast content for political advertising revealed some interesting similarities and differences between the stable governments analyzed. The evolving democracies examined in this volume are in many ways less stable, and they provide an opportunity to examine both progressive and hesitant attempts to embrace democracy. The campaign laws found in these countries appear to restrain these developing democracies from embracing in full what Gurevitch and Blumler (1990, p. 311) have termed "American-style 'video-politics.'"

As democratic political and media system characteristics emerge in countries like the Czech Republic and Bulgaria, and transform in lands like Greece and Germany, it is interesting to see what features of American-style video politics they adopt and which they reject or reconstruct. The gradual adaptation of the American model for electoral campaigns has been referred to and documented by several scholars as "Americanization" (Gurevitch & Blumler, 1990; Holtz-Bacha & Kaid, 1995; Johnson & Elebash, 1986; Kaid & Tedesco, 1993). The key features of the American model identified by Gurevitch and Blumler (1990) include (1) dominance of television as the primary form of campaign communication, (2) prevalence of image and character qualities, and (3) professional political public relations and consultant-dominated candidate actors. These three factors point to the manifest decline in the role of political party institutions in the candidate selection process in the U.S. Holtz-Bacha and Kaid agree with Blumler (1990) that it is important to question whether presence of the key criteria in the American model signifies "Americanization" or a "more general trend of political systems in the Western world" (1995, p. 9). Blumler (1990) termed this the "modern publicity process," and suggests that "Americanization" may result more from a widespread circumstance of mass mediated political communication than an American-centered trend. However, it does appear that American media characteristics are the most favorable for development of Blumler's publicity process. In either case, the American political system appears to be the pacesetter for modern political campaigning.

The "modern publicity process" has demonstrated that political parties are being replaced by political campaigns that employ "active media management" (Holtz-Bacha & Kaid, 1995, p. 9). Aggressive advertising and public relations campaigns with specialized marketing tools are using sophisticated audience segmentation techniques to target highly specialized pockets of an erratic voting population. However, as *Western Democracies* revealed, not all stable and reasonably evolved democracies exhibit the same candidate image-centered characteristics symbolic of the "modern publicity process." Factors such as public versus private broadcast regulations, restrictions on the number and length of candidate spots, allocation of broadcast time, and sponsorship of spots contribute greatly to our understanding about media and political system restraints on political advertising, which is at the center of the modern publicity process.

Underlying the American model of political campaign communication are the U.S. Constitutional guarantees of free speech and freedom of association which secure the rights of citizens to band together to support political candidates of their choosing and express that support in various forms from bumper stickers to electronic advertising (*Buckley*, 1976). As the evolving democracies examined here move from regimes of political repression toward political systems capable of and willing to tolerate genuine political pluralism, it is useful to keep in mind the extent to which their election laws and regulation of political broadcasting incorporate "or not" international norms of free expression and fair elections.

Although each of the chapters that follows provides a detailed historical context of the media and political system characteristics for the individual countries presented in this book, there are several important distinctions that are presented here for the reader to bear in mind as each chapter unfolds. As Johnston and Gerstlé (1993) note, in order "to understand the role of broadcasting to promote presidential candidates, it is also important to understand the diversity of factors and history that influence the state of affairs" (p. 13). Thus, a brief synopsis will be presented in this chapter with some tables designed to illustrate key media and political structural differences.

The objectives of this chapter are to describe first the general principles of international law and treaties to which the countries in this study are obligated to adhere and which pertain to protection of political speech, political advertising, and free and fair elections. Second, this chapter presents an overview of the new post-Communist political and media systems of the evolving democracies included in this study. Third, this chapter summarizes and reports on the precise restrictions which each country concerned imposes on the place, manner, length, and content of political broadcasts.

THE INTERNATIONAL LAW CONTEXT: POLITICAL TELEVISION REGULATION, DEMOCRACY, AND HUMAN RIGHTS

The mention of international human rights law in the context of Central and Eastern Europe typically evokes images of genocide, mass graves, torture, rape, and refugees such as those most recently observed in the conflicts in the Yugoslavian province of Kosovo and in Bosnia-Herzogovina. The reach of international human rights law is not restricted to the more extreme forms of physical violence, but it also encompasses civil and political rights relating to freedom of political expression and rights to free and fair elections. Each country included in this study is to a greater or lesser degree a political system in transition from some form of totalitarian government to a genuinely functioning democratic state. One of the many marked changes in post-Communist Europe is the degree to which international legal structures now seek to ensure pluralistic political systems, free political expression, and access to the broadcast media by political opponents. Indeed, a study of political advertising in elections carried out in the subject countries is only possible or relevant because of these changes.

International norms concerning free expression and fair elections appear in a number of legal instruments, the most important of which for present purposes are the Council of Europe's 1950 "Convention for the Protection of Human Rights and Fundamental Freedoms," better known as the European Convention on Human Rights (ECHR), and certain constitutive treaties and case law of the European Community (EC), now also generally referred to as the European Union (EU).[1] In addition, the United Nations International Covenant on Civil and Political Rights (19 December 1966) is a binding declaration of international law which has many similarities to the ECHR (Voorhoof, 1995, p. 28). Accordingly, no separate discussion of the UN Covenant will be offered here. The Council of Europe, distinct from the EU, also has a recently amended (1989 and 1998) European Convention on Transfrontier Television (ECTT), that contains provisions protecting trans-frontier broadcasting and advertising.

The pertinent treaties relating to the EC or EU are the Treaty of Rome (1957), as amended, the Treaty on European Union ("Maastricht Treaty") (1991), and the Treaty of Amsterdam (1997), which came into force in 1999. The countries included in this study (except Russia) are all either current or hopeful members of the EU who are or likely will be bound by EU law concerning human rights and television broadcasting. Secondary EU legislation which governs certain aspects of television broadcasting and advertising includes the recently amended "Television Without Frontiers" (TWF) Directive (1989 and 1997), which is quite similar to the ECTT of the Council of Europe.

The European Union Treaties

The various EC treaties are of great importance to the legal framework of political advertising because they give the evolving democracies of central and eastern Europe powerful economic and political incentives to implement and enforce the principles of free expression and fair elections. These countries covet membership in the EC in part because they wish to replicate the economic, social, and political successes of the democracies of Western Europe. The West European democracies, in turn, condition participation of the evolving democracies in the EC on adherence to political freedom as well as creation of market-based economic systems.

While the EC Treaty of Rome (1957) itself did not expressly incorporate human rights principles, the European Court of Justice (ECJ), the judicial organ of the EC, has long considered the ECHR as stating human rights principles common to the legal systems of the Member States (*Nold*, 1974). In *E.R.T.* (1991), a case dealing with whether the Greek public monopoly on television broadcasting was consistent with certain provisions of EC law, the ECJ explained the relevance of the ECHR to Community law and the ECJ's activities:

> Fundamental rights form an integral part of the general principles of law, the observance of which it [the ECJ] ensures. For that purpose the Court draws inspiration from the constitutional traditions common to the member states and from the guidelines supplied by international treaties for the protection of human rights on which the member states have collaborated or of which they are signatories (see, in particular, the judgment in case c-4/73 *Nold v Commission* [1974] ECR 491, paragraph 13). The European Convention on Human Rights has special significance in that respect . . . the Community cannot accept measures which are incompatible with observance of the human rights thus recognized and guaranteed. . . .[Greece's justifications for the television monopoly] must be appraised in the light of the general principle of freedom of expression embodied in Article 10 of the European Convention on Human Rights.

While the incorporation of human rights principles into EC law may have begun with the ECJ, subsequent Treaty amendments have adopted and strengthened this approach. The Maastricht Treaty (1991), as amended by the Treaty of Amsterdam (1997), provides in Article 6 that:

> 1. The Union is founded on the principles of liberty, democracy, respect for human rights and fundamental freedoms, and the rule of law, principles which are common to the Member States.

> 2. The Union shall respect fundamental rights, as guaranteed by the European Convention for the Protection of Human Rights and Fundamental Freedoms signed in Rome on 4 November 1950 and as they result from the constitutional traditions common to the Member States, as general principles of Community law.

Article 7 of the Maastricht Treaty, as amended, further provides for penalties including suspension to be imposed on Member States who allow a "persistent and serious breach" of these principles to occur. Article 49 of the Maastricht Treaty, as amended at Amsterdam, explicitly limits membership to a state which "respects the principles set out in Article 6(1)." Hence, evolving democracies which do not secure freedom of expression and fair elections to their citizens may not enjoy the benefits of joining the EU.

Greece (since 1981) and the former "East" German Democratic Republic (now reunited with the "West" Federal Republic of Germany since 1990) as Member States are already fully bound by all EU treaties and directives. Negotiations for the accession of Hungary, Poland, and the Czech Republic, among others, to the EC Treaty (Rome) are now underway. It is expected that accession negotiations for Romania, Bulgaria, and hopefully ultimately Yugoslavia[2] will begin after the current negotiations have concluded, provided these candidates satisfy the conditions for membership. Even those prospective EU members who are not yet ready to commence accession negotiations for the most part have entered into "Association agreements" or "Accession Partnerships" with the EU to begin to conform their laws and practices to EU standards. Table 2.1 summarizes the status of the subject countries with regard to these legal and contractual instruments.

Table 2.1 - Adherence to Treaties and Conventions

Country	EU[a]	Assoc./Candidate[b]	ECHR[c]	ECTT[c]
Bulgaria	N	Y	Y (1992)	Y (1999)
Czech Republic	N	Y	Y (1992)	S[d]
Germany (ex E.)	Y	n/a	Y (1990)	Y (1994)
Greece	Y	n/a	Y (1974)	S[d]
Hungary	N	Y	Y (1992)	Y (1997)
Poland	N	Y	Y (1993)	Y (1993)
Romania	N	Y	Y (1994)	S[d]
Russia	N	N	Y (1998)	N
Turkey	N	Y	Y (1954)	Y (1994)
Yugoslavia	N	N	N	N

[a] Includes all treaties and secondary legislation.
[b] Has signed an association agreement or applied for membership in EU.
[c] Date is that of ratification or entry into force.
[d] Signed, but not yet ratified or in force.

The Council of Europe's Convention on Human Rights

All of the subject countries, with the exception of Yugoslavia, are Members of the Council of Europe. The Council of Europe, not to be confused with the "European Council" or the Council of the European Communities (which are related to the EU), is a political organization established in 1949 to promote democracy and human rights in Europe as well as to respond to cultural, social, and legal challenges among its members. At present, it has 41 members, making it far broader in scope than the European Union. The ECHR is adhered to by substantially all of its members, although the ECTT is in force in 19 member states and signed but not yet in force in another 13 states.

The ECHR was opened for signature in 1950 and entered into force in September, 1953. The object of its authors was to take the first steps for the collective enforcement of certain of the rights stated in the United Nations Universal Declaration of Human Rights of 1948. In addition to laying down a catalogue of civil and political rights and freedoms, the Convention set up a system of enforcement of the obligations entered into by Contracting States. Three institutions were entrusted with this responsibility: the European Commission of Human Rights (set up in 1954), the European Court of Human Rights (set up in 1959), and the Committee of Ministers of the Council of Europe, the latter organ being composed of the Ministers of Foreign Affairs of the member States or their representatives.

The original enforcement structure involving proceedings before the European Commission on Human Rights, further proceedings in the European Court of Human Rights, and enforcement by the Committee of Ministers of the Council of Europe ultimately proved too slow and cumbersome. This system was revised to streamline the process and render it completely compulsory. The new European Court of Human Rights came into operation on November 1, 1998 with the entry into force of Protocol No. 11 and the Commission was abolished except for a one-year period (until October 31, 1999) to deal with cases which had been declared admissible before the new system came into force.

Under the new system, both individuals and member states may complain to the Court of Human Rights of alleged violations of the ECHR. Complaints are screened by committees composed of three judges or by chambers composed of seven judges. In certain cases, a grand chamber of all judges will hear a case. A decision is first rendered as to whether a case is admissible; if so, a chamber or the grand chamber will decide the merits. A decision that the ECHR has been violated results in a judgment by the Court. Relief may include the awarding of damages and legal costs to the applicant, as well as requirements that the infringing State conform its laws or behavior to the terms of the ECHR. All final judgments of the Court are binding on the respondent States concerned regardless of contrary national laws.

Article 10[3] of the ECHR deals with freedom of expression which includes the right to receive and impart information and ideas "without interference by public authority and regardless of frontiers." Restrictions on this freedom must be both "necessary in a democratic society" and in furtherance of certain specified objectives, such as protection of health or morals or in the interests of public safety in order to comply with the Convention.

The European Court of Human Rights has applied Article 10 to broadcasting in several cases (*Groppera*,1990; *Autronic*; 1990; and *Informationsverein Lentia*, 1994), and in the most recent *Lentia* decision the Court unanimously held the Austrian public broadcasting monopoly incompatible with Article 10 of the ECHR. In so doing, the Court said:

> The Court has frequently stressed the fundamental role of freedom of expression in a democratic society, in particular where, through the press, it serves to impart information and ideas of general interest, which the public is moreover entitled to receive. . . . Such an undertaking cannot successfully be accomplished unless it is grounded in the principle of pluralism, of which the State is the ultimate guarantor. This observation is especially valid in relation to audio-visual media, whose programmes are often broadcast very widely (¶ 38).

It has been said that Art. 10 of the ECHR provides the fundamental framework for media and information law in Europe both within the scope of the European Union and the Council of Europe (Voorhoof, 1995, p. 28). It must be considered together with Article 3 of Protocol No. 1 to the ECHR, which provides that the member states undertake to hold free elections at reasonable intervals by secret ballot, under conditions which will "ensure the free expression of the opinion of the people." Accordingly, a country's election laws must protect free expression in the form of broadcasting of political views in election campaigns. Moreover, Article 14 of the ECHR provides that states must secure the enjoyment of the rights protected by the Convention, including rights of free expression, without discrimination on grounds, among others, of language, religion, political or other opinion, or association with a national minority. This means that political opposition must have non-discriminatory access to the broadcast media during election campaigns.

However, the rights provided by the ECHR are not absolute. The approach used by the Court in applying the Convention was described in the *Observer & Guardian* case (1991), in which the Court ruled that the court injunctions obtained by the U.K. government against publication of Peter Wright's memoirs of intelligence work ("Spycatcher") violated Article 10. According to the European Court of Human Rights, the major principles established in its case law are that "freedom of expression constitutes one of the essential foundations of a democratic society" but this freedom "is subject to a number of exceptions which, however, must be narrowly interpreted and the necessity for any restrictions must be convincingly established." A restriction on free expression may only be considered justified as "necessary in a democratic society" (Art. 10, ECHR, para. 2) where a "pressing social need" is shown to exist (*Observer/Guardian*, 1991).

The free expression rights secured by Article 10 apply to advertising of both a commercial and political nature, as the European Court of Human Rights stated in *Casoda Coca* (1994):

> The Court would first point out that Article 10 guarantees freedom of expression to "everyone." No distinction is made in it according to whether the type of aim pursued is profit-making or not . . . and a difference in treatment in this sphere might fall foul of Article 14 . . . . Article 10 does not apply solely to certain types of information or ideas or forms of expression ... , in particular those of a political nature; it also encompasses artistic expression . . ., information of a commercial nature. . . and even light music and commercials transmitted by cable (see the *Groppera Radio AG and Others v. Switzerland* judgment of 28 March 1990. . . .

While Article 10 has been construed to apply to commercial advertising, there has yet to be a case in which the European Court of Human Rights has declared restrictions on such advertising not to be sufficiently justified. There are no cases on broadcast political advertising yet, but it seems that the Court is likely to give greater weight to the importance of political expression. There have not yet been any cases decided by the Human Rights Court involving the evolving democracies examined in this book, but there is a recent case from the UK addressing government limits on political expression in the election context (*Bowman*, 1998).

In *Bowman* (1998), the applicant was prosecuted for printing and distribution of some 1.5 million leaflets throughout the United Kingdom. Mrs. Bowman was charged under English law with the offense of expending more than five pounds sterling (about $8 at current exchange rates) by an "unauthorized person" (she was not the election agent for any candidate) on conveying information to electors with a view to promoting the election of a candidate.

Mrs. Bowman argued that English law amounted to a restriction on freedom of expression which was not "necessary in a democratic society." The Court ruled by a vote of 14 to 6 that the rule operated for all practical purposes as a total barrier to publishing information designed to influence voters to support a candidate and violated Article 10. In particular, the Court thought it was unnecessary and disproportionate to limit her expenditure to five pounds in order to protect the equality of expenditures by candidates when the press were free to support particular candidates and political parties and their supporters were free to advertise so long as the ads were not directed to particular candidates in particular constituencies (districts).

The *Bowman* judgment suggests that restrictions on political advertising which have the effect of preventing political expression will be subject to a critical review and possible invalidation where they are not proportionate to a legitimate aim and are thus not "necessary in a democratic society." Some restrictions appearing in the election laws of some of the evolving democracies which could come under scrutiny in the future include rules which ban electronic advertising for certain offices, during election periods, on government-controlled "public" channels, or on private channels as the case may be.

Other international legal instruments and institutions also support and reinforce the principles contained in the ECHR. The Council of Europe's Convention on Transfrontier Television (ECTT), previously mentioned, requires that the parties "ensure freedom of expression and information in accordance with Article 10 of the ECHR . . ." (ECTT, Art. 4, 1989 and 1998). The very similar Television Without Frontiers Directive of the EU refers in the preamble to "the freedom of expression of Article 10 of the ECHR" (TWF,

1989 and 1997). In principle at least, the evolving democracies are now as never before required to adhere to international norms of political communication in their campaigns and elections.

COMPARISON OF POLITICAL AND MEDIA STRUCTURES IN EVOLVING EUROPEAN DEMOCRACIES

Before presenting the comparison of media and political systems, it is important to provide a brief overview of the general political landscape surrounding these evolving democracies. With the exception of Greece and Turkey (and Germany considering the agreement of the former East Germany to adopt the West Germany political model), the countries explored in this book inaugurated transitional governments following the demise of Soviet control over much of Eastern Europe. The economic devastation throughout the Soviet Union and the countries under its grip led to mass social movements in the Eastern European countries, particular evident through the Polish Solidarity trade union movement. However, the Solidarity movement in Poland was unique in that it and its leader (Lech Walesa) were highly visible throughout the world. This movement developed throughout the 1980s and provided Poles with a powerful, organized movement to embrace. Change throughout many of the other Soviet-controlled countries was much more rapid and characterized by more limited political organization. Furthermore, as demonstrated by Ceausescu's dictatorship in Romania, citizens throughout the former Soviet bloc had reason to be weary and fearful of untested or unrecognizable leaders or organizations. One important point to note is that although the changes in most of these countries were born out of desire to abolish communism, the roots of change were unique in each country. Many of the pre-communist traditions were vastly different, and, as this manuscript unfolds, readers will see that the paths to change reflect some of the social and cultural differences of each country.

The pre-communist era for the countries reported here is not uniform. As reported in Chapter 4, Poland embraced democracy in its Constitution of 1791. However, years of rule by Russia, Prussia, and Austria-Hungary were to follow. Although democracy was restored in 1918, the Soviets ruled Poland in the years following World War II. Turkey presents another interesting example of political unrest. Although a parliamentary system was established in Turkey during 1923, numerous military coups throughout the 20th Century point to its instability. Adding to the mix is a reunited Germany with residents of its former western land accustomed to economic prominence and stability and its former eastern inhabitants reeling from political oppression and economic devastation. Given the turbulent pasts of these evolving states, constructing new governments undoubtedly will be a long and often arduous task.

Each of the countries has chosen democracy as its governing framework. However, central chords heard throughout the continent include economic instability, social unrest, and growing tension and conflict between ethnic factions. These economic and social problems will certainly impede smooth political evolution. Nevertheless, incentives for democratic progress are in place. The European Union offers the hope of economic stability and world trade power as an incentive to the non-member countries discussed in this book. The media systems are perhaps harbingers of the willingness to accept the privatization that seems indivisible from American-style video politics.

Political System Differences

As reported in *Western Democracies* (Kaid & Holtz-Bacha, 1995), the political system and electoral system characteristics are strongly linked with the strength of political party organizations. Whereas the party organizations in the United States continue to suffer in terms of the numbers enlisted in their membership roles, the European party organizations maintain a very strong presence. However, as evidenced in the 1997 British election, content analysis of the party election broadcasts showed an increased tendency to focus on individual candidate characteristics (Hodess & Tedesco, 1998). Despite the recent findings in Britain, the party organizations throughout Europe continue to play an influential role in the political process. As Table 2.2 shows, the strength of the political parties in the evolving democracies is supported by the fact that the party is the dominant sponsor of political advertising in each of the countries. In fact, with only two exceptions (Poland and Russia), parties are the sole financiers of political spots. Even in Poland and Russia the party is the controlling force in parliamentary elections. In Russia, political party organizations are the largest sponsor of spots in parliamentary campaigns due to the fact that most individual candidates do not have the funds to produce spots. Russia is unique on the presidential level since there has been no real substantial development of national parties to promote and support presidential candidates, with the exception of the Communist Party of the Russian Federation. The Polish parliamentary campaigns are funded by parties, while presidential campaigns are funded by the candidate's electoral committee.

One thing all of the countries share is a multi-party system. Even Germany, which had a long-standing, dominant two-party system has developed into a multiparty system with a number of parties banding together to establish a ruling coalition. Likewise, in Romania a center-left coalition (Party of Social Democracy in Romania - PDSR) and a center-right coalition (National Peasant Christian and Democratic Party - PNTCD) have developed through allegiances by a number of parties on both sides of the political spectrum. In the Serbian Parliamentary elections in Yugoslavia, more than 20 parties presented themselves, and 10 parties came up with political commercials. In Poland, the 1991 and 1993 Parliamentary elections produced four strong parties, the SLD (Democratic Left Alliance), the Post-Solidarity formations, the Polish Peasants' Party and the Confederation of Independent Poland. In Bulgaria, the Bulgarian Socialist Party, the Union of Democratic Forces, and the Bulgarian Agrarian People's Union have emerged as the strongest parties. In Hungary, more than 15 political parties attempted to establish marketable images, including the Hungarian Socialist Party, the Alliance of Free Democrats, the Hungarian Democratic Forum, the Independent Smallholders' Party, the

Christian Democrat People's Party, and the Alliance of Young Democrats. The Hungarian Socialist Party and the Alliance of Free Democrats were most successful. The 1995 Russian Parliamentary elections proved the most bizarre in view of the fact that no less than 43 parties registered for the elections, including the Beer Lovers Party. While only four parties were able to obtain the 5% threshold needed to produce seats in the Parliament, under Russian law, all 43 parties were granted equal broadcast time. The Motherland Party (ANAP), True Path Party (DYP), and the Welfare Party (RP) have shown strength in Turkey.

Table 2.2 - Sponsorship of Spots

Country	Sponsorship
Bulgaria	Party
Czech Republic	Party
Germany	Party
Greece	Party
Hungary	Party
Poland	Party + Candidate[a]
Romania	Party
Russia	Party + Candidates[b]
Turkey	Party
Yugoslavia	Party
(Serbia and Montenegro)	Not available.

[a]Parliamentary campaigns are funded by parties and presidential campaigns are funded by the candidates electoral committee.
[b]Party is the largest sponsor of spots, particularly in parliamentary campaigns due to the fact that most individual candidates do not have the funds to produce spots.

The instability of the electorate (and the ruling governments) in many of these evolving countries is reflected in the changes in names of political parties (and coalitions) from one election to the next. Furthermore, the increased diversity of parties that appear to gain support from specialized interests demonstrates that the ruling parties are failing to command large, loyal segments of the electorate. In several of the European countries the leading parties must form allegiances with specialized smaller parties, which are beginning to attract larger percentages of the electorate. For example, in the Czech Republic, the Civic Democratic Party and the Czech Social Democratic Party (the two largest parties) lost voters to the specialized interests of the Christian Democratic Union-Czechoslovak People's Party (8% on an anti-crime platform), the Assembly of the Republic-Czechoslovak Republican Party (8% on an anti-German, anti-Romania stance), and the Civic Democratic Alliance led by Trade and Industry Minister Vladimir Dlouhy (6% on appeals to young professionals). Despite the turbulence of the party organizations, for the most part the parties continue to present a much stronger influence than individual candidates, despite the increased presence of U.S. political consultants working in many of the countries.

The electoral systems of the countries presented in this book are in most cases much more complex than in the U.S. The majority vote system in the U.S. (with the exception of the more complex electoral college system on the presidential level) is fairly simplistic. However, as Table 2.3 shows, the electoral process for the executive branch of government is quite mixed among the countries. The ruling presidents, prime ministers, or chancellors come to power either through popular vote or through appointment from the president.

Table 2.3 - Electoral Procedure for the Executive Branch*

Bulgaria	President and Vice President elected on the same ticket by popular vote for five-year terms. Chairman of the Council of Ministers (Prime Minister) nominated by the President.
Czech Republic	President elected by Parliament for a five-year term. Prime Minister appointed by the President.
Germany	President elected by the Federal Convention including members of the Federal Assembly and an equal number of members elected by the Land Parliaments for a five-year term. Chancellor elected by an absolute majority of the Federal Assembly for a four-year term.
Greece	President elected by the Chamber of Deputies for a five-year term. Prime Minister appointed by the President.
Hungary	President elected by the National Assembly for a four-year term. Prime Minister elected by the National Assembly on the recommendation of the President.
Poland	President elected by popular vote for a five-year term. Prime Minister appointed by the President and confirmed by the Sejm.
Romania	President elected by popular vote for a four-year term. Prime Minister appointed by the President.
Russia	President elected by popular vote for a four-year term. Premier appointed by the President with approval of the Duma.
Turkey	President elected by the National Assembly for a seven year term. Prime Minister appointed by the President.
Yugoslavia	Not available.
(Serbia and Montenegro)	President elected by the Federal Assembly for a four-year term. Prime Minister nominated by the President.

*Much of the information provided in Table 2.3 was obtained through information available in *The World Factbook 1998* published by the U.S. Central Intelligence Agency. *The World Factbook 1998* is in the public domain and information is made available through the Central Intelligence Agency web site at http://www.cia.gov.

Table 2.4 - Electoral Procedure for Legislative Branch(es)*

Bulgaria	Unicameral National Assembly. Members are popularly elected to serve four year terms.
Czech Republic	Bicameral Parliament. Consists of Senate (elected by popular vote to serve staggered two-, four-, and six-year terms) and Chamber of Deputies (popular vote to serve for four years).
Germany	Bicameral Chamber (no official name as a whole). Federal Assembly elected by direct popular vote under a system combining direct and proportional representation for a four year term (a party must win 5% of the national vote or three direct mandates to gain representation. In the Federal Council state governments are directly represented by voters depending on population. Members from each state are required to vote as a bloc. No fixed terms.
Greece	Unicameral Parliament. Members are elected by direct popular vote to serve four-year terms.
Hungary	Unicameral National Assembly. Members are elected by popular vote under a system of proportional and direct representation to serve four-year terms. A 5% threshold is imposed for party representation.
Poland	Bicameral National Assembly consisting of the Sejm (proportional representation for a four-year term) and the Senate (majority vote for a four-year term).
Romania	Bicameral Parliament consists of Senate and a Chamber of Deputies. Members of both houses are elected direct popular vote on a proportional representation to serve four-year terms.
Russia	Bicameral Federal Assembly. Federation Council consists of four-year terms for top executive and legislative officials in each of the 89 federal administrative units. In the State Duma, half of the members are elected in single-member districts and half are elected from national party lists. Members are elected by direct popular vote to serve four-year terms. A 5% threshold for the 225 party list seats applies.
Turkey	Unicameral Grand National Assembly of Turkey. Members are elected by percentage of vote by party.
Yugoslavia (Serbia and Montenegro)	Not available. Bicameral Federal Assembly. Members distributed on the basis of party representation in the Chamber of Republics to serve four-year terms. In the Chamber of Citizens half of the members are elected by constituency majorities and half are elected by proportional representation for four-year terms.

* Much of the information provided in Table 2.4 was obtained through information available in *The World Factbook 1998* published by the U.S. Central Intelligence Agency. *The World*

Factbook 1998 is in the public domain and information is made available through the Central Intelligence Agency web site at http://www.cia.gov.

The electoral systems on the legislative level are far more complex. For example, as Table 2.4 shows, legislators in the various countries are elected through either majority vote, proportional representation to party percentages, or through a mixture of majority vote and proportional representation. In some cases, parties must acquire at least a 5% threshold in order to gain representation. Furthermore, the Czech Republic has a complex system in which terms for Senators are staggered at two-, four-, and six-year intervals. In Bulgaria, Poland, Romania, and Russia the president is elected by the people, whereas in the Czech Republic, Germany, Greece, Hungary, Yugoslavia (Serbia and Montenegro), and Turkey, the national leader is either appointed by the president or elected by the parliament.

Media System Differences

In addition to the political system differences, the media system differences have a strong impact on the function and importance of political spots. The broadcasting systems of the countries in this book not only have a remarkably different history, but also have distinct stages of growth and development. Germany began privatization of the media in the West during the mid-1980s, while most of the other countries in this book are experiencing a much more recent private broadcasting environment.

The former Czechoslovakia took the necessary steps to become the first former East Bloc nation to adopt and implement a new broadcasting law in October 1991. However, the first private station did not obtain its channel until February 1994. Meanwhile, privatization began in Turkey in 1991. Since television was used as a tool of Soviet propaganda, television developed a high penetration rate throughout the former Soviet Union. Today, there are three private and three public channels in Russia, with two of the public and one of the private stations reaching the entire nation. In Romania and Bulgaria, media systems are still undergoing changes as television systems transform from state-controlled to private institutions. Poland's Polsat TV became the first private station in that country.

Although it is now possible for candidates and parties to reach the public through private stations, the regulatory environment is not always completely permissive for uncontrolled or unlimited access. However, with the exception of Turkey and the Czech Republic, candidates and parties are allowed some form of political advertising on private stations. In Bulgaria, advertisements were allowed for parliamentary candidates only.

Political Advertising Rules

There are disparities in political advertising practice and regulation among the ten countries examined in this book. This is not surprising given these countries' lack of experience with the abstract concept of democracy and one of its concrete manifestations, a more open media system. The tables provided here offer some general guidelines to political advertising practice and regulations with the text providing further, more specific explanation for individual countries. It should be noted that information from Turkey applies to practices as they stood for the 1995 elections.

Table 2.5 illustrates the variety of broadcast outlets in which political spots can be found in these developing democracies. Many allow spots on both public and private stations, probably reflective of the long history of public or state-owned television having to coexist with emerging private media. What is perhaps more interesting is that the countries which only allow spots on one of the systems choose the public outlets for allowable broadcast. The logic of this policy is clear considering that, in countries such as Turkey and the Czech Republic, political time is given free of charge. Poland allows paid advertising on the public stations but not private ones. This policy would seem to adhere to the philosophy that paid or free political advertising is related to public service matters and should be separated from capitalistic concerns.

Table 2.5 - Where Spots Are Broadcast

Bulgaria	Public and Private[a]
Czech Republic	Public
Germany	Public and Private
Greece	Public and Private
Hungary	Public and Private
Poland	Public and Private
Romania	Public and Private
Russia	Public and Private
Turkey	Public
Yugoslavia	Public and Private
(Serbia and Montenegro)	Not available.

[a]Paid ads allowed on private television since 1997 for parliamentary elections.

Because the public/private media dichotomy remains important in many of the countries, the remaining tables will try to take this relevant distinction into account. Table 2.6, dealing with broadcast allocation time, shows this disparity nicely. For the public systems in most of the countries, allocation centers on either proportional party strength or equality of time between the parties. Free purchase of time is more common for the private media systems.

Table 2.6 - Method of Political Broadcast Allocation

	Public	*Private*
E. Germany	According to party strength	free purchase
Poland	Free: Equal time/number for all parties; Paid: Free purchase with restrictions	N/A
Bulgaria	According to party strength	free purchase
Romania	Various proportional criteria	free purchase
Hungary	Free: Equal time for parties; Paid: Free purchase	free purchase
Yugoslavia	Proportionate to party strength	same as public
Serbia and Montenegro)	Not available.	Not available.
Russia	Equal time for all parties	Equal time for all parties
Turkey	According to party strength	N/A
Greece	Purchase of equal time	Purchase of equal time
Czech Republic	Equal time for all parties	N/A

The proportional criteria can be fairly complicated. For example in Romania, presidential candidates get equal time, but parties represented in parliament receive time based on their share of seats. Parties which hold no seats in parliament receive half the time. In Turkey "visual propaganda" cannot account for more than 50% of the total time allotted to each party, which is determined by parliamentary strength. Parties with 20 or fewer deputies in parliament were given equal time which was shorter than that enjoyed by the larger parties, and they could not use any of it for visual propaganda. Hungary offers limited and equal time on public television with the party determining the amount of paid time on public and private television. In Greece, public and private stations provide 5 free minutes to each party in addition to time available for purchase.

Table 2.7 provides an overview of limitations imposed on the number of ads. Given the information provided in Table 2.6, it is important to note that the "limitation" on number of ads can be the result of an overall time limit on allocations, as is the case in Russia. Of course, limitation can also center on the actual number of ads, as is the case with German public television. An interesting twist to the possibilities is provided by Romania, which allows free purchase of time on private stations, but those stations still have to abide by the allotment rules mentioned in the earlier discussion. This in essence limits what happens even with paid ads. The reader can see from Table 2.7 that much of the time on public stations, while free, is limited. Overall there seems to be more opportunity for unlimited ads on the private stations, which of course often have to be purchased.

Table 2.7 - Number of Political Spots

	Public	Private
E. Germany	Limited	Unlimited
Poland	Paid: Unlimited	N/A
	Free: Limited	
Bulgaria	Limited	Unlimited
Romania	Limited	Limited
Hungary	Free: Limited	Unlimited
	Paid: Unlimited	
Yugoslavia	N/A	N/A
(Serbia and Montenegro)	Limited	Limited
Russia	Limited	Limited
Turkey	Limited	N/A
Greece	Limited	Limited
Czech Republic	Limited	N/A

A few examples illustrate the disparity in particular countries' limitations. In Russia, paid time is not supposed to exceed free time provided by the government, but enforcement of the rule is lax. In 1996 in the Czech Republic the total time split between the parties was 14 hours in the two weeks prior to the election. In free limited time, Poland allowed each candidate to be seen in 16 spots in the first round of elections and 6 spots in the second round. The clear trend to note in Eastern Europe is that despite particular regulatory differences concerning time allocation, virtually every country limits the number of ads some way.

Table 2.8 illustrates the differences in political spot length. This comparison is of interest given the concern about the American propensity for ads in the 30 second range and American "influence" in the media practices of such countries as the ones discussed in this book. Oftentimes this criticism is offered as a negative commentary on the American system, though short political ads can and do contain important information. While it is difficult to ascertain any real pattern among the 10 Eastern European countries, some specific examples may certainly point to a situation in which free, regulated ads are longer while paid ads are shorter, more in the American style.

Table 2.8 - Length of Political Broadcasts

	Public	Private
E. Germany	2:30	Variable
	(1998)1:30	MC, :30-:45
Poland	(1995)Free:3:30 & 5:10; Paid: MC,:30;	N/A
Bulgaria	3-5:00	Variable
Romania	Variable	Variable
	Presidential	Presidential
	MC,1:00-2:00	MC,1:00-2:00
Hungary	Variable	Variable
Yugoslavia	Not available.	Not available.
(Serbia and Montenegro)	Variable	Variable
Russia	Variable	Variable
	MC, :30 or <	MC, :30 or <
Turkey	At least 2:00; 10:00 or < per day	N/A
Greece	Variable	Variable
Czech Republic	Variable	N/A

MC – Most common

Germany provides an interesting example since "free" ads are allowed on public stations and paid ads are only carried on private stations. While there is no legal regulation, public stations determine the length of ads on their programming. Historically that length has been 2 minutes and 30 seconds but for the 1998 national elections length was set at 1 minute 30 seconds. In contrast the paid ads varied in length, with 30-45 seconds being the normal range. Likewise in the 1995 Polish election, free ads lasted 3 minutes and 30 seconds and 5 minutes and 10 seconds while paid advertisements were in the (U.S.) standard 30 second range.

Again, it would be tempting for some readers to use these examples as evidence for the "Americanization" of Eastern European politics, a process presumably reliant on exploiting, if not creating, short attention spans through superficial discussion of issues in short spots. Of course, an equally viable explanation of what is happening is economic. What is true in America is almost certainly true in developing democratic and capitalistic states. Shorter ads are used because they cost less to produce and run.

Assessment of the restrictions on political spot content across the countries (Table 2.9) shows there is still some split between those that have granted that content protected political speech status similar to the United States and those that have been more cautious in this regard. Even in Germany and Poland, which have no content restrictions per se, political ads must be labeled as such. Several factors probably come into play for countries such as Bulgaria, Romania, and Russia as they set content restrictions. The idea of total freedom of expression might be difficult to comprehend in countries with a long history of oppressive, state owned media systems. There may also be the feeling that this type of freedom may not really be in the best interest of the political system. The citizenry may want restrictions on political speech for fear that total "freedom" will result in powerful groups left over from repressive regimes utilizing propaganda to maintain and expand their influence. Governments in power may believe that the best way to stay there is to limit their opponents' access to electronic campaign advertising.

Table 2.9 - Restrictions on Content of Political Broadcasts

	Public	Private
E. Germany	No	No
Poland	No	N/A
Bulgaria	No commercial topics in ads	No commercial topics in ads
Romania	Detailed criteria	Detailed criteria
Hungary	No	No
Yugoslavia	Not available.	Not available.
(Serbia and Montenegro)	Not available.	Not available.
Russia	Cannot commit libel or incite racism	Cannot commit libel or incite racism
Turkey	No	N/A
Greece	Not available.	Not available.
Czech Republic	No	N/A

Several strategies have been employed by countries choosing the regulatory route. Bulgaria's content restriction (of no commercial topics) points to the aforementioned concern of trying to maintain some separation between politics and economics. Romania offers the most extensive and conservative approach to content regulation. According to material produced by the National Council of the Audiovisual (1996) candidates in their broadcasts cannot contest "the lawful order and the principles of the constitutional democracy," endanger the "public order and safety of persons and goods," or commit libel or slander. In addition, Romanian regulation forbids use of national symbols, international organization symbols, or symbols from religious cults (National Council of the Audiovisual, 1996). This concern over the negative impact of nationalistic presentations may be reflected in Russia's regulation against inciting racism. The marriage of nationalistic appeals with inflammation of ethnic differences seems an all too common political strategy.

REFERENCES

Autronic AG v. Switzerland. (1990). 178 Eur. Ct. H.R. (ser. A), 12 EHRR 485.

Blumler, J. G. (1990). Elections, the media and the modern publicity process. In M. Ferguson (Ed.), *Public communication. The new imperatives. Future directions for media research* (pp. 101-113). Newbury Park, CA: Sage.

Buckley v. Valeo. (1976). 424 U.S. 1.

Casado Coca v. Spain. (1994). Case No. 8/1993/403/481 Eur. Ct. H.R.

Commission of the European Communities. (1999). *Commission communication on the stabilisation and association process for countries of southeastern Europe.* 26 May. COM(99)235.

Council of Europe. (1950). *European Convention on Human Rights and Fundamental Freedoms .* 213 U.N.T.S. 222 (ECHR).

Council of the European Union. (1997). *Council conclusions on the application of conditionality with a view to developing a coherent EU-strategy for the relations with the countries in the region.* Luxembourg: Office of Official Publications of the European Communities.

E.R.T. v. D.E.P. (1991). Case C-260/89. [1991] E.C.R. I-2925.

Groppera Radio AG v. Switzerland. (1990). 173 Eur. Ct. H.R. (Ser. A), 12 EHRR 321.

Gurevitch, M., & Blumler, J. G. (1990). Comparative research: The extending frontier. In D. L. Swanson & D. Nimmo (Eds.), *New directions in political communication: A resource book* (pp. 305-325). Newbury Park, CA: Sage.

Hodess, R., & Tedesco, J. C. (1998). *The Party Election Broadcasts in Britain: A comparison of the 1992 and 1997 broadcasts and their coverage in the media.* Paper presented at the American Political Science Association Convention, Boston.

Holtz-Bacha, C., & Kaid, L. L. (1995). A comparative perspective on political advertising: Media and political system characteristics. In L. L. Kaid and C. Holtz-Bacha (Eds.), *Political advertising in Western democracies* (pp. 8-18). Thousand Oaks, CA: Sage.

Informationsverein Lentia v. Austria. (1994). 17 EHRR 93.

Johnson, K. S., & Elebash, C. (1986). The contagion from the right: Americanization of British political advertising. In L. L. Kaid, D. Nimmo, & K. Sanders (Eds.), *New perspective on political advertising* (pp. 293-313). Carbondale: Southern Illinois University Press.

Johnston, A., & Gerstlé, J. (1993). Uloga televizijskih programa u promicanju francuskih predsjednickih kandidata [The role of television broadcasts in promoting french presidential candidates]. *Informatologia,* 25(1-2), 13-22.

Kaid, L. L., & Holtz-Bacha, C. (1995). *Political advertising in Western democracies.* Thousand Oaks, CA: Sage.

Kaid, L. L., & Tedesco, J. C. (1993). Usporedba televizijske politicke promicbe tijekom Britanske i Americke kampanje 1992 [A comparison of political television advertising from the 1992 British and American campaigns]. *Informatologia, 25*(1-2), 1-12.

Nold v. Commission. (1974). Case 4/73, [1974] ECR 491.

Treaty Establishing European Economic Community (Treaty of Rome), March 25, 1957, 298 U.N.T.S. 3.

Treaty on European Union. (1992). ("Maastricht Treaty").

Treaty of Amsterdam Amending the Treaty on European Union, the Treaties Establishing The European Communities And Certain Related Acts. 1997. ("Treaty of Amsterdam").

Voorhoof, D. (1995). *Critical perspectives on the scope and interpretation of Article 10 of the European Convention on Human Rights.* Strasbourg: Council of Europe Press.

NOTES

1. As of January 1, 1995, there are fifteen Member States. In order of accession, they are France, Germany, Italy, Belgium, The Netherlands, Luxembourg (the original "Six"), the United Kingdom, Ireland, Denmark, Greece, Spain, Portugal, Austria, Sweden, and Finland.

2. At this writing, Yugoslav forces have withdrawn from the Kosovo province, NATO forces have ceased bombing, and multinational peacekeeping units have entered the province. Yugoslavia has a badly damaged infrastructure resulting from NATO bombing in the spring of 1999, including destroyed broadcasting facilities. Conditions for NATO and EU reconstructive aid which at this time are unfulfilled include the removal from power of Slobodan Milosovic, cooperation with international war crimes tribunals, restoration of democratic principles, and respect for human rights and the rule of law. In particular, the conditions laid down by the EU include a representative government with an accountable executive, a government acting in accordance with the constitution and law, separation of powers, free and fair elections at reasonable intervals by secret ballot, freedom of expression, including independent media, rights of assembly and demonstration, and access to courts and right to a fair trial, among others (Commission, 1999; Council of the European Union, 1997). Much depends on events to come, but it is likely that Yugoslavia is more than a decade away from membership in the EU.

3. The text of Article 10 ECHR reads:

(1)Everyone has the right to freedom of expression. This right shall include freedom to hold opinions and to receive and impart information and ideas without interference by public authority and regardless of frontiers. This Article shall not prevent States from requiring the licensing of broadcasting, television or cinema enterprises.

(2)The exercise of these freedoms, since it carries with it duties and responsibilities, may be subject to such formalities, conditions, restrictions or penalties as are prescribed by law and are necessary in a democratic society, in the interests of national security, territorial integrity or public safety, for the prevention of disorder or crime, for the protection of health or morals, for the protection of the reputation or rights of others, for preventing the disclosure of information received in confidence, or for maintaining the authority and impartiality of the judiciary.

Chapter 3

POLITICAL ADVERTISING IN EAST GERMANY

Christina Holtz-Bacha

After forty years of separation, Germany was reunited on October 3, 1990. The "peaceful revolution" that started in the former German Democratic Republic in the fall of 1989 and finally led to the unification paralleled political change in other East European countries. However, East Germany is a special case compared to the other East European countries represented in this book. What East Germany has in common with its neighboring countries is the changed political system. The majority of today's voting age population in East Germany underwent political socialization during a socialist and authoritarian regime dominated by a single state party. These citizens, among them many who had never experienced another political system, were at some point in their lives confronted by a fundamental change of the political structures which also had far-reaching consequences for their everyday lives.

What East Germany does not have in common with other East European countries is that it did not develop its own new system. Instead, the West German political system was simply extended to the east. *Technically*, the unification was accomplished by rebuilding five federal states on the territory of the GDR that then joined the Federal Republic of Germany (11 federal states that made up West Germany). Thus, the German Democratic Republic ceased to exist in October 1990 when the five new states joined the Federal Republic, and German unity was officially sealed. Only two months after the unification, the first all-German parliamentary election took place on December 2, 1990.

Since the events of fall, 1989, the East German party system underwent a structural change. The former GDR state party SED (Sozialistische Einheitspartei Deutschlands) was renamed PDS (Partei des Demokratischen Sozialismus). The East German Christian Democrats and Liberals joined with their West German sister parties, the Christian Democratic Union (CDU) and the Free Democratic Party (FDP). Several new parties emerged. The East German Social Democratic Party, founded in November 1989, merged with its West German sister party SPD. The Deutsche Soziale Union (DSU) was founded as a counterpart to the Bavarian CSU (Christlich-Soziale Union).[1] A couple of small left-wing groups joined Bündnis 90 that cooperated with West Germany's Green Party, Die

Grünen. The two groups later merged to a single party now called Bündnis 90/Die Grünen (Jesse, 1994).

THE ELECTORAL SYSTEM AND
REGULATION FOR POLITICAL ADVERTISING

The first all-German election took place under the rules of the West German electoral system which is a "personalized proportional election." It gives each voter two votes: With the first vote a party candidate in the constituency is elected, and the second vote is given to a party list. Given that only the bigger parties have the chance to win the constituency, the second vote is more important, particularly for the smaller parties. The first vote given to a small party can therefore be regarded as a lost vote. Since the 1960s, more and more people in West Germany have split their ticket, giving their first vote to one of the big parties and their second vote to a smaller party. During the campaign all parties aim to solicit the second votes.

The party receiving the majority of votes, or a coalition of two or more parties, nominates the chancellor who is the head of the government and proposes the ministers who are then elected by the parliament (Bundestag). While the president is a representative and therefore comparatively powerless position, the chancellor is the most important figure in the German political system. As neither the president nor the chancellor is elected directly by the people, the Bundestag is the only institution to be voted for on the national level.

The parties play a central role in the German political system. Their task of "participating in the formation of political opinion and political will" is laid down in the constitution. In order to be represented in parliament, parties have to get more than 5 percent of the votes.

While political advertising on radio has a long tradition in Germany going back to the twenties, electoral advertising on television was broadcast for the first time during the (West German) national election campaign of 1957.

Political advertising on radio and television is only allowed during election campaigns. It is broadcast within certain limitations and under conditions that differ for public and for commercial television. Parties are allotted free time for a certain number of ads on public television, while they can purchase additional time on commercial television where they have to pay the prime costs which in 1994 was interpreted as 55 to 60% of the usual advertising prices. Equal opportunity holds for all parties that are registered for the upcoming election. However, the Federal Constitutional Court in several cases has approved a system of graded allocation of broadcasting time with smaller parties getting less time (fewer spots) than the larger ones. On public television the spots, one or two at a time, are usually included before or after prime time programs. On private television the ads are part of the general advertising blocs.

The political parties produce the television spots themselves and are responsible for their contents. The broadcasting stations can refuse spots only if they obviously do not contain electoral advertising or contravene criminal law.

Though spots receive high viewer exposure, very little research has been done on political advertising in Germany. Discussion of legal aspects has been prevalent in publications on party broadcasts (Becker, 1990; Bornemann, 1992; Franke, 1979; Gabriel-Bräutigam, 1991). Several studies describing single, or comparing different, campaigns have usually presented accounts of the advertising campaign and thus, among the other means of electoral advertising, also considered TV spots. However, only a few German studies have specifically addressed questions of creation, content, formal features, or effectiveness of party spots. Dröge, Lerg, and Weissenborn (1969) presented a description of contents and styles of the commercials broadcast during the 1969 parliamentary election campaign. Martin Wachtel (1988) analyzed the argumentation content of the 1987 parliamentary election spots. He determined that communicating trustworthiness and competence was the major goal of the political parties in their television spots and that visual qualities of the commercials played an important role in communicating these qualities. Christina Holtz-Bacha (1990) analyzed survey data on the 1989 European Parliamentary election in West Germany and found that watching party commercials also correlates with a positive opinion about the campaign and also with an improvement in the attitude toward the European Community, the German membership in the EC, and the attitude toward the European Parliament. Tobias Klein (1992) presented a long-term analysis comparing the electoral spots of the most important German parties between 1972 and 1990. Using continuous computer-assisted measurement, Lynda Lee Kaid (1996) provided a step-by-step analysis of the reception process of spots during the 1994 campaign.

PARTY SPOTS DURING THE 1990 AND 1994 NATIONAL ELECTION CAMPAIGNS[2]

During the 1990 campaign, 67 spots of 21 parties were broadcast per public channel, with the two largest parties, Christian Democrats (CDU) and Social Democrats (SPD), receiving 8 spots each. Six parties, among them the smaller partners of the then-governing coalition, the Christian Social Union (CSU) and the Free Democrats (FDP), were allotted 4 spots each. The 13 smaller parties received 3 or 2 spots. This arrangement was made for the two national public television stations ARD (Arbeitsgemeinschaft der öffentlich-rechtlichen Rundfunkanstalten der Bundesrepublik Deutschland) and ZDF (Zweites Deutsches Fernsehen). The ads were identical for both stations, only the order of the spots was different. Only the CDU produced a spot to be shown several times on commercial television.

As the parties did not always produce different spots for each time slot, some spots were repeated several times. Thus, 38 different spots could be seen during the 1990 campaign, all were 2 1/2 minutes in length as prescribed by the stations.

As in 1990, party commercials in 1994 were broadcast during the last four weeks of the election campaign. While 22 of 24 parties registered for the election produced spots to be broadcast on ARD and ZDF for free, only the bigger parties bought additional air time on private channels. Altogether 31 different spots were broadcast on public television. In addition, another 22 different spots were shown on commercial channels.

In 1990, three East German parties ran in the election: PDS, DSU, and Bündnis 90/Grüne. Each of these parties was allotted four time slots per public station. The PDS produced four different spots, Bündnis 90/Grüne three, and DSU only one spot. Four years later, for the parliamentary election in 1994, only the PDS was left after Bündnis 90/Grüne had merged with the West German Green Party. The DSU, though still running for the election, was of no further significance. This time the PDS only produced 1 spot which was repeated 3 times on each public channel.

Given that the parties of East German origin produced electoral advertising for the first time in 1990, their spots were highly professional. Table 3.1 shows the formats that were used by these parties in comparison to the results for all parties together. Due to the relatively high number of small parties that on the whole, probably because of the low production costs, preferred this format, the candidate statement was the most popular format of all spots taken together. The East German parties however, like the bigger West German parties, used the candidate statement less frequently. Instead they employed formats, like staged scenes or videoclip, comparatively more often than the West German parties. Of 8 spots 3 were filmed outdoors, another 3 showed a studio production, and 2 used a special production technique. In 1994, the PDS also applied an unusual format when it used a staged scene for its only spot.

Table 3.1 - Formats of Party Spots in 1990

	All parties		East German parties
	n (%)		n (%)*
Candidate statement	12 (32)		2 (25)
Issue presentation	9 (24)		2 (25)
Documentary	4 (10)		-
Testimonial	4 (10)		-
Staging	3 (8)		2 (25)
Issue dramatization	3 (8)		-
Videoclip	2 (5)		1 (13)
Question and answer	1 (3)		1 (13)

* Percentages add up to 101% due to rounding error.

In 1990, campaign advertising of all parties was overwhelmingly image-oriented and so were the majority of the spots of the East German parties. Appeals made in the spots were mainly emotional; this is true for the spots altogether as well as for the East German parties' advertising. The 1990 TV ads in general were less negative than earlier campaigns (Klein, 1992). However, the negativity of the ads of the East German parties was even below average. The PDS ad in 1994 was coded as balanced between issue- and image-orientation, and it included a combination of different kinds of appeals. This spot also did not use any direct negative attacks but criticized other parties more in an indirect and ironic way.

The PDS was the only one of the East German parties that prominently featured its top candidate. In 1990, the party leader Gregor Gysi was presented in a personality spot. He also was the one who, in another spot, spoke about a finance scandal of the party as a consequence of inheriting the property of the former GDR state party. In 1994, Gysi appeared at the end of the spot encouraging viewers to "dare" to vote for the PDS.

It comes as no surprise that unification was the main issue of the 1990 campaign with 55% of all 38 spots addressing this topic. It is more of a surprise that 4 out of 8 East German party spots did not deal with German unity in their TV advertising. Though the DSU presented itself as "the party of German unity," it also stressed being the sister party of the Bavarian CSU and also included a testimonial by the CSU chairman. The PDS, in a vocal music (sung) spot, addressed differences between East and West Germany and warned of the domination of the West over the East.

In 1994 again, unification appeared among the 15 most important issues of the advertising campaign on TV though less prominent than in 1990. This time, the PDS did not address the topic in its spot. Instead, employing irony and humor which is unusual for German political advertising, it recommended itself as a left alternative to the other parties.

In contrast to the other German parties, the PDS, in 1990 as well as in 1994, also addressed women's issues. While this topic was only mentioned in 21% (1990) and 13% (1994) of all spots,[3] the PDS in 1990 dedicated one spot to five female candidates who also dealt with women's policy. The topic was addressed again in a 1994 PDS spot.

MEASURING THE EFFECTS OF THE SPOTS

The first all-German parliamentary election in 1990 also seemed to be an interesting setting for a comparison of the potential different effects of the party commercials on viewers from West and East Germany. Although East Germans might have seen party spots before because West German television could be received in the GDR, 1990 was the first time these spots had any significance for them in terms of voting decisions. Differences in the reactions of East and West Germans could be expected due to a different political socialization and different experiences in contrasting political systems.[4] Also, attitudes towards advertising in general differ considerably between people in East and West Germany: In 1990, 67% of the West Germans compared to only 59% of the

East Germans held positive attitudes towards advertising. About one year later the difference was even more distinct when 71% in the West and 50% in the East expressed a positive opinion about advertising (Werbung in Deutschland, 1993, p. 50).

Thus, an experimental study was carried out to determine the effectiveness of the spots (Holtz-Bacha & Kaid, 1993). This experiment was repeated in 1994 (Holtz-Bacha & Kaid, 1996; Holtz-Bacha, Kaid, & Chanslor, 1995). In 1990, the sample consisted of 171 voting-age students representing a broad cross-section of university students enrolled in mass communication and journalism at two universities in West Germany and 73 who were enrolled in a major university in an East German state. Among the students were 104 women and 66 men, the average age was 23.5 years. In 1994, the sample consisted of 202 voting-age students at two universities in West Germany and two universities in East Germany. Among the students were 93 women and 108 men (one answer was missing on this variable); the average age was 22.4 years. In both cases, the experimental sessions were conducted shortly before the election date.

The study employed a pre-post research design involving the administration of pre- and post-test questionnaires. In between, the respondents were shown four television spots of the most important German parties, two spots of the Christian Democrats (CDU) and two of the Social Democrats (SPD). All ads focussed on the parties' top candidates.

The pretest questionnaire started with an open-ended question asking for the characteristics of the ideal chancellor for Germany. In addition, the questionnaire consisted of demographic information, political interest measures, media use variables, a thermometer scale to ascertain the general feelings towards each party chancellor candidate, and a semantic differential scale, evaluating the candidates. The post-test questionnaire repeated the thermometer and the semantic differential scale on each candidate and also included several open-ended questions on issue, image, and visual recall and other rating questions on emotional responses and learning.

The semantic differential scale used to evaluate candidate image consisted of 12 sets of bi-polar adjectives (e.g., qualified-unqualified), each rated on a 7-point range. This scale was derived from earlier scales used to measure candidate image (Kaid, 1991; Kaid & Boydston, 1987; Kaid, Downs, & Ragan, 1990; Sanders & Pace 1977).

In order to allow for a comparison with earlier results the 1994 experiment used the same design as the 1990 study. However, while the CDU top candidate still was the incumbent chancellor Helmut Kohl, the SPD in 1994 presented a new candidate. In 1990 the SPD had nominated Oskar Lafontaine as chancellor candidate; four years later the party started its campaign with the SPD leader Rudolf Scharping at the top. All three were politicians from West Germany. Helmut Kohl had been chancellor since 1982 and, on the West German side, also had the main responsibility for the unification in 1990. The SPD candidates both were state prime ministers and as such probably better known to the West German than to the East German electorate.

FINDINGS FROM THE EXPERIMENTS

The introductory question asking for the most important attributes the ideal chancellor for Germany should have, produced considerable differences between East and West German respondents. In 1990, honesty/integrity ranked first among the East Germans while in West Germany an ecological attitude was seen as most important for the ideal chancellor. The biggest difference for the attributes mentioned was for tolerance which ranked third in East Germany and last in West Germany among 13 attributes mentioned by more than 10% either in the East or in the West (Kaid & Holtz-Bacha, 1993, p. 190).

Evaluations on the thermometer scale express the more general feelings towards the candidates. Table 3.2 compares the pre- and post-test ratings of East and West Germans for each candidate in 1990 and 1994.[5] In general the results confirm the greater popularity of the SPD candidates in both groups, though the difference in 1994 was not as high as in 1990.[6] Watching the spots obviously affects East Germans more than West Germans: In 3 of 4 cases East Germans change their evaluation after having seen the spots while West Germans only show a significant change for the SPD candidate in 1994.

Table 3.2 - General Feelings towards the Candidates (Thermometer Scale)

	East Germans		West Germans
Helmut Kohl 1990			
pretest	19.5		26.4
posttest	20.2		25.1
Oskar Lafontaine 1990			
pretest	62.9		54.7
posttest	65.3**		53.9
Helmut Kohl 1994			
pretest	30.2		26.8
posttest	28.0**		26.6
Rudolf Scharping 1994			
pretest	37.1		45.5
posttest	40.7*		46.7*

* $p \leq 05$ ** $p \leq 00$

In order to ascertain the factors influencing the more detailed evaluation of the candidates on the 12 attribute scales resulting from the semantic differential, multiple variance analysis was applied. In 1990 as well as in 1994, main effects were produced for the candidate, the regional origin of the subjects (East/West) as well as for the spots (pre-/post-test). So, ratings for Kohl and Lafontaine and Scharping respectively were not only

influenced by the personalities of the candidates but also by the spots, and these evaluations were different in East and West Germany. This proves that subjects in the East and
in the West indeed react differently to the presentation of the candidates in the party
advertising. (cf. Holtz-Bacha, 1993; Holtz-Bacha & Kaid, 1993; Holtz-Bacha, Kaid, &
Chanslor, 1995)

Tables 3.3 and 3.4 take these findings from the multiple variance analysis into
account and presents a comparison of the candidate images of East and West German
subjects before and after the spots were shown.[7] Besides the individual evaluations two
things are remarkable here. East Germans change their ratings more often than their West
German counterparts which confirms the finding from the thermometer scale that
subjects in the East seem to be more affected by the spots than in the West. Also, there is
much more change in the ratings for the challengers from the SPD than for the incumbent
chancellor. It seems plausible to attribute these findings to the fact that Helmut Kohl as
the incumbent in 1990 and 1994 was more visible in the media and thus much better
known than Lafontaine and Scharping who, as prime ministers of West German states, do
not get that much attention outside the campaign.

Table 3.3 - Candidate Image Before and After Presentation of Spots: 1990

	1990				1990			
	Helmut Kohl				Oskar Lafontaine			
	East		West		East		West	
	pre	post	pre	post	pre	post	pre	post
Qualified	3.5	3.8*	3.2	3.5*	5.2	5.5*	4.8	4.8
Sophisticated	3.8	3.7	2.8	2.9	5.0	5.3	4.9	5.0
Honest	2.8	2.9	3.5	3.5	5.1	5.4*	4.8	4.9
Believable	3.1	2.9	3.4	3.2	5.0	5.1	4.6	4.7
Successful	5.6	5.5	5.6	5.5	3.8	4.2**	3.7	3.9*
Attractive	2.5	2.6	2.4	2.3	4.3	4.4	4.0	3.9
Friendly	3.8	3.9	4.2	4.2	5.1	5.4*	4.8	4.9
Sincere	4.8	5.0	4.8	4.7	5.4	5.5	4.9	4.8
Calm	4.3	4.0*	4.5	4.6	3.4	3.2	3.3	3.3
Not aggressive	4.2	4.0	4.4	4.3	4.1	4.2	3.5	3.5
Strong	4.4	4.2	4.3	4.6	4.7	5.1*	4.7	4.6
Active	4.6	4.8	4.2	4.2	5.8	5.9	5.5	5.3*

* $p \le .05$ ** $p \le .00$

Table 3.4 - Candidate Image Before and After Presentation of Spots: 1994

| | Helmut Kohl | | | | Rudolf Scharping | | | |
| | East | | West | | East | | West | |
	pre	post	pre	post	pre	post	pre	post
Qualified	4.5	4.4	4.2	4.2	4.2	4.3	4.5	4.5
Sophisticated	4.2	4.3	3.8	3.9	4.1	4.1	4.1	4.1
Honest	3.3	3.2	2.9	2.9	4.4	4.6	4.4	4.7**
Believable	3.7	3.4	3.5	3.1*	4.2	4.2	4.3	4.3
Successful	5.4	5.3	5.2	5.3	4.0	4.2	3.8	3.7
Attractive	3.0	2.9	2.6	2.5	3.5	3.6	3.7	3.8
Friendly	3.8	4.1	3.4	3.5	4.7	5.1**	4.7	4.9
Sincere	5.0	4.7**	5.1	4.8**	4.6	5.0**	5.2	5.0
Calm	3.6	3.5	4.0	4.0	4.7	4.9	4.7	5.1**
Not aggressive	4.0	3.6*	3.6	3.7	4.5	4.9**	4.6	5.1**
Strong	4.9	5.1	4.9	5.0	4.0	4.0	3.7	3.7
Active	4.7	4.7	4.4	4.4	4.7	4.6	4.5	4.2**

* $p \leq .05$ ** $p \leq .00$

The answers to an open-ended question asking subjects to describe which aspects in the design of the spots stood out show that it is not only the candidate to whom respondents in East and West react differently. In both studies West Germans, more often than East Germans, mentioned the use of national symbols as the flag and the national colors and referred to them in a negative way.

CONCLUSION

Different from the East European countries presented in this book Germany provided the opportunity of a quasi natural experiment with the possibility of comparing subjects from East and West. West Germans, familiar with the style of electoral advertising as used in the campaigns of 1990 and 1994 and also more familiar with the candidates, on the one side, and East Germans, socialized in a different political system, on the other. While the parties with East German origin at once adapted to the West German style of electoral advertising and presented highly professional spots, significant differences between East and West German respondents stand out in the reactions to the spots and to the candidates. The instruments measuring the impact of the ads on the image of the top candidates have shown that East Germans reacted more sensibly to the presentation of the spots and changed their evaluation of the candidates more than West Germans. This is particularly true for the images of the challenger candidates who probably, due to less visibility in the news media, were less known to subjects in the East. Their images might have been less distinct than the image of the incumbent chancellor and were therefore more open to change.

The comparison of 1990 and 1994 also shows that the differences between East and West are continuous. This can be attributed to a long-term effect of political socialization that is not quickly outweighed by new political experiences in unified Germany. Several studies have proved considerable differences of East and West Germans in political culture and media use (cf. for example Bergem, 1993; Schmitt-Beck, 1994) which are also reflected in the findings of this study. The findings suggest a particular interest in analyzing subsequent elections and to determine whether differences in East an West in reactions to spots can be seen in the 1998 and future elections.

REFERENCES

Becker, J. (Ed.). (1990). *Wahlwerbung politischer Parteien im Rundfunk. Symposium zum 65. Geburtstag von Ernst W. Fuhr* (pp. 31-40). Baden-Baden, Germany: Nomos.

Bergem, W. (1993). *Tradition und Transformation. Zur politischen Kultur in Deutschland.* [Tradition and transformation. Political culture in Germany.] Opladen, Germany: Westdeutscher Verlag.

Bornemann, R. (1992). Ideenwerbung im Rundfunk. [Ideological advertising in broadcasting.] In Bayerische Landeszentrale für neue Medien (Ed.), *BLM Jahrbuch 92. Privater Rundfunk in Bayern* (pp. 127-138). München, Germany: R. Fischer.

Dröge, F., Lerg, W. B., & Weißenborn, R. (1969). Zur Technik politischer Propaganda in der Demokratie. Analyse der Fernseh-Wahlwerbesendungen der Parteien im Wahlkampf 1969 [The technique of political propaganda in a democracy. Analysis of the TV party ads during the 1969 election campaign.] In *Fernsehen in Deutschland. Die Bundestagswahl 1969 als journalistische Aufgabe* (pp. 107-142). Mainz, Germany: v. Hase & Koehler.

Feist, U., & Liepelt, K. (1994). Auseinander oder miteinander? Zum unterschiedlichen Politikverständnis der Deutschen in Ost und West. [Separately or together? The different political culture of the Germans in the East and in the West.] In H.-D. Klingemann & M. Kaase (Eds.), *Wahlen und Wähler. Analysen aus Anlaß der Bundestagswahl 1990* (pp. 575-611). Opladen, Germany: Westdeutscher Verlag.

Gabriel-Bräutigam, K. (1991). Wahlkampf im Rundfunk. Eine Beitrag zur Problematik von Drittsendungsrechten. [The campaign in broadcasting. A chapter on the problem of the right to broadcast ads.] *Zeitschrift für Urheber- und Medienrecht, 35*, 466-478.

Holtz-Bacha, C. (1990). Nur bei den Wasserwerken Effekte? Eine Studie zur parteipolitischen Spot-Werbung vor Europawahlen. [Only effects at the water works? A study on party spots during the European election campaign.] *medium, 20*, 50-53.

Holtz-Bacha, C. (1993, May). *Television spots in the German elections: Content and effects.* Paper presented at the conference of the International Communication Association, Washington, DC.

Holtz-Bacha, C., & Kaid, L. L. (1993). Wahlspots im Fernsehen. Eine Analyse der Parteienwerbung zur Bundestagswahl 1990. [Electoral spots on TV. A analysis of party advertising during the 1990 election campaign.] In C. Holtz-Bacha & L. L.

Kaid (Eds.), *Die Massenmedien im Wahlkampf. Untersuchungen aus dem Wahljahr 1990* (pp. 46-71). Opladen, Germany: Westdeutscher Verlag.

Holtz-Bacha, C., & Kaid, L. L. (1995). Television spots in German national elections: Content and effects. In L. L. Kaid & C. Holtz-Bacha (Eds.), *Political advertising in Western democracies: Parties and candidates on television* (pp. 61-88). Thousand Oaks, CA: Sage.

Holtz-Bacha, C., Kaid, L. L., & Chanslor, M. (1995, May). *Audience reactions to election campaign spots in Germany. A comparison of 1990 and 1994*. Paper presented at the Convention of the International Communication Association in Albuquerque, NM.

Jesse, E. (1994). Institutionelle Rahmenbedingungen der Bundestagswahl vom 2. Dezember 1990. [The institutional framework of the Bundestag election on December 2, 1990.] In H.-D. Klingemann, & M. Kaase (Eds.), *Wahlen und Wähler. Analysen aus Anlaß der Bundestagswahl 1990* (pp. 15-41). Opladen, Germany: Westdeutscher Verlag.

Kaid, L. L. (1991). The effects of television broadcasts on perceptions of political candidates in the United States and France. In L. L. Kaid, J. Gerstlé, & K. R. Sanders (Eds.), *Mediated politics in two cultures: Presidential campaigning in the United States and France* (pp. 247-60). New York: Praeger.

Kaid, L. L. (1996). "Und dann, auf der Wahlparty..." Reaktionen auf Wahlwerbespots: Computergestützte Messungen. ["Und dann, auf der Wahlparty..." Reactions to electoral spots: Computer-assisted measurements.] In C. Holtz-Bacha, & L. L. Kaid (Eds.), *Wahlen und Wahlkampf in den Medien. Untersuchungen aus dem Wahljahr 1994* (pp. 208-224). Opladen, Germany: Westdeutscher Verlag.

Kaid, L. L., & Boydston, J. (1987). An experimental study of the effectiveness of negative political advertising. *Communication Quarterly, 35*, 193-201.

Kaid, L. L., Downs, V. C., & Ragan, S. (1990). Political argumentation and violations of audience expectations: An analysis of the Bush-Rather encounter. *Journal of Broadcasting and Electronic Media, 34*, 1-15.

Kaid, L. L., & Holtz-Bacha, C. (1993). Der Einfluß von Wahlspots auf die Wahrnehmung der Spitzenkandidaten. [The influence of electoral spots on the perception of the top candidates.] In C. Holtz-Bacha & L. L. Kaid (Eds.), *Die Massenmedien im Wahlkampf. Untersuchungen aus dem Wahljahr 1990* (pp. 185-207). Opladen, Germany: Westdeutscher Verlag.

Klein, T. (1992). *Zum Wandel des Kommunikationsstils in Wahlwerbespots von 1972 bis 1990*. [The change of the style of the electoral ads from 1972 until 1990.] Diplomarbeit Universität Erlangen-Nürnberg, Germany (unpublished manuscript).

Sanders, K. R. & Pace, T. J. (1977). The influence of speech communication on the image of a political candidate: "Limited Effects" revisited. In B. Ruben (Ed.), *Communication Yearbook I* (pp. 465-474). New Brunswick, NJ: Transaction.

Schmitt-Beck, R. (1994). Vermittlungsumwelten westdeutscher und ostdeutscher Wähler: Interpersonale Kommunikation, Massenkommunikation und Parteipräferenzen vor der Bundestagswahl 1990. [Communicative environments of West and East German voters: Interpersonal communication, mass communication and party preferences before the Bundestag election in 1990.] In H. Rattinger, O. W. Gabriel, & W. Jagodzinski (Eds.), *Wahlen und politische Einstellungen im vereinigten Deutschland* (pp. 189-234). Frankfurt a. M., Germany: Peter Lang.

Wachtel, M. (1988). *Die Darstellung von Vertrauenswürdigkeit in Wahlwerbespots: Eine argumentationsanalytische und semiotische Untersuchung zum Bundestagswahlkampf 1987*. [The presentation of trustworthiness in electoral spots: A study analyzing the argumentational and semiotic style during the 1987 campaign for the Bundestag election.] Tübingen, Germany: Max Niemeyer.

Zentralverband der deutschen Werbewirtschaft (1993). *Werbung in Deutschland 1993*. Bonn, Germany: Zentralverband der deutschen Werbewirtschaft.

NOTES

1. The CSU (Christlich-Soziale Union) only exists in the state of Bavaria. It forms a permanent coalition with the CDU, that in turn does not run for election in Bavaria.

2. The author would like to thank Andreas Weiß (University of Mainz) for his help with the data analysis and Sonja Jürschik (University of Mainz) who made transcriptions of the ads of the East German parties.

3. Percentages refer to the spots shown on public TV only.

4. Several accounts of the differences of the political culture in East and West Germany have been published in the meantime. Among others cf. Bergem, 1993; Feist & Liepelt, 1994.

5. Asterisks indicate significant differences between pre- and post-test ratings within a group and not between groups (East/West).

6. The overall higher popularity of the SPD candidate among the sample is of no relevance to the study. Because the experiment aimed at studying how the spots and the presented issues and candidates were perceived, and whether the spots led to changes in the candidate images, the good or not so good evaluation of the candidates is less important.

7. Asterisks indicating significant differences refer to the comparison of pre- ad post-test ratings and do not show differences between East and West Germans.

Chapter 4

TELEVISION SPOTS IN POLISH PRESIDENTIAL ELECTIONS

Wojciech Cwalina, Andrzej Falkowski, and Bohdan Roznowski

Social, political, and economic changes in Poland after 1989 had a strong impact on Polish life in all respects. Pointing toward democracy forced authorities to accept the necessity of the co-existence of different, sometimes contradictory, political ideas and programs. This pluralistic approach to democracy influenced also the public thinking on the completely different worlds of the economy and politics. In some respects, such as political advertising in national elections, the new born Polish political system grew more similar to established Western democracies. In other respects, there were differences due to the leftover elements of communism that still influence Polish social, political, and economic life. This chapter analyzes political advertising in Poland, looking at both the strategies used by political parties and at the public reactions. First, the political structures and media system characteristics are described, followed by results of the analysis of empirical research on the effects of political spots in the 1995 Polish presidential election.

TRADITIONS AND STRUCTURE OF POLISH DEMOCRACY

Although many observers point to 1989 as the birth of democracy in Poland, this is not strictly true. The year 1989 can be treated only as a revival of democracy in Polish history. Therefore, it is worthwhile to recount the basic Polish traditions of democracy and the social-political system.

Poland is the second country in the world (the U.S.A. being the first one), and the first one in Europe, in which democratic rules were adopted. When the famous 3rd May Constitution of 1791 was established, new national institutions were brought into being in the First Polish Republic. Pioneer Poland's work in the propagation of democracy had a short life, however. Over the next hundred years Poland was removed from the world map and was partitioned into three separate parts governed by Russia, Prussia, and the Austro-Hungarian Empire, respectively. A democratic renaissance took place when the Second Polish Republic (RP) of 11 November 1918 began (not counting the Constitutional Principality of Warsaw in Napoleonic times). In this year Poland regained its independence. After the elected parliament (Seym + Senate, both forming the National Assembly) proclaimed the constitution, Gabriel Narutowicz was appointed the first President of RP for a seven year term; one week later he was assassinated. Between the wars Poland had two more presidents: Stanislaw Wojciechowski (1922-1926) and Ignacy Mosicki (1926-1939).

After the outbreak of the Second World War the formal democratic institution of the Polish President existed in exile until December 22, 1990, when the insignia of presidential power were handed over to the elected President of the Third Polish Republic, Lech Walesa. During part of this intervening period, the presidency existed in a duality in which there was a "president in exile" out of the country and a Communist Party president who functioned as a puppet for the Soviet Union. Later, as a result of both the democratic changes and an agreement between the Solidarity and Communist Party (PZPR or the Polish United Workers' Party), the Parliament appointed general Wojciech Jaruzelski as President. He held the office until the first general election in which Solidarity leader Lech Walesa won.

As a result of intense economic crisis in 1989, social disquiet and a wave of strikes inspired by the still illegal Solidarity Movement heightened concerns about needed reforms. In this same time Michail Gorbachev started the reconstruction (so called *perestroika*) of the U.S.S.R. These as well as some others factors forced the Communist authorities in Poland to negotiate with the opposition possible changes in the Polish political system. New agreements on the parliament and procedures for presidential elections were finalized in 1989 (Gebethner, 1992; Skórzynski, 1995). In the parliamentary elections following these reforms, Polish voters gave resounding support to the Solidarity candidates (Skórzynski, 1995); the Parliament re-appointed General Jaruzelski, leader of communistic party, as President of RP. One of the sign of evolving democracy was the dissolving of the PZPR party (the Polish United Workers' Party) and founding in its place the SdRP party (the Social-democracy of the Polish Republic) in January, 1990.

Current Parliamentary System in Poland

Under the current parliamentary system, legislative authority is controlled by a two-chamber Parliament that constitutes the National Assembly of 560 parliamentarians with terms that last four years: Seym (lower chamber) with 460 members; Senate (higher chamber) with 100 members.

The costs of electoral campaigns are covered by parties, and then partially reimbursed by the government's budget for winning parties. The election campaign starts the day of its announcement by the president and ends 24 hours before the vote day. From the twelfth day before the election day, no electoral publicity is allowed.

Since 1989 there have been two general parliamentary elections (1991 and 1993) that have been conducted according to two different sets of electoral rules. The elections of October 27, 1991, were general elections in which everyone over 18 with Polish citizenship or who had lived in Poland at least 5 years (active franchise) could vote. To be elected to Seym (passive franchise), one had to be at least 21 years old (Dziennik Ustaw, 1991a). The elections of September 19, 1993, were also general elections, but different sets of rules governed Parliamentary selection and voting. Members of the Seym were selected from regional and general lists of candidates, and minimum percentages were placed on parties in order to achieve representation. On the other hand, elections to the Senate were completely democratic (Dziennik Ustaw, 1991b, 1994).

These changes in electoral rules resulted in destabilization of the Polish political scene. Gebethner (1995) states that every election would cause a perverted arrangement of forces in Parliament in comparison to votes received by political parties. The main reason for this state of affairs was the election rule to maintain both a proportionality and electoral thresholds (5% for parties and 8% for coalitions). As a result, 34.35% of voters were not represented in the Seym. One clear result of these rules was that right-oriented parties (originating from Solidarity) suffered from these changes.

Presidential Elections

As mentioned earlier, on July 19, 1989, the Parliament appointed General Wojciech Jaruzelski as President of the Polish People's Republic (PRL). Although he was the only candidate for the office, his election was not assured until the last moment. The Communist leader was chosen thanks to the electoral exclusion of Solidarity representatives. Seven of them cast invalid votes, four did not take part in the election, and one voted for Jaruzelski. For the second time since Parliamentary elections, the opposition did not take advantage of their political domination (Skórzynski, 1995).

The first general election for president took place in November (first ballot) and in December (second ballot) of 1990, according to new established, electoral rules which are still in place. Under these rules, presidential elections are general elections. Every Polish citizen over 18 and everyone who has lived in Poland for at least 5 years regardless of citizenship is entitled to vote. To be a candidate for president, one must be supported by at least 100,000 potential voter signatures. The costs of the campaign of a particular candidate are covered by the candidate's electoral committee. Presidential campaigning is banned on the voting day and in the 36 hours before that day (so called "pre-election silence"). The process of the election is overseen by a special appointed institution, called the "National Electoral Committee." The president of the RP is elected for a 5-year term (Dziennik Ustaw, 1990). The presidential office in Poland is modeled after those in Finland and France (Gebethner, 1992).

In 1990 in this first true presidential election, six candidates competed. They fought very aggressively using negative advertisements frequently. Although the electoral turnout was relatively high, the first vote was not conclusive. In the second vote, which pitted the two top vote getters against each other, Solidarity leader Lech Walesa was the winner.

During Walesa's five years in the presidency the political-economic situation changed considerably. Political parties that had originated from Solidarity underwent both subdivision and polarization, partly as a result of investigations designed to uncover officials who had collaborated with the Communist regime. In this environment, post-communists were committed to remaking themselves in the hope of hiding their communist past from society.

Therefore, the results of the 1995 presidential election were uncertain from the beginning. Seventeen candidates declared their candidacies initially, but four resigned, leaving thirteen candidates in the first ballot (Olszewski, 1995). As in 1990, there was a high election turnout in 1995 for the first vote, but no candidate received a majority. The two leading candidates advanced to the second vote: incumbent President Lech Walesa, supported by most post-Solidarity and rightist parties, and Aleksander Kwašniewski, supported by the post-communist party, the SLD (Democratic Left Alliance). At this point, the political campaigning changed from relatively soft into a sharp and brutal battle. The result was not clear until the last moment when Kwašniewski won with 51.7% of the vote.

For many Poles it seemed like a personal defeat. The election results caused a wave of protests as people insisted that the election be invalidated because Kwašniewski had lied about having a higher education degree. Almost 600,000 electoral protests were filed in the courts which ruled eventually that the 1995 election was valid. The court verdict was that the presidential election of November 19, 1995 was valid, although a number of judges dissented (Kesicka & Jachowicz, 1995).

Televised Political Advertisements and Regulations

Political advertisements were not a part of the Polish political scene before 1989. Until then television was completely controlled by the existing Communist Party; thus, there was no need to inform citizens about opposition alternatives as they officially never existed (Koralewicz, 1990).

In Poland today there are two public TV channels that reach all Polish areas, TV1 and TV2 controlled indirectly by the Seym and the President. In addition, there is a well developed network of regional TV consisting of eleven centers located in the following cities: Warszawa, Lublin, Katowice, Lódz, Szczecin, Gdansk, Bydgoszcz, Wroclaw, Poznan, Kraków i Rzeszów. Within their reach are about 17.5 million viewers, 45% of the Polish population (Olejniczak, 1996). These TV centers, including the satellite channel "TV Polonia" which has existed since 1993, form a single company of the Treasury, "Polish Television Inc., S.A." with the Minister of Finance as the only shareholder. There is also one private TV entity that reaches all of Poland, Polsat TV. It obtained rights for broadcasting from the National Council of Broadcasting Corporation founded by the government.

The use of TV for electoral campaigns is strictly regulated. For parliamentary election, the candidate's electoral committee is entitled to cost-free broadcasting of election programs on public channels TV1, TV2, and on regional channels. The election programs are broadcast starting 15 days before the election day (until 1993 for one month before this day). Table 4.1 shows the allocation of such time in the 1991 and 1993 parliamentary elections.

Table 4.1 - Time Offered for Free Election Broadcasts in 1991 and 1993 Polish Parliamentary Elections

	Seym		Senate	
	1991	1993	1991	1993
Electoral programs within all-Polish reach (TV1 and TV2)	25-30 h.	15 h.	25-30 h.	5 h.
Electoral programs within regional reach (regional TV)	8-10 h.	10 h.	3-5 h.	6 h.

Source: Dziennik Ustaw 1991a, 1991b, 1993, 1994

Apart from the free time offered for parties to broadcast election programs, one can buy additional time, up to a limit of 15% of the free time given for the particular electoral committee (until 1993 the limit was 10%).

In September, 1993, between two and four election programs prepared by parties were broadcast daily. Each party was allowed to present itself for about 3 minutes in each allocated slot. In addition, there were special one-hour programs in which three members of different parties took part. Similarly, the programs were broadcast by regional TV. Each program started and ended with the message that the television channel was not responsible for its content.

Political advertisements in presidential campaigns appeared for the first time in 1990. Access to TV is equal and free for every registered candidate. The National Electoral Committee determines in detail the rules for broadcasting time in agreement with the National Council of Broadcasting Corporation. Furthermore, electoral committees of the parties/candidates can buy additional broadcasting time. Paid political advertisements are broadcast along with other product commercials within the ad block (Dziennik Ustaw, 1990).

On October 29, 1990, Polish Television broadcast the first electoral block "Candidates for RP Presidential Office." Each electoral committee had equal broadcasting time, 5 minutes within a half-hour program transmitted either by TV1 or TV2 during the highest audience times (from 6:30 to 7:30 p.m. and from 8:00 to 8:30 p.m.). In this first round of broadcast slots, Lech Walesa's spots stood out as high quality productions. The common element in all candidate programs was the assumption that the social and economic reality in Poland was in deep crisis. However, different candidates emphasized different sources or causes of this crisis, as well as different policies for economic recovery. The second common element related to the method of persuasion. Spots were filled with content designed to awaken feelings of fear and anxiety. This negative presentation of the current economic crises was used by the candidates to discredit their opponents. Each candidate focused on different aspects in their spots: Roman Bartoszcze stressed his peasant origins; Wlodzimierz Cimoszewicz promised help for poor, unemployed, and young people; Tadeusz Mazowiecki emphasized the "force of silence," caution, and dignity; Leszek Moczulski focused on patriotism and anti-communism; Stanislaw Tyminski presented himself as a successful businessman; Lech Walesa stressed the necessity to continue policies originated ten years before by Solidarity (Winiarska-Maziuk, 1991).

Since no candidate received a majority in the first ballot on November 25, 1990, the next series of election programs preceding the second ballot started on November 28. Broadcasting time was similar to that for first vote with the exception that programs lasted 20 minutes each and were divided into two equal 10-minute parts, each one for one candidate. The 1990 election climaxed with the direct meeting of the two candidates, Tyminski and Walesa, in a television debate. At the end of the 1990 election, of course, Lech Walesa took office as the first nationally-elected president in post-communist Poland.

In 1995 the presidential campaign on television started on October 20; TV1 broadcast 14 blocks of spots, TV2 aired 6 blocks, and TV Polonia which reaches many countries of the world provided 2 blocks. Each block consisted of 13 spots in the first round of the election (at the beginning it was 17 spots until 4 candidates resigned) and of 2 spots in the second round. The broadcast spots had two different lengths: 3 minutes, 30 seconds, and 5 minutes, 10 seconds. In the first round, each candidate had 16 time slots, and in the second round the final 2 candidates each received an additional 6 spots. In addition, 2 candidates purchased time for additional 30 seconds spots: Jan Olszewski for 2 spots and Waldemar Pawlak for 10 spots. Regional television and Polsat TV were not allowed to broadcast political advertisements.

Furthermore, discussion shows with candidates were presented throughout the week, except on Sunday, each day with one candidate, in both the first and the second rounds of the election. These discussion programs lasted 20 minutes in TV1 and one hour in TV2. They took place also in Polsat TV one time in a week.

With this background on the political and media system in Poland, the remainder of this chapter reports the results of research on television advertising from the 1995 presidential election. An analysis of the content and strategies used in the spots is followed by experimental findings about the effects of exposure to the spots on images and evaluations of the candidates.

APPROACH TO ESTABLISHING CONTENT AND MEASURING EFFECTS

For the content analysis of the spot content and strategies, the researchers selected 81 of the total of 220 spots broadcast by three channels of public television. Spots were drawn for all candidates who received at least 5% of the votes in the first election round. There were four such candidates: Aleksander Kwašniewski (35%), Lech Walesa (33%), Jacek Kuron (9%) and Jan Olszewski (7%). All of them together received 84% of the votes. Other candidates are grouped together under the "other" classification in the analysis. The spots were coded by three trained coders, and the coding instrument for the spots was based on earlier studies of Western democratic systems (Kaid & Holtz-Bacha, 1995b; Kaid & Johnston, 1991).

The experiments designed to measure the effects of exposure were also adopted from similar research carried out in other countries, including the U.S., Germany, France, and Italy (Kaid & Holtz-Bacha, 1995a). The objective was to study the reception of the spots and the changes in the candidate images. The research involved the administration of pretest questionnaires, the showing of television broadcasts, and the subsequent administration of a posttest questionnaire. The sample consisted of 203 voting-age students, representing a broad cross-section of university students at three universities in Poland: University of Lódz (Central Poland), Catholic University of Lublin, and M. Curie-Slodowska University in Lublin (Eastern Poland). Among the subjects were 39% male respondents and 61% female respondents; the average age was 21 years. The experimental sessions were conducted between November 10 and November 18, 1995 (after the first and before the second vote of presidential national election on November 19).

Between the pretest and posttest questionnaires the respondents were shown four television spots, two from Kwašniewski's and two from Walesa's electoral committees (the remaining two candidates in the second ballot vote). The pretest questionnaire consisted of demographic information, a thermometer scale to ascertain the general feeling toward each candidate, and a semantic differential scale, evaluating the candidates. The posttest questionnaire repeated the thermometer and the semantic differential scale on each candidate and also included several open-ended questions on issue, image, and visual recall.

The semantic differential scale consisted of 14 sets of bipolar adjectives, each rated on a 7-point range (see Table 4.3). This semantic differential scale was similar to those used in studies of political advertisements in other countries by Kaid (1995) and Kaid and Holtz-Bacha (1995a, 1995b).

CONTENT AND STRATEGIES IN THE SPOTS

Examination of the content of the spots indicates that a majority of spots were candidate-positive focused (93%). Only 7% of spots were opponent-negative focused: four for Olszewski and one for Walesa. Table 4.2 presents details of appeals and strategies used. The dominant type of appeal was emotional (67%). The logical appeal was used relatively rarely (21%). Interestingly, Walesa who was the incumbent president, did not rely on ethical or source credibility appeals in his spots.

Table 4.2 - Appeals and Strategies Used in Spots (N=81)

	All n (%)	Kwašniewski (n=7)	Walesa (n=6)	Others (n=68)
Focus:				
Candidate-positive focused	75(93) 6(7)	7	5	63
Opponent-negative focused		-	1	5
Dominant type of appeal:				
Logical	17(21)	-	2	15
Emotional	54(67)	7	4	43
Source credibility/ethos	10(12)	-	-	10
Dominant type of content:				
Partnership	3(4)	-	2	1
Issue concerns	41(50)	6	-	35
Policy preference	3(4)	-	-	3
Policy proposals	2(2)	-	-	2
Personal characteristics	24(30)	1	4	19
Group affiliations	8(10)	-	-	8

Content in the spots was dominated by issue concerns (50%), a finding that puts the Polish spots in line with those in most other Western democracies (Kaid & Holtz-Bacha, 1995b). Personal or image characteristics were dominant in 30% of the spots and were relied upon heavily by Walesa. Among the principal candidates, only Walesa appealed strongly to partisanship, and his spots were never dominated by issue concerns.

As the nonverbal behavior seems to be a significant one in the communication processes (Argyle, 1988; Dunckel & Parnham, 1990; Eichler, 1993; Pease, 1990; Watzlawick, 1967), its analysis in the spots is particularly interesting. Only 31% of the spots featured the candidate himself as the main speaker, and, interestingly, neither of the two major candidates (Walesa and Kwasniewski remaining in the second ballot) produced any spots in which he was the main speaker. This was partly due to the more sophisticated production techniques used by these candidates. Their spots were professionally produced and contained a number of special effects techniques designed to get and hold audience attention. Most candidates sought to maintain eye contact with the audience (37%) to create a sense of sincerity and credibility. Only Kwašniewski seemed to avoid this form of behavior. Candidates rarely smiled in their spots (22%) and in general showed little body movement. The exception to the movement category was the spots of Kwašniewski who often appeared dynamic and energetic in his presentations.

EFFECTS OF THE SPOTS

Results from the experiments in which audiences were shown spots and asked their opinions toward the candidates indicated that the Social-democracy of the Polish Republic (SdRP) candidate Aleksander Kwašniewski was rated more positively than the incumbent president Lech Walesa. Before presentations of the spots Walesa was rated at an average of 36.4 on the feeling thermometer (range of 1 to 100); Kwašniewski achieved an average rating of 46.0. After watching the spots, evaluation of both candidates increased to 39.3 for Walesa and 47.4 for Kwašniewski.

Effects on Candidate Evaluations

A multiple variance analysis was applied to ascertain the factors influencing the classification of the two politicians on the thermometer scale. The time (pretest vs. posttest separately for each candidate) and the candidate (Walesa vs. Kwašniewski) as independent factors were included in the analysis.

The results shows that the candidate variable proves to be the significant main effect, $F(1,202)=6.83$; $p=.01$). Also watching the spots influenced the evaluation of the candidates as the analysis provided another significant main effect for time (pretest vs. posttest), $F(1,202)=17.63$; $p<.001$). Figure 4.1 shows the overall picture of evaluating candidates on the thermometer scale.

The evaluation of both Lech Walesa and Aleksander Kwašniewski increased with the presentation of the spots which means that the spots helped both candidates in a positive way. The interesting finding is that Kwašniewski was substantially better evaluated in the pretest as well as in the posttest, than Walesa, which seems intriguing in the light of Kwasniewski's Communist Party origins and in the context of general rejection of the political communistic system by the Polish people. One can hypothesize that Kwašniewski was better evaluated by those who voted for him than Walesa was by his own voters. Therefore, we attempted to provide further analysis by splitting the subjects into groups according to how candidates were rated on the thermometer scale. Figure 4.2 confirms this hypothesis, showing that the difference in thermometer ratings of Walesa and Kwašniewski was greater for Kwašniewski's electorate than for the electorate of Walesa. Furthermore, Kwašniewski was better evaluated by his electorate than Walesa was evaluated by his own electorate.

Figure 4.1

Thermometer Ratings of Candidates Before and After Spot Viewing

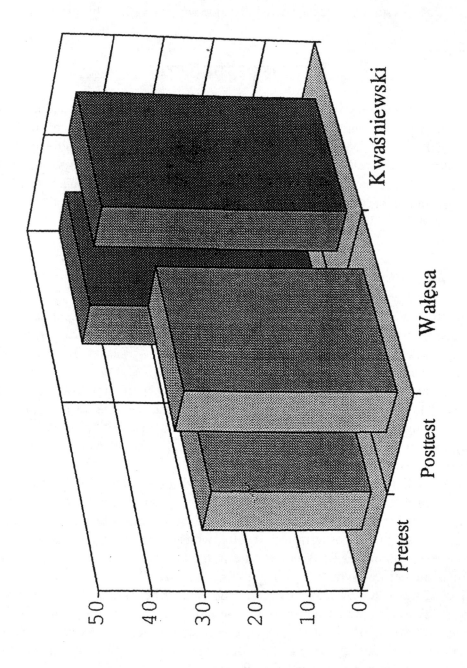

Figure 4.2

Thermometer Ratings of Both Candidates by their Separate Electorates

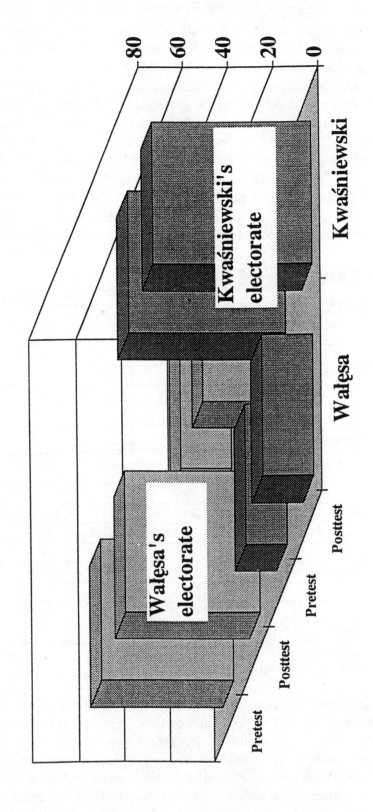

A similar method was used for the analysis of the candidate evaluations on the semantic differential. As for the thermometer scale,. a multiple variance analysis (MANOVA) with 14 attributes scales was chosen. The reliability coefficient (Cronbach's alpha for pretest and posttest for both candidates is $\alpha=0.87$. The MANOVA procedure produced significant main effects for the *candidate*, F(1,189)=16.7; $p<.0001$), but for Kwašniewski *time* was not significant, F(1,190)= 0.35, $p=.553$), although it was significant for Walesa, F(1,194)=5.01, $p=.03$). Additionally, the t-test was applied to find significant differences between the evaluation of candidates in pretest and posttest for each of 14 attribute scales. Table 4.3 shows these results for Lech Walesa and Aleksander Kwašniewski before and after presentation of the spots. All attributes are coded with a high value representing a more positive attitude, but in the questionnaire the attributes were alternately given on the right and left side to prevent a uniform response behavior.

Table 4.3 - Candidate image before and after viewing of spots

	Kwašniewski		Walesa	
	Pretest	Posttest	Pretest	Posttest
Qualified	5.29	5.56**	3.21	3.49**
Open for World	5.27	5.41	4.01	4.26*
Honest	3.84	4.05*	4.26	4.57*
Believable	3.96	4.21*	3.55	3.97**
Successful	4.73	4.91	3.56	3.95**
Attractive	5.09	5.11	2.89	3.17**
Respectable	5.27	5.39	3.00	3.46**
Calm	5.43	5.44	2.12	2.55**
Not aggressive	5.01	5.18	2.78	2.85
Strong	5.14	5.13	4.47	4.57
Active	5.71	5.64	4.74	4.76
Believing Christian	3.21	3.28	5.87	5.76
Sophisticated	3.62	3.73	4.30	4.21
Friendly	4.72	4.89	3.93	4.15*
Overall image	66.29	67.93	52.69	55.72

* t-test between pretest and posttest is significant at 0.05
** t-test between pretest and posttest is significant at 0.01

Aleksander Kwašniewski received better evaluations than Lech Walesa on almost all attributes in both the pretest and posttest. Only on three items did Walesa receive better ratings: "honest", "believing Christian", and "sophisticated." For Lech Walesa the difference between pretest and posttest was much larger than for Aleksander Kwašniewski which indicates that evaluation of the latter candidate was more stable, and the spots did not influence his evaluation in any significant way. This results seems to be compatible with Blumler and McQuail's (1968) conclusion that advertisements do affect some voters' opinions when the voters are undecided while deep-seated attitudes remain impervious. The voter is more undecided when the difference in thermometer ratings of the two candidates is small while a big difference indicates that the voter already has clear opinions about the candidates. In the first case, which applies to the Walesa electorate, the voter is susceptible to persuasion, while in the second case, corresponding to the electorate of Kwašniewski, the voter opinions of the candidates are already well polarized. In general this analysis shows that spots can change the image of candidates, and, in this case, the change always stands for an image enhancement.

Recall from the Television Spots

Another way of evaluating the effects of the spots was to determine what voters remembered from them. Respondents were asked in open-ended questions to indicate what they liked and disliked about Walesa and Kwašniewski. Similar to previous research in other countries (Kaid & Holtz-Bacha, 1995a), the answers were categorized according to subject matter and were also classified as to whether each item mentioned was an image characteristic of the candidate or a reference to an issue position or stance. The results are shown in Table 4.4.

Table 4.4 - Comparison of Likes and Dislikes from Polish Political Spots

		Walesa	Kwašniewski
Likes	Image characteristics	85%	66%
	Issues	15%	34%
Dislikes	Image characteristics	66%	69%
	Issues	34%	31%

Include only those attributes that were mentioned by at least 10% of subjects.

After viewing the spots, recall about both Kwašniewski and Walesa consistently focused on likes and dislikes related to their image characteristics. However, recall about Kwašniewski focused more on likes and dislikes related to his position on issues. This pattern, to some extent, is reinforced when examining the specific issues recalled about each candidate from the spots. For example, many more different issues were recalled from Kwašniewski's spots than from those of Walesa. In addition, Kwašniewski's issues concentrated around present and future problems (e.g., unemployment, entry to European Union) while Walesa's issues concerned the past (e.g., fight against communism in the past and in the present). The issues recalled from Kwašniewski's spots were also more concrete in nature while Walesa were more vague and general. There was only one issue common to both candidates in their spots, "Entry to NATO."

In addition to the issues in the broadcasts, the respondents were also asked to list the personal characteristics of the politicians they felt had been stressed in the spots. Kwašniewski generated far more personal image mentions than Walesa.

SUMMARY AND CONCLUSIONS

The results of the experiment and of the content analysis allow some conclusions about the Polish political scene. It is important to remember that the current form of democracy in Poland is very young and came into being after 40 years of a totalitarian system. Thus, it seems reasonable to expect considerable differences, compared with Western societies. In terms of spot content, however, there were many similarities to other countries, including a high concentration on issues and a positive, rather than negative, focus (Kaid & Holtz-Bacha, 1995b). The first noticeable difference in the Polish political spots, compared to findings in other countries, is that the spots helped both the candidates in a positive way. In most of the studies and countries where this experiment has been performed, only one of the candidates has been affected (i.e., Bush in 1988 and 1992 in the U. S., Lafontaine in eastern Germany in 1990, etc.), and sometimes it has been in a negative way (Chirac, 1988, France) (Kaid & Holtz-Bacha, 1995a, 1995b). This intriguing result might be related to the relative "newness" of television spots in the electoral system in Poland.

The experiment also showed that Kwaśniewski's electorate evaluated their candidate more positively than Walesa's electorate evaluated him. Furthermore, the difference in both thermometer as well as in overall image ratings of Walesa and Kwaśniewski was greater for Kwaśniewski's electorate than for the electorate of Walesa. Thus, one can ask why was this so? The answer may lie in the mentality of the Polish people who spent most of their lives under the Communistic totalitarian system. If one takes into account that Kwaśniewski belonged to the Communist Party and was a minister in the Communist government before 1989, the answer seems to be clear in the context of the cognitive theory of affect. Namely, it has been empirically proved that a relationship exists between repeated exposure to an event and liking of the event. This interesting phenomena, known as the "mere exposure" effect, was described by Zajonc (1968) who explicitly stated that the liking for and attractiveness of a stimulus increases as the number of exposures increases. Exposure builds a feeling of familiarity that individuals interpret as affect for the stimulus, even in those cases in which the stimulus is subconsciously processed. Thus, the exposure effect is a significant factor in forming an individual's preferences for objects and events. Something which is repeatedly experienced seems to be close, liked, and attractive while something which is seen for the first time seems to be distant, neutral, and unattractive. In addition, the previous five years of Walesa's presidency decreased positive feelings toward him and dispelled his myth as a great leader.

REFERENCES

Ajnenkel, A. (Ed.) (1991). *Prezydenci Polski*. Warszawa: Wydawnictwo Sejmowe.

Argyle, M. (1988). *Bodily communication*. London: Methuen

Blumler, J.G., & McQuail, D. (1968). *Television in politics*. London: Faber and Faber.

Dunckel, J., & Parnham, E. (1990). *Effective speaking for business success*. St-Laurent, Quebeck: M&A Marketing Communications Inc.

Dziennik Ustaw RP (1990). 2 pazdziernika, Nr 67, 933-940. Warszawa: Urzad Rady Ministrów.

Dziennik Ustaw RP (1991a). 19 sierpnia, Nr 72, 993-1056. Warszawa: Urzad Rady Ministrów.

Dziennik Ustaw RP (1991b). 3 lipca, Nr 59, 777-792. Warszawa: Urzad Rady Ministrów.

Dziennik Ustaw RP (1993). 2 czerwca, Nr 45, 841-864. Warszawa: Urzad Rady Ministrów.

Dziennik Ustaw RP (1994). 27 kwietnia, Nr 54, 1045-1056. Warszawa: Urzad Rady Ministrów.

Dziennik Ustaw RP (1995a). 10 listopada, Nr 126, 2809-2815. Warszawa: Urzad Rady Ministrów.

Dziennik Ustaw RP (1995b). 23 listopada, Nr 131, 2885-2888. Warszawa: Urzad Rady Ministrów.

Eicher, J. (1993). *Making the message clear*. Grinder, Delozier & Associates.

Gebethner, S. (1992). Political institutions in the process of transition to a postsocialist formation: Polish and comparative perspectives. In W. D. Connor & P. Ploszajski (Eds.), *Escape from Socialism: The Polish route* (pp. 231-254). Warszawa: IFIS Publishers.

Gebethner, S. (1995). System wyborczy: Deformacja czy reprezentacja?. In S. Gebethner (Ed.), *Wybory parlamentarne 1991 i 1993*. Warszawa: Wydawnictwo Sejmowe.

Jasiewicz, K. (1992). Polish elections of 1990: Beyond the "Pospolite Ruszenie." In W. D. Connor & P. Ploszajski (Eds.), *Escape from Socialism: The Polish route* (pp. 181-198). Warszawa: IFIS Publishers.

Kaid, L. L. (1995). Measuring candidate images with semantic differentials. In K. Hacker (Ed.), *Candidate images in presidential election campaigns* (pp. 131-134). New York: Praeger.

Kaid, L., L., Johnston, A. (1991). Negative versus positive television advertising in U.S. presidential campaigns, 1960-1988. *Journal of Communication, 41(3)*, 53-64.

Kaid, L., L.,& Holtz-Bacha, C. (Eds.). (1995a). *Political advertising in Western democracies*. Thousand Oaks: Sage Publications.

Kaid, L., L. & Holtz-Bacha, C. (1995b). Political advertising across cultures: Comparing content, styles and effects. In L. L. Kaid & C. Holtz-Bacha (Eds.), *Political advertising in Western democracies* (pp. 206-227). Thousand Oaks: Sage Publications.

Kesicka, K., & Jachowicz, J. (1995). Prezydent, ale.... *Gazeta Wyborcza*, 11 grudnia, Nr 287.1975, p.1.

Koralewicz, J. (1989). Autorytaryzm a poglady polityczne Polaków. In J. Reykowski, K. Skarzynska, & M. Ziólkowski (Eds.), *Orientacje spoleczne jako element mentalnosci* (pp. 77-92). Poznan: Nakom.

Olejniczak, H. (1996). Wotwarte karty. *Businessman Magazine*, luty, Nr 2(59), pp.108-109.

Olszewski, K. (1995). Kandydaci w wyborach prezydenckich'95. *Rzeczpospolita*, 29 wrzeznia, Nr 226(4179), p.3

Pease, A. (1990). *Body language. How to read others' thoughts by their gestures.* London: Sheldon Press.

Rocznik Statystyczny 1990 (1990). Warszawa: Glówny Urzad Statystyczny.

Rocznik Statystyczny 1995 (1995). Warszawa: Glówny Urzad Statystyczny.

Skórzynski, J. (1995). *Ugoda i rewolucja. Wladza i opozycja 1985-1989.* Warszawa: Presspublica.

Watzlawick, P. (1967). *Pragmatics of human communication.* New York: Norton.

Winiarska-Maziuk, A. (1991). Kampania wyborcza w telewizji. In M. Grabowska & I. Krzeminski (Eds.), *Bitwa o Belweder* (pp. 145-163). Warszawa: Wydawnictwo Literackie, Wydawnictwo Mysl.

Zajonc, R. B. (1968). Attitudinal effects of mere exposure. *Journal of Personality and Social Psychology Supplement, 9 (June),* 1-27

Chapter 5

POLITICAL ADVERTISING IN BULGARIAN TELEVISION, 1990-1997

Lilia Raycheva

The collapse of the totalitarian regime in Bulgaria brought about profound changes throughout the whole social system of the country. For more than four decades *The Communist Party* dominated the functions of the State, curtailing the rights and liberties of the people. An atmosphere encouraging social obedience in line with the propaganda requirements reigned in the country and freedom of expression was limited. Normal political life was practically non-existent in Bulgaria. Only two parties, *The Bulgarian Communist Party*, and its satellite, *The Bulgarian Agrarian People's Union*, were legal in the country. Paradoxically, membership of the Agrarians in their own organization had to be approved by the Communist apparatus. There were no election campaigns, because there were no opposition parties, nor were any worthy sociological surveys carried out. Any monitoring of the public's mood catered to a tight circle of ruling party officials and never made its way into the media. The recurring result of 99 per cent electoral participation and support for the political *status quo* naturally aroused doubts in all thinking people. However, any reliable information demonstrating whether these data coincided with the actual vote was absent.

The ideas of *glasnost* and *perestroyka* launched after 1985 opened the doors for political discussions in Bulgaria. The first dissident associations, however small, found a willing audience among the public. The most prominent of them were: *The Committee for Ecological Defence of Rouse* (a town on the Danube, suffering for a long time from suffocating gases drifting along from a chemical plant across the river in neighboring Romania), *The Independent Society for Protection of Human Rights*, *The Club for Glasnost and Perestroyka*, *Ecoglasnost* (Ecological Publicity), and *The Podkrepa* (Support) *Trade Union*.

Several party leaders felt the threat of social unrest and tried to preserve the monopoly on power by reforming the party according to the Soviet *perestroyka*. They staged a coup on November 10, 1989, removing Todor Zhivkov from his post as a

General Secretary of the Party and Chairman of the State Council. The political activity of the population surged, and its legality was no longer questioned. Political rallies and demonstrations became the events of the day. Encouraged by the landslide of totalitarian collapse throughout Central and Eastern Europe, the opposition set up *The Union of Democratic Forces* (UDF) on December 7, 1989. This was a coalition of 16 pro-democratic parties and organizations which became the driving force of the real opposition against the ruling *Communist Party*. Although fragile, inexperienced, and with an obscure political profile, the opposition of that period immediately filled the gap of a public reform position needed for the functioning of democracy. One of the major political achievements, provoked by the new forces in society during that hot winter, was the abolishment of Article I in the Constitution, which had guaranteed a leading role to the *Communist Party* in societal and state affairs.

On June 10 and 17, 1990, elections were held for Grand National Assembly and the *Socialist Party* (successor of the former *Communist Party*) won the majority. The Grand National Assembly then adopted a new Constitution on July 12, 1991. It was the first constitution of a Western type in any of the former Eastern Bloc countries. Although it had imperfections, it proclaimed that Bulgaria is governed by the rule of law and set up the fundamental principles of a civil society in Bulgaria. Zhelyu Zhelev, the leader of the *UDF* and a long-time dissident, was elected President by the Grand National Assembly on August 1, 1991. Thus, he became Bulgaria's first non-communist head of state since 1944.

As the country approached elections for a new parliament in October, the mass media brought about high political involvement for the Bulgarian people. Political advertising telecasts and strong press and radio activity aided voters as they narrowed their choices in the pre-election campaign. In the October 1, 1991 new parliamentary elections, the majority of votes went to the *Union of Democratic Forces*, and with the former *Communist Party* no longer in power, Zhelev was elected President by the people in January, 1992. These elections were considered historic because they were the first Presidential elections since Bulgaria's liberation from Ottoman bondage in 1878.

In a period of eight years two presidential elections (in 1992 and 1996), four parliamentary elections (in 1990, 1991, 1994, and in 1997) and two local elections (in 1991 and 1995) were held, eight governments were appointed' and as a result of the fierce political fights all the legislative and economic processes advanced at a slow pace. This resulted in new social and economic problems with solutions nowhere in sight. Thus, the country lost its momentum generated by the quick start of the democratic reforms, missed the chance to get integrated with the Central European countries into the important European structures, and may very likely enter the 21st century under the already launched Currency Board.

EVOLUTION OF THE MASS MEDIA SYSTEM

Bulgaria's democratization processes strongly influenced mass media development. The liberalization and deregulation of the whole mass media system led to its decentralization and to the emergence of a pluralistic press and alternative electronic media. The establishment of the mass media market stimulated the development of new formats and styles of expression, thus fostering the higher selectivity standards of the audiences.

For forty years the mass media in Bulgaria were monotonous, instructive, and politically controlled (Raycheva & Tedev, 1996). The censoring institution prompted the development of self-censorship in journalism, the lack of information entailed misinformation, the absence of an alternative press and broadcasting resulted in newspapers, magazines, radio, and television programs of a marginalized nature. There were some meek attempts to diversify the journalistic landscape, but as a rule the mass media at that time were carefully monitored by the party headquarters.

In the early 1990s a tremendous shift in the press industry heralded the age of deregulation of print media. In a short period of time the tight *Communist Party* control mechanisms over the mass media were switched over to economically based principles. According to the information of the National Statistical Institute, 1,053 newspapers totalling 454,200,000 in circulation, were issued in 1996, compared to the 381 newspapers with a total distribution of 879,663,000 in 1988 (National Statistical Institute Reports, 1995). In the same year there were 635 magazines and bulletins with a total circulation of 12,200,000, while the year 1988 saw the highest circulation: 69,599,000 of 873 magazines and bulletins, a tendency indicative of the concentration processes unfolding in that period (National Statistical Institute Reports, 1995).

In a very short time, without gatekeeping or ideological control, the style and content of the press departed very much from its former patterns. Political pluralism brought about the establishment of different party organs. For the first time after more than four decades the public enjoyed increased choice between political press outlets. The emergence of the independent press was a new phenomenon in the national media landscape. The greater part of the new periodicals declared themselves independent, even though their financial sources remain unreported. Large press corporations emerged under the auspices of privatization and commercialization. Instead of indulging in political rhetoric, the main popular independent newspapers attracted broader audiences because of their pragmatic, down to earth approach to current issues. While the political press was preoccupied with ongoing power clashes, the independent periodicals focused their attention on economic interests. The formation and development of an independent, diversified, and pluralistic press in this period is a sign of the emergence of a Fourth Estate (the mass media) within the power structure (Petev, 1995).

Because they were funded mainly from the state budget, radio and television in Bulgaria followed the state policy very closely for a long time. Another factor for their slow transformation was the related restrictive legislature. Currently, the Bulgarian National Radio (BNR) and the Bulgarian National Television (BNT) are the only two broadcasting institutions whose programs cover the entire territory of the country. By a decision of the Grand National Assembly of March 6, 1991, they also are proclaimed to be independent institutions, financed mostly out of the State budget. Since the early 1990s BNR and BNT have been allowed to earn extra financial income from advertising and co-production contracts. This marks an attempt to transform these state-controlled institutions into public ones. The liberalized rules for licensing of local radio and television stations marked the onset of a rapid development of private radio (Ordinance No. 1, 1992). The advent of private television came nearly two years later. Despite several years of reform attempts, the television system lacks a stable organizational system, although there now exist several licensed local TV stations and numerous cable television operators who are gaining popularity among their subscribers (Report of the Committee for Postal Services, 1995). Radio broadcasting, on the other hand, has developed into a broader system of public and private entities, providing the public with a wide array of programming choices.

From an election standpoint, the first political advertising appeared in 1990. Since that time, marketing and election campaigns have become quite common on the TV screen (Raycheva, 1995). Of additional historical significance was the fact that on January 10, 1992, the first presidential debate was televised "live." National Radio and National Television maintained a high degree of audience credibility. According to different sociological surveys, their ratings were much higher than the deeply polarized press sources and the main state institutions of the Presidency, National Assembly, government and police (Political and Economic Index, 1995).

POLITICAL SYSTEM STRUCTURE IN BULGARIA

Under the terms of its Constitution, Bulgaria is a Republic with a parliamentary system of government. The National Assembly is composed of 240 deputies each elected for a term of four years. Any Bulgarian citizen (who does not hold a second citizenship, is 21, is not under judicial disability, and is not imprisoned) is eligible to run for Parliament. Members of Parliament represent not only their constituencies, but also the entire nation.

The president is the head of state of the Republic of Bulgaria. He is assisted in his work by a vice-president. The president is elected directly by the people for a term of five years. Every Bulgarian citizen by birth (who is 40, who is eligible for Parliament, and has lived in the country in the last five years) is eligible to run for President. The latter condition was added to frustrate any possible claims on the part of Tsar Simeon II, the Bulgarian monarch in exile who lives at present in Madrid, to run for head of state. The President of the Republic schedules the elections for a National Assembly and for the local administrative bodies, as well as the national referenda decided upon by the National Assembly. After consultations with the parliamentary groups, the president asks the candidates for a prime minister, nominated by the largest parliamentary group, to form a cabinet. If the prospective prime minister fails to compose a cabinet in the course of seven days, the president assigns this task to another candidate for the prime ministerial post, nominated by the second largest parliamentary group. If that candidate also fails to form a cabinet, the president, again in a term of seven days, asks the next parliamentary group to nominate a candidate for prime minister. Upon a successful completion of this task, s/he proposes to the National Assembly that they elect the candidate as prime minister. At a subsequent failure to have a cabinet formed, the president selects a Functional Cabinet, dissolves the National Assembly, and schedules new elections, after appointing a Central Electoral Commission. The act by which he dissolves the National Assembly also schedules the election date for a new National Assembly.

Legislation created a number of normative documents that regulate various activities of the political parties in any pre-election period. Financing of the political parties and their campaigns was a sensitive and difficult issue. From the outset of democratization the public had difficulties in accepting the role of private financial involvement in politics. This is why the governmental institutions were entrusted with the procedure and control of this kind of activity. This was particularly true for the political campaigning on the national electronic media, where firm rules were instituted and strictly observed. After 1992, with the emergence of the private radio and TV stations, at first timidly and then more confidently in the 1997 elections, purchase of broadcasting time by candidates/parties became possible under the regulations.

In line with other democracies, financing of the election campaigns in Bulgaria has been carried out by two major groups; government and non-government funding. Government funding is realized chiefly in the following forms: (1) partial advance subsidizing from the state budget of the parties and coalitions represented in the Parliament, in proportion to the votes cast for them in the previous elections, (2) short-term crediting, usually interest-free, of the registered extra-parliamentary forces and independent candidates, and (3) post-election levelling of the funds received by the parties, coalitions, and independent candidates, in proportion to the votes cast for them.

These financial rules, although seemingly clear at the beginning, showed their weak spots in actual campaign situations. In practice the State outwardly tolerated the parliamentary represented forces and especially the two leading ones, *The Bulgarian Socialist Party* and *The Union of Democratic Forces*. It tolerated them indirectly, too, by granting them access to the material facilities and the national electronic media (Pachkova, 1996). Contrary to this, the extra-parliamentary forces and independent candidates faced enormously complex hardships. These further complicated their already difficult race with the larger, dominant parties.

By the letter of the law, candidates for elected offices, in the parliamentary, presidential, and local administration elections, have to report publicly to their constituencies and the respective election commissions on how they fund their election campaigns (An Election Act, 1990). No such thing has happened in practice. Parties can also raise funds through membership fees and private contributions. However, foreign sponsorship is the most delicate component of pre-election party funding; legislation is adamant that candidates for president, members of parliament, mayors, and municipal councilors should not receive foreign aid, donations, and contributions from foreign countries, nor from foreign legal bodies or independent persons (An Election Act, 1990). But this clause of the election law is most frequently violated and seldom sanctioned, irrespective of the fact that it provides for canceling the election returns and confiscation of the received sums by the state. Furthermore, it is important to realize the large number of participating parties who have never submitted financial reports to the Control Commission of the National Assembly. For instance, in 1994, of the 154 legal parties, only 19 submitted reports; and in 1995, of 188 legal parties, only 71 had submitted reports by March of 1995. In spite of the fact that the control commission of the National Assembly has repeatedly invited candidates to submit their reports, over 60% of them have not fulfilled their legal obligations. Conversely, an analysis of the submitted reports made in 1995 by The National Statistical Institute indicated most were incomplete and unsatisfactory.

ELECTION ACCESS TO THE NATIONAL ELECTRONIC MEDIA

The right of access to the national electronic mass media is a central issue in the preparation and unfolding of the election campaigns. The principle on which the procedures rest has been modeled after contemporary practices in other countries. Thus, broadcasting time is divided between the participating parties and coalitions according to their parliamentary representation in the previous parliament. Under the transitional and final provisions of the Constitution, until the development of a new legislative regulation of the Bulgarian National Television, Bulgarian National Radio, and Bulgarian Telegraph Agency; the National Assembly has been charged with enforcing the rights of the Grand National Assembly with respect to these national institutions. Immediately after the political changes in 1989, some major principles on the provisional status of the Bulgarian National Television and the Bulgarian National Radio were adopted, which represented an attempt to regulate the legal status and activity of the national electronic media by means of legislation (Zankova, 1997). A special decision of the Grand National Assembly of August 21, 1991, on the access to the national mass media during election campaigns determines the parameters of this activity: twice weekly thematic debates by the parties and the coalitions, according to their representation in the Parliament (90 minutes of telecasts and 120 minutes of broadcasts on both radio programs), a 90 minute introductory and a 90 minute final discussion of the parliamentary parties and coalitions on the TV and on the radio. Twice during the entire election period, debates will be held by the extra-parliamentary parties and coalitions, if they have registered lists in at least one-third of the constituencies. On the first and on the last electioneering day Bulgarian Radio and Bulgarian Television shall broadcast (under equal program conditions and for five minutes each) the election addresses of all parties and coalitions which have registered lists in at least one-third of the constituencies. The *First* program of Bulgarian Television and the *Horizont* program of Bulgarian Radio shall beam twice weekly, in the same hours, clips or reports made by teams of Bulgarian Television and Bulgarian Radio under supervision of the parties and coalitions, which have registered lists in at least one-third of the constituencies. The clips and reports should not exceed three minutes and should detail the platform of the respective political parties. The expenses incurred by Bulgarian Radio, Bulgarian Television, and the Bulgarian Telegraph Agency for the coverage of election campaigns are shouldered by the State Budget.

TELEVISION IN THE 1990 PARLIAMENTARY CAMPAIGN

The Parliamentary elections in 1990 were the first to be held in a post-totalitarian situation. They were organized in an atmosphere of vigorous political activity. Numerous rallies and meetings were held during this period. Daily, people filled the central streets and squares of the big cities to express spontaneous support for some of the three competing political formations, the *Bulgarian Socialist Party*, the *Union of Democratic Forces*, and the *Bulgarian Agrarian People's Union*. These public efforts were accompanied by dramatic changes in the printed media. Political pluralism brought about various party organ newspapers and party propaganda. These were the means by which in early 1990 political advertising and campaigning were re-established in Bulgaria after an interruption of more than forty years. As a matter of fact, 1990 marks the outset of the history of television advertising in Bulgaria. The elections were held in two days, on June 10 and on June 17, 1990. Two electoral systems were applied, majority vote and proportional representation. While political campaigning in newspapers was practically uncontrollable, the Parliamentary Commission for Radio and Television set the rules for this activity on National Radio and National Television (there were no private broadcasting stations at that time). Political advertising campaigns on television started approximately fifty days prior to the first round of the elections. TV managers canceled all journalistic programs and replaced them with entertainment or feature films. Political events were covered only in the news slots, where there were certain regulations for ensuring representative balance between the activities of the different parties.

According to a preliminary agreement, the political advertising campaign on television was organized in two forms, party video ads and a studio debate, named *The Open Studio*. Both were aired in prime time every working day, for nearly an hour, under the heading, *Pre-Election Studio*. The campaign totalled more than thirty two hours of political advertising, organized in thirty seven program blocks.

The party video ads were broadcast on Mondays, Wednesdays, and Fridays. The two biggest political parties, the *Bulgarian Socialist Party* and the *Union of Democratic Forces*, had 20 minutes of screen time each for every program, and the *Bulgarian Agrarian People's Union* got 15 minutes for each of its video ads. Every political formation had chosen its own color; the traditional red for the *BSP*, blue was the color of hope for the *UDF*, and the traditional orange for the *BAPU*. Each had also its own slogan (1) "SPoluka (Success) for Bulgaria" for the *BSP*, the first two letters of the word *SPoluka* were emphasized, suggesting an abbreviation of the name of the party as a connotation to the word success, (2) "Time is on our side" for the *UDF*, and (3) "Peace, bread and sovereignty of the people" for the *BAPU*. The *BSP* chose as a mascot the image of a little boy, named Nachko, with his thumb up, and a rose bud. The mascot of the *UDF* was a cartoon lion with fingers raised in a V-sign.

One characteristic of the first television advertising campaign was that all programs were produced without any substantial preliminary preparation. The pace of production was hectic, and the election strategies of the political formations took shape in the process of shooting and editing the programs. However, each political organization managed to create a specific image based on its propaganda messages to the public. The *BSP* programs were addressed to its adherents who were thought to reaffirm the views of its members. The Socialists were still in power, and they had to face a real opposition for the first time in forty years; they were not aware of how quickly the *UDF* was gaining popularity. The *Socialist Party* programs focused on an improvement of the socialist system in the *perestroyka* spirit. The guilt for the disastrous ruling of the country over the course of decades and the former *Communist Party's* share of responsibility for the severe economic crisis, including the deficit in the State Budget, were naturally overlooked. Instead, the emphasis was on the conservative preference of the people to remember a "not so bad" past as the alternative to an unknown and frightening future. The *Union of Democratic Forces* was a political formation without a past. It comprised some member-parties who had been banned by the Communist rulers decades before. Some of the leaders of these parties, who had survived the concentration camps, helped restore the parties and took leadership positions. They emerged as resurrected prosecutors of the communist deeds at a time when the totalitarian regime was established in the country. The image of an enemy as well as intolerance to the reconstruction of the socialist system became the trademark of the *UDF* ads. A young and beautiful girl, who opened each program, was used as a symbol of innocence and hope. Another strong symbol was a metronome which was counting out the last minutes of the communist era. In a state of severe confrontation between the two main political formations, the *BSP* and the *UDF*, the chances of the *Bulgarian Agrarian People's Union* were not very promising. A former dedicated ally of the Communist Party subordinated totally to the communist rules and regulations for nearly fifty years, the *BAPU* attempted to distinguish between the Communists and the Agrarians in things they had actually done together in the past in order to improve the latter's electoral chances in a new political atmosphere. This strategy certainly repulsed those natural supporters of *BAPU's* ideas, who had suffered under the previous Communist regime, and they preferred the *UDF*. The *BAPU* programs were built around specifically agrarian issues and their messages were presented in a folklorist tradition. Bread, land, wheat fields, and agricultural values were the major symbols in these programs.

Although the three political rivals were each following their own advertising strategies and their crews worked separately, all three had to use the facilities of Bulgarian National Television. There were several occasions on which the *BSP* and the *UDF* engaged in some televised blows-swapping. The most significant clash occurred during the week between the two rounds of elections, and everyone became aware that this political game could have a serious and dramatic ending. Until then the *BSP* programs were basically tolerant and moderate, but then it aired an aggressive piece, a crosscutting of one of the young *UDF* leaders with footage from Bob Fosse's film

Cabaret that showed the rise of *Hitler Jugend (Youth)* in Germany. The allusion was transparent, and the comparison more than clear. In its next scheduled program the *UDF* fired back. It showed an accidentally videotaped remark uttered by the then Bulgarian President Petar Mladenov, who served many years as Minister of Foreign Affairs under Zhivkov, to the Minister of Defence at a December 1989 anti-Communist rally in which he states, "Maybe it's better to call the tanks." The controversial remark later ignited a students' strike that provoked Mladenov's resignation. For the first time television manifested its power to be a catalyst for fundamental shifts in political life. It also plainly showed, as with the 1989 Romanian revolution, how easily the electronic media could become a political instrument in times of turmoil. Another form of political advertising on television for the first Parliamentary elections after 1989 was the *Open Studio*. Every Tuesday and Thursday it presented hour-long live debates on various political, economic, and social issues between representatives of the three rival formations.

The returns of the run-off (or second ballot) on June 17 showed the Socialist Party winning a majority of 400 seats in the Parliament (Election Results, 1990). A Government of National Consensus was formed with representatives of all the political forces in the Grand National Assembly and the Chairman of the Election Commission Dimitar Popov as Prime Minister. According to a survey among 200 journalists, conducted by the School of Journalism and Mass Communications of The St. Kliment Ohridsky University of Sofia, the television advertisements played a significant role in determining the final choice of undecided voters. Twenty-five per cent confirmed that the programs of the pre-election TV studio had definitely influenced votes, while sixteen per cent thought that the voters' decisions were not influenced by TV ads. Over half (55%) shared the opinion that these programs influenced the political vote to a certain extent, and 4% did not respond to this question (Mass Media Behavior, 1990). The sociological agency *SIGMA* undertook a survey of how the viewers evaluated the televised political campaigning. It asked the question, "Which political party did best on the TV screen?" ten days prior to the first round and ten days after the second round of the elections. The answers were as follows; 39% to 34% for the *BSP*, respectively before and after the elections; 20% to 25% for the *UDF*; and 14% to 16% for the *BAPU*. *SIGMA* went even further in an attempt to poll the credibility of the media in the eyes of the public. National Television topped the standings before and after the elections. The respective figures were 60% and 39% for television, followed by the *BSP* press with 45% and 36%, National Radio with 31% and 34%, and the *UDF* press with 25% and 27% (Raykov, 1990). The high credibility of television after the elections slid by about 20%. This dramatic drop reflected the rejection of the over-politicized programs by the audience. In the summer of 1991, in accordance with an earlier agreement between the political forces in the country, the Grand National Assembly was dissolved after it adopted the new Constitution. The date October 13, 1991, was appointed as the day for new Parliamentary elections.

TELEVISION IN THE PARLIAMENTARY
ELECTIONS OF 1991, 1994, AND 1997

Since the dissolution of the Grand National Assembly the country has had three parliamentary elections. Economic instability and political uncertainty made the 36th and 37th National Assemblies unable to complete their legally fixed mandate. Parliamentary crises entailed early elections. During this period, there were both political election reforms and new regulations on the access to the national mass media during the campaigns. The 1995 Local Elections Act introduced thirteen articles regulating the appearance of the political parties in the national media during the campaigns (A Local Elections Act, 1995). The concrete problems in each pre-election situation were to be settled by the Central Electoral Commission and the Council of Ministers (Archive of the CEC). The dynamics of development of these decisions deserves mention. In 1991 the duration and form of political advertising was strictly fixed and could be aired only by the central national medium and was fully financed by the State Budget. In the 1994 elections, new rules made it possible for the regional radio and television centers to join in but only by observing fixed regulations in the campaigning of the candidates, who must have registered lists in their respective constituencies. Again, funding came from the State Budget. The order of appearances on the national screen was determined by a random drawing. CEC introduced another important point in its decision in the 1997 elections, the TV and radio stations and cable televisions owned by actual persons and legal entities can assign air time for the parties, coalitions, and the independent candidates under the same, preliminary set conditions and prices (Decision of the CEC, 1997). **For the first time it became possible to buy air time for political TV advertising, although only at the local TV centers.**

Political Turmoil and Instability

The elections for the 36th Parliament on October 13, 1991 were held in a very strongly politicized atmosphere. The political arena was restructured. While the electorate of the *Socialist Party* remained comparatively monolithic, significant shifts and changes took place in the camps of the *UDF* and the *BAPU*. The *Union of Democratic Forces* was a political formation of different parties and organizations. At first, their unity was built on the mutual grounds of opposing a major antagonist, the *Socialist Party*. However, the differences and misunderstandings between them gradually became intolerable and led to secession of various fractions. On the eve of elections the *Union of Democratic Forces* split into three fractions; the *Union of Democratic Forces*, the *Union of Democratic Forces (Centre)*, and the *Union of Democratic Forces (Liberals)*. The situation was significant in that no one wanted to abandon the name *Union of Democratic Forces*, which had already gained popularity and success among the voters. There was also friction among the agrarians. Some of them united and formed the *Bulgarian Agrarian People's Union (United)*, others opposed that formation and formed a new one, the

Bulgarian Agrarian People's Union (Nikola Petkov). This was followed later by other agrarian political formations. During that restructuring of political space the *Movement for Rights and Freedoms*, which had won 5.75% in the previous elections, was strengthening its ranks. Though this was not mentioned officially, it was generally known that this was the party of the ethnic Turks, a population of about one million people.

In the meantime, the economic crisis deepened further. Consumer goods and food gradually disappeared from shelves, and a severe shortage of foodstuffs was experienced by the population. Food rationing was introduced for several months but without success. During the harsh winter months prices were released and increased tenfold, while salaries increased only three times. The economy was collapsing. Profiteering spread widely. Beggars emerged on the streets. The first strikes began. Crime was increasing quickly. Almost all shop-windows were barred in iron, and the wail of alarms pierced the night. The well educated and highly qualified young people were lining up in front of foreign consulates for émigré or working visas for abroad.

A significant feature of the 1991 Parliamentary elections was the fact that the nominees were divided into three groups; Parliamentary political formations (i.e., those who had deputies in the Grand National Assembly), Non-parliamentary political formations, and Independent candidates. Permission for political advertising on TV was issued to eight Parliamentary formations, nineteen Non-parliamentary formations, and six Independent candidates. The 36th National Assembly was dissolved before it finished its term. It began work with 240 members, who were organized in three parliamentary groups; the *Union of Democratic Forces* (110 members), the *Bulgarian Socialist Party and Coalition* (106 members), and the *Movement for Rights and Freedoms* (24 members). However, three years later, on October 17, 1994, it had 237 members organized in new groups: the *Parliamentary Union for Social Democracy* (the former Bulgarian Socialist Party and Coalition with 99 members), the *Union of Democratic Forces* (57 members), the Parliamentary group of the *Democratic Party* (28 members who had split from the *UDF*), the *Movement for Rights and Freedoms* (19 members), the *Democratic Alternative for the Republic* (11 members), and *Nov Izbor*, the New Option (10 members). There were also 13 members who declared themselves independent. Two of the members of Parliament were stripped of their parliamentary immunity. One of them, a former Prime Minister and a long-time high-ranking official under the Communist regime, was even imprisoned for six months and, later, in 1996, assassinated in front of his home.

Shortly after the elections in 1991, with the *UDF* gaining power, the political friction between the parties within the *UDF* increased, and certain centrifugal processes began in the coalition. Along with other reasons, this led to a governmental crisis which aggravated the economic situation in the country. The government of the *UDF* (the first non-communist administration in more than four decades) had to step down in less than an year after a non-confidence vote. The next government, that of Professor Lyuben Berov (elected with the ballot of the *Movement for Rights and Freedoms*, but backed by the Socialist Party), resigned in about twenty months. Among the important reasons for this decision by the Prime Minister were the severe economic crisis, the grave social problems, the misunderstandings between the institutions, and the malfunctioning Parliament. This is why, during that period, the political space was totally restructured resulting in a reality quite different from the vote of the people. The Parliament made one final effort to elect a new government. The ensuing failure of that attempt clearly showed the deep political crisis and the path to the next Parliamentary elections was already underway.

The President then appointed Mrs. Reneta Indjova (a former Chairman of the *Agency for Privatization*) to form a Functional Cabinet with the task of preparing the forthcoming elections. Mrs. Indjova was the first woman in Bulgarian history to be appointed in such a high position, and she coped commendably with her duties. A sociological survey conducted by *BBSS Gallup International* showed that within a single month confidence in Reneta Indjova had dramatically increased, from 36% on October 25, 1994, to 61% on November 29, 1994 (Political and Economic Index, 1994). Election day was set for December 18, 1994, and the electoral system again envisaged proportional representation. Disintegration in Parliament directly reflected political re-allocation in the country. Eleven coalitions and 38 parties and movements registered for participation in the elections. The *Bulgarian Socialist Party* formed a coalition with the *Bulgarian Agrarian People's Union"Alexander Stamboliyski"* and the *Political Club "Ecoglasnost"*. The *Union of Democratic Forces*, after some dramatic discussions, rechecked the registration of its members. Eleven political formations were active participants in the *Union* and another fifteen signed a political agreement of support. Another coalition, the *National Alliance*, was formed by two comparatively important parties, the *Democratic Party* and the *Bulgarian Agrarian People's Union*, who had left the *UDF*. The *Political Union "Democratic Alternative for the Republic"* combined the efforts of four different former parliamentary formations. The *"New Option" Union* was also constituted of former MPs who were dissatisfied with the policy of their previous parties.

Though much rested on these elections, most political formations did not have a clear-cut campaigning strategy. A survey was carried out by *ASSA-M* in late October of 1994. The question, "Have you read the platforms of the political formations for the previous elections?" drew the following answers" "Yes, several of them"--25%; "Yes, two of them"--12%; "Yes, one of them"--16%; and 46% responded negatively (Sociological Survey, 1994).

The 37th National Assembly elected in the 1994 campaigns was also dissolved before it finished its term. The 240 deputies were organized at the beginning in five parliamentary groups; *The Bulgarian Socialist Party and Coalition* (125 seats), *The Union of Democratic Forces* (69 seats), *The National Alliance* (18 seats), *The Movement for Rights and Freedoms* (15 seats) and *The Bulgarian Business Block* (13 seats). After the turbulent events of January 10, 1997 (aired throughout the world) when the MPs were besieged in the Parliament by the social unrest and the Parliament building itself was violated, it became clear that the political space needed to be rearranged yet again. The political crisis was explosive, and every day peaceful protest marches and meetings were organized on the streets of Sofia and other Bulgarian cities, but the tension gradually escalated. On the initiative of the President, on February 4, 1997, a Declaration on the Principles for Escaping from the Crisis was signed by the leaders of the five groups represented in Parliament and the independents who had split from them. One of the immediate steps to be undertaken was the scheduling of new parliamentary elections. In little more than two years, on February 13, 1997, the 37th National Assembly held its final meeting, but political instability continues.

Televised Political Advertising

The campaign of 1991 was shorter than that of 1990. It lasted less than a month and was launched in three major forms: video ads, debates, and addresses. Strict regulations were in force regarding the proper usage of TV time.

Prior to dissolving the 36th National Assembly in 1994, the Parliamentary Commission for Radio and Television failed to suggest any rules for the state-owned electronic mass media during the upcoming campaign. The rules, voted earlier by the Grand National Assembly had to be applied, no matter how outdated they were. Thus, National Television was in good technical shape well in advance of the on-air political fights. A special commission was charged with accepting the submitted video ads 48 hours prior to broadcast.

The campaign lasted one month and was developed in two major forms, video ads and debates. The video ads were organized into blocks aired three times weekly (on Mondays, Wednesdays and Fridays). Tuesdays and Thursdays were left for debates. The weekends were free from television campaigning.

As mentioned earlier, by the time of the 1997 elections, more specific rules for party and candidate use of television time had been adopted, and it was possible to buy time on the regional private channels. The 1997 parliamentary election campaign lasted under one month and was held in three major forms, addresses, campaign news, and debates. Campaign news was organized into blocks aired four times weekly (on Mondays, Tuesdays, Thursdays and Fridays). Debates were aired on Wednesdays.

Addresses. An important form of the televised 1991 and 1997 campaigns were the addresses of the Parliamentary and Non-parliamentary formations to the public. Each address could not exceed five minutes in length. It was usually made by the leader of the political formation. The visual and graphic layout of the recorded addresses was made by the Bulgarian National Television and was visually uniform for each party, while the succession of their airing was determined by drawing lots. In 1977 addresses of the parties and coalitions which had registered lists at least in eleven constituencies were aired on the first and last day of the pre-election campaign, which some thought became a tiring and dreary marathon race.

Video ads. The video ad was one of the formats of political campaigning during the 1991 and 1994 campaigns. The video ads became the hit of the 1991 campaign. It was then that the political video ad in Bulgarian television was born. Though lacking in prior experience, the production crews worked with great inspiration and produced some good political pieces in terms of screen aesthetics. According to the rules, each clip could not exceed three minutes in length. The parliamentary formations were given the opportunity to air five video ads each, and the non-parliamentary groups two each. However, not all parties took advantage of the opportunity to construct original productions. Some of the ads were repeated. Most of the basic formations continued to use their prime colors, slogans, and symbols of the previous elections, but some new designs were also introduced.

The tendency in the video ads of the *BSP and Coalition* was again to reach those voters who shared party views. The symbols of Biblical faith, hope and love were also widely used. A strong emphasis was put on mutual tolerance. Though blamed for the failures in its 45-year rule, the BSP tried to recall all positive achievements throughout the years, as well as to warn of a "blue" repetition of its own deeds. Video sequences of the Assembly House set on fire in 1991, of monuments stained with red paint, resembling blood, and of uncontrolled facial expressions of hatred were added to the pictures symbolizing eternity, peace, and love.

The video ads of the *UDF* were by far more aggressive. All successful symbols of the previous elections were used again, with many new ones added (the dismantled pentacle from the roof of the Communist Party House in the heart of the city, the long lines in front of the grocery stores in the harsh winter of 1990-1991, the former Communist leader Todor Zhivkov kissing and hugging the current BSP leader Alexander Lilov, the grotesque figure of Karl Marx begging an excuse from the proletariat). "Tomorrow starts today" was the new slogan. Anti-Communism was the leading idea of all the pieces. For over a year, songs with political content topped the popularity charts. One of them, "The Last Waltz," addressing the Socialist Party's stepping down from power, became the core theme in one of the most popular ads of the *UDF*.

While the *UDF* retained all symbols of the *Union* as it was initially formed at the previous elections, the *UDF-Center* and the *UDF-Liberals* formations attempted to stake on their own political personality. The *UDF-Center* was a coalition of the *Bulgarian Socialist Democratic Party* and the *Ecoglasnost Movement*. Their symbol was a rose stem intertwined with a pine twig, their basic slogan read, "With the ballot for the *UDF-Center* you vote for your present and your future." The *UDF-Center* staked professionalism as a major virtue in contrast to the political fragmentation of the country. The egg was used as the main symbol of the *UDF-Liberals*; their color was yellow. In their video ads they put a strong emphasis on the individuality and personal qualities of their leaders. Their main slogans were, "You will succeed" and "Give us a chance."

Though the video ads of the *UDF-Center* and the *UDF-Liberals* were professionally produced, the two formations failed to pass the established
4% limit of votes to enter the Parliament. (*UDF-Center* won 3.2% of the ballots and *UDF-Liberals* 2.8%). The basic reason for this was probably that time was too short for them to develop their own political profile and their own political symbols. The blue color and the anti-Communist pattern ("the blue idea" versus "the red garbage") were strong enough to attract those who wanted to vote for a radical political change.

A similar fate befell the Agrarians. While they were squabbling among themselves, their traditional orange color was usurped by a small and insignificant party. Split into two separate coalitions, the *BAPU-United* and the *BAPU-Nikola Petkov*, they shared similar political programs and similar election symbols. The bread, the land, the popular folk music and symbols were insufficient to compensate for their discord, and they ended up failing to secure a place in the Parliament (*BAPU-United* won 3.9% of the vote and *BAPU-Nikola Petkov* got 3.4%).

While the large political formations were fighting to divide the electorate between themselves, a small party managed to weave into its way in the political struggle, winning almost 8 per cent of the vote. This was the *Movement for Rights and Freedoms*. Although this organization did not offer a clear political platform and symbols, it united big masses of the voters, mainly from the Turkish and Gypsy minorities.

Some video ads of the non-parliamentary parties and the Independent candidates were comparatively well made, while others were naive and declarative. Nevertheless, they failed to bring success to their creators due to the lack of a political and propaganda infrastructure in the country and to the very nature of proportional representation used in the elections.

In the 1994 campaign, a public drawing of lots, televised live, determined the order of the broadcasting of video ads. According to the decision of the Central Electoral Commission, the candidates were divided into two groups, parliamentary formations (i.e., the six formations constituted as separate groups at the closing of the former Parliament) and non-parliamentary formations. The rules determined that each video ad should not exceed three minutes in length. Almost all candidates concentrated their efforts on attracting some skilled cinematographers able to produce attractive video ads with their crews. The gratuitous enthusiasm of the previous elections was absent this time, and the political formations were trying to outdo each other in generous offers to famous pop-singers and football players for endorsements.

The *BSP and Coalition* followed their old strategy of trying to attract left-oriented voters. The white, green, and red colors of the national flag were used to represent the three coalition partners, though the ballot itself was red. The major slogan of the Coalition was "Change, justice, confidence." Some of the primary ideological issues in the *BSP* platform, presented by a coalition's speaker, were interwoven with thematically edited sequences in their video ads. A strong emphasis was put on mutual tolerance and concerted efforts for the renovation of the country.

The *UDF* video ads were cinematographically superior to those of the *BSP*. Their messages were emotional rather than ideological. A remake of a successful video ad ("The Last Waltz") used in the previous elections was included in the campaign. The main color remained blue, and the slogan was "Victory, Bulgaria!" The anti-Communist theme (aimed against political opponents from the *BSP*) was the dominant feature of the *UDF* campaign. An interesting detail was included in the ads of both rivals aired on the same evening, a slow-motion take of a shabby, ailing man. The shot was taken from the regular news program and used by both coalitions to accuse their opponents.

After some fighting about the distribution of ballots, the *National Alliance* got the use of the traditional orange color of the Bulgarian Agrarians. The Alliance was led by two well-known politicians (the leader of the *Democratic Party* and a former Chairperson of Parliament, Stefan Savov, and Anastasiya Dimitrova-Mozer, leader of the *Bulgarian Agrarian People's Union* and daughter of Dr. G.M. Dimitrov, an Agrarian leader persecuted by the Communists who died in exile). They called the political platform of their alliance "A Program for Saving Bulgaria." This formation maintained a reasonable campaign tone, embodied in their main slogan which was, "Vote reasonably."

Similar to earlier campaigns, the *Movement for Rights and Freedoms* emphasized human rights in its ads. Their slogan was "Bulgaria for all!"

The Political Union "Democratic Alternative for the Republic" based its ads on the joint efforts of the leaders of the four political forces who formed it, directed to the future perspective of the country. This Union succeeded in attracting many pop-singers to its campaign.

The "New Option" Union earned a permanent place in the history of Bulgarian political advertising because of its attempt to suggest something different in political reality but also because of the famous poster of naked bottoms in reference to its political rivals. The text beneath the picture read, "Which option: old or new?" The world-famous football star Hristo Stoichkov, winner of the Golden Ball for 1994, took part in video ads for the Union. George Ganchev, leader of the *Bulgarian Business Block* (subsequently dismissed from Parliament for carrying dual citizenship) based the video ad of his formation on one of his songs. The slogan of this formation was, "Bulgaria, God and Business Block."

For various reasons, some political formations could not produce their own video ads. Instead, these groups used the allotted time for addresses to the voters.

Debates. One basic format for all campaigns was the debate focusing on some of the country's important political, social, and economic issues. According to the rules, approved by the Grand National Assembly, the length of the debates was determined to be 90 minutes per debate. The Parliamentary groups for the 1991 elections were entitled to six. The six topics of the debates were: the Social Politics under the Reform, the Land and Its Owners, Education and Culture in Changing Bulgaria, What Type of Market Economy, Bulgaria and the World, and the Society for Which We Aspire. The Non-parliamentary parties were entitled to one discussion on the topic "The Future Society of Bulgaria", divided into two parts (each 90 minutes long).

This format provided an opportunity for the experts and representatives of the different parties and coalitions to display their views on the issues. However, even though the speakers were introduced to the public with captions of their names and also with their ballot colors, the discussions resembled a friendly conversation rather than real debates. This was especially true for the Non-parliamentary formations in which the participants were so numerous that there was no time for any real debate.

According to a decision of the Central Electoral Commission, eight televised debates were organized during the 1994 pre-election campaign. The Parliamentary groups (with which the former Parliament had started its existence) participated in six 120-minute TV discussions. The *Bulgarian Socialist Party* and the *Union of Democratic Forces* were entitled to up to 45 per cent of the allocated time, and 10 per cent was assigned to the *Movement for Rights and Freedoms*. The discussions were anchored by four famous press journalists with various pre-set topics.

The *Bulgarian Socialist Party and Coalition* devoted some of its time (3.25 minutes) to the *Political Union "New Option"* (Discussion No. 5) and to the *Patriotic Union* (Discussions No. 5 and 6). Two other formations flatly refused to use the same amount of time for presentation. Their objection was the organization of these debates. Since all the statements were strictly time limited (with an electronic clock ticking in the camera eye), no real discussion took place. Moreover, many voters were disgusted by this form of TV propaganda, finding it boring and tiresome.

The 1997 debates were similar. As per the agreement of the political forces on the rules for air time distribution during the 1997 parliamentary election campaign, the parties and coalitions represented in the preceding National Assembly were to take part in three thematic public debates. The other parties and coalitions, which had registered election lists in all constituencies and were enjoying higher public credibility according to sociological surveys, were eligible as well. CEC determined the participants in that block. These were; *the Democratic Left*, *the Joint Democratic Forces*, *the Euroleft*, *the Alliance for National Salvation* and the *Bulgarian Business Block*. The remaining parties and coalitions, which had registered lists in at least one-third of the constituencies, took part in two debates throughout the pre-election period. They shared equal time slots in the 90 minutes of air time after drawing lots for order of appearance. The debates were held before an audience and each political force was entitled to an equal number of places in the auditorium. The debate themes were: (1) a short-term program for a way out of the crisis, (2) foreign policy and national security, and (3) Bulgaria after the parliamentary elections. The two debates of the extra-parliamentary parties were held on the basis of questions taken from the first and third above-mentioned themes.

Campaign news. In the 1997 parliamentary election campaign another format was added to political advertising, campaign news. This type of presentation conditioned a more equal presentation of the parties and coalitions, especially of those which lacked the sufficient intellectual and material capacity to produce video clips. In line with the agreement of the political forces on the rules for distribution of media air time, the campaign news was aired on Mondays, Tuesdays, Thursdays, and Fridays. Up to twenty minutes of coverage, but no longer than a minute and a half daily, was fixed per party or coalition campaigning for the entire pre-election period. The campaign news of the political parties which had registered election lists in at least eleven constituencies were aired after the central news on both channels of Bulgarian National Television and of the other parties and coalitions after the late news. Particular attention was attached to the observance of the principles of objectivity and equal standing.

The campaign news reported the marches, meetings, concerts, and other events organized by the respective parties and coalitions, as well as personal functions of their candidates for MPs related to the campaign. They were aired in an order following the succession of the election addresses according to the lots drawn before CEC. In spite of all equality provisions, however, there was a certain discord in the presence of the political forces on screen. For instance, in block A (the parliamentary represented parties) *The Euroleft* had the greatest number of televised pieces (22), followed by *the Joint Democratic Forces* (21), *Alliance for National Salvation* (19), *Democratic Left* (18), and *Bulgarian Business Block* (17). While the *Joint Democratic Forces*, *the Euroleft* and the *Bulgarian Business Block* appeared 14 days on screen, the *Alliance for National Salvation* did 12 days, and the *Democratic Left*, 11. Of the 29 political forces of block B (the non-parliamentary parties) the *Liberal Forum* had the greatest number of reports

(14), followed by the *Democratic League* (13) and two parties with 10, three with 9, one with 8, two with 7, three with 6, one with 5, three with 4, two with 2, one with 1, and another six parties did not air campaign news. The election returns showed that it was hardly the number of the aired reports that swayed the popular vote, but it was a fact that the conjectured equality was strongly disrupted. The four parties without a single vote had not been on TV. They were ineligible for access to the TV screen, while all others which appeared on television had registered votes in their favor. There was a party which did not take part in the televised appearances, but managed to receive 670 votes or 0.2 per cent of the valid ballot. This only seems to reconfirm the view that information from TV affects the audience in reaffirming its convictions and intents (Velikova, 1997).

The campaign news had an informative rather than a propaganda character. The fascination and fantasy of the political advertising clip were unfortunately replaced by the rigidity of the news.

PRESIDENTIAL CAMPAIGNS IN 1992 AND 1996

Besides developing and adopting the new Constitution of the Republic of Bulgaria, the Grand National Assembly completed another important task. On August 1, 1991, after heated debate and negotiation, it elected a President, Zhelyu Zhelev, the then-leader of the *Union of Democratic Forces*. Under the newly adopted constitution, elections had to be held as soon as possible so as to let the people choose the head of state. Since that time, Bulgaria has managed to conduct successful presidential elections twice, in 1992 and in 1996.

By a decision of the Grand National Assembly, the first presidential elections in the country were slated to be held in early 1992. *The Union of Democratic Forces* was still euphoric with its parliamentary victory. The parties whose candidates failed to attract enough votes were taking their defeat seriously and analyzing its causes. The *Socialist Party* reconciled itself to the loss of power.

In the meantime newspapers were privatized quickly, although the Radio and the Television were still under State monopoly. However, the National Assembly appointed new chairmen in these institutions. A large-scale loyalty purge was carried out, allegedly blamed on the budget cuts, especially in the television industry. Hundreds of qualified workers lost their jobs, some of them for political reasons. Many of the old departments were closed and new ones were created.

Thus, the presidential campaign opened in a tense atmosphere of restructuring in the media and the political arena. A two-round electoral system was adopted, allowing the two nominee pairs (a president and vice-president) with the highest number of votes in the first round to run for the second and final round.

Once more, regulations were introduced for the TV campaign. Every nominated pair was entitled to two short public addresses of up to five minutes each. The two finalists were expected to have a one-hour televised debate. A significant point of this advertising campaign was the fact that most candidates were politically, psychologically, and professionally unprepared for such a task. There was much confusion and misunderstanding concerning the constitutional rights and responsibilities of the President. Some candidates lacked a mature approach to important administrative issues, others had behavioral problems in front of the TV camera.

There was a lot of naiveté and non-professionalism in this campaign, which explains why only four nominated pairs managed to collect over 2% of the vote in the first round. These candidates were Zhelyu Zhelev/Blaga Dimitrova (*Union of Democratic Forces*) with 44.6% and Velko Vulkanov/Roumen Vodenicharov (Independent backed by *Bulgarian Socialist Party*) with 30.44%. Georgy Petrushev/Peter Beron (*Bulgarian Business Block*) with 16.77%, and Blagovest Sendov/Ognyan Saparev (Independent Candidates) with 2.23%.

The first presidential debate on television was held "live" on January 10, 1992. The opponents were Dr. Zhelyu Zhelev, the candidate of the *UDF*, and Professor Velko Vulkanov, an independent candidate, backed by the *BSP*. The debate was anchored by long-time journalist Dimitry Ivanov. Both candidates were supposed to have equal time. The result however, was 44 minutes for Professor Vulkanov and 17 minutes for Dr. Zhelev (Pesheva, 1992). This imbalance was the fault of the anchorman who was charged with watching the time. On the whole, the performance of Professor Vulkanov was aggressive, while the behavior of Dr. Zhelev was restrained. According to some sociological surveys, the offensive behavior of Professor Vulkanov probably earned him an extra 16.61% of votes in the second round of elections. However, in the long run, Dr. Zhelev won the elections on January 12, 1992, with 52.85% of the votes against 47.15% for Professor Vulkanov, thus becoming the first democratically elected President in Bulgaria.

The 1996 presidential elections were preceded by the escalation of social tension as a result of the failures of the Socialist government. On the eve of the election campaign an MP, a former Prime Minister and a well-known figure in the socio-political life of the country, Andrey Loukanov, was assassinated in front of his home. Contrary to the expectations of some, his tragic death postponed the start of the campaign, but not the elections. Five new articles regulating the campaign on the national electronic media were voted in the addenda to the Presidential Elections Act. A decision of the Central Electoral Commission (CEC) created the rules for running the campaign on the radio and on TV in the following forms: (1) an introductory and closing address of the candidates for President and Vice President registered in the lists at the CEC, (2) debates, and (3) coverage of the demonstrations and meetings, concerts and other events organized by the parties, coalitions and independent candidates.

The regional radio and TV centers and the local and municipal radio stations could assign up to two hours a week to presidential campaigning, including the time for debates. Moreover, TV and radio stations and cable televisions owned by physical and legal entities could sell time to all candidates at the same, preliminary fixed prices. Thus, it became possible to purchase radio and TV air time for political promotion, although on the local level.

Thirteen nomination pairs for President and Vice President filed. A two-round electoral system was again used, allowing the two running nominees with the highest number of votes to run for the second round. Voting on October 27, 1996, failed to produce a President and Vice-President, as none of the candidates polled more than one-half of the valid votes cast. Only four pairs managed to collect over 1% of the votes. These were; Petar Stoyanov-Todor Kavaldjiev (*Joint Democratic Forces*) with 44%, Ivan Marazov-Irina Bokov ("Together for Bulgaria" coalition) with 27% per cent, George Ganchev-Arlin Antonov (*Bulgarian Business Block*) with 22%, and Hristo Boychev-Ivan Koulekov (*Movement in Defense of Pensioners, Unemployed and Marginal-Income Citizens*) with 1%.

The candidate of the *Joint Democratic Forces* was the favorite in these elections, because of the public mood in the country. The first candidate of the *Socialists*, Georgi Pirinski, was disqualified 40 days prior to the elections because he was not a Bulgarian by birth. The strong presentation of George Ganchev, with his well-schooled behavior in front of the TV cameras marked the first attempt at breaking up the bipolar model in the country. Hristo Boichev and Ivan Koulekov were a tandem of writers of comic works who ran in the presidential elections to challenge the high political passions in the country. Their TV addresses voiced the mocking corrective of the Bulgarian people who have characteristically displayed a healthy common sense awareness of the political spectacles being performed. Although the pair did not actually want power, they collected 57,668 votes.

According to the adopted rules, all presidential pairs of candidates were entitled to free introductory and concluding addresses (of 7 minutes each) in the first round. On the last day of the election campaign they were allotted ten minutes; the order was determined by drawing of lots organized by the Central Electoral Commission.

The debates were televised once a week, in 120 minutes of air time altogether, and participation in them was prepaid according to tariffs set by the Council of Ministers. For the regional centers the sum was 80 per cent of the funds paid to Bulgarian National Television. The time allocations of the debates were determined by the parliamentary strengths of the registered candidates/parties, and the topics were pre-set. Although the debates offered a platform from which the political forces could most pointedly voice their program message to their voters, its regulation apparently was not very clear. The rigid structure frustrated real discussion. In the period between the two rounds a 90-minute debate between the major contenders was held, funded by the State Budget. It was dedicated to the theme, "President as Unifier of the Nation." The coverage of campaign events of the candidates was also free as it was funded by the State Budget. There was also a requirement for equal duration, the use of the same journalistic means and forms of coverage, and a changing succession of televising of events.

Runoff polls between the two top-scoring candidate lists were held on November third. Petar Stoyanov won with a majority of 59.73%. His carefully built media image during the campaign had certainly contributed to his success.

CONCLUSION

In the period of transition to a democratic society and a market economy political life in Bulgaria continues to face many social and economic difficulties. Encouragment comes from the fact that the political processes and changes in the country are carried out peacefully and in spite of significant differences between political forces, their reasonable behavior has so far not allowed any display of violence.

On the one hand, practically all the existing mass-media institutions continue to undergo changes in their management, structure, and professional programs. On the other hand, it is disturbing that the legislative regulation of the mass media in Bulgaria is very limited. Problems pertaining to intellectual property rights over the artistic and cultural media products, copyright and distribution rights, have not been settled yet.

Mass media also brought about a high-level politicization of the people in Bulgaria. Journalism operates as a mirror, frequently distorting the political processes in the country, and yet exerting considerable influence on public opinion. In such a situation the Bulgarian National Television maintains a peculiar position. While the printed media is no longer under State monopoly, the national electronic media still depends almost entirely on the State Budget. BNT is still the only available national medium for audio-visual advertisement. In line with the regulations it successfully carried eight campaigns at various levels between 1990 and 1997. Thus, in the process of political fighting for democracy, the foundations of televised political advertisement were laid down in Bulgaria. This reserved for television the great responsibility of molding public opinion, especially since sociological surveys have found Bulgarians maintain greatest confidence in television as compared to the other mass media.

The analysis of political advertising in pre-election campaigns on Bulgarian Television during the period of transition prompts the following inferences and conclusions:

1. Political pluralism was established in the country after four decades of one-party rule.
2. Privatization of the press is fully in progress.
3. Liberalization of radio and television is already under way, though not yet legally regulated.
4. Political advertising has made its advent, and television has become the most important media for political campaigning with new TV genres (such as political video ads, political addresses, and political debates) being introduced.
5. For the first time in Bulgarian history a public debate between two candidates for President was held and aired live on television.

An analysis of the TV political campaign programs shows some interesting characteristics. Only the big political formations, such as the *BSP*, the *UDF*, the *MRF*, the *BAPU*, had the financial and creative opportunities to produce and participate in all the forms of TV propaganda, video ads, addresses and debates. The smaller formations had to restrict themselves mainly to addresses. Gradually, a significant success in terms of creativity was achieved in producing the video ads. However, they still last too long, up to three minutes. The addresses to the electorate of most of the speakers were pretty boring due to the considerable lack of public speaking and television performance experience. A lot more needs to be achieved in the area of the political debates, since there was little discussion on air but very often stiff statements and clumsy declarations.

Bulgaria still experiences the difficulties of the transitional period. The political status quo remains undetermined and unstable. Economic life is left in crisis. The state of culture is problematic and Americanized. The mass media, and especially television, often operate as the Fourth Estate, strongly influencing the political, economic, social, and cultural leanings of public opinion.

A sociological survey, "Mass Media Credibility and Journalistic Ethics", was carried out by *NOEMA LTD.* in July of 1994. This study showed some interesting tendencies. It demonstrated that most Bulgarians would rather trust the national mass media, the Bulgarian National Radio (74%) and the Bulgarian National Television (71%), as sources of reliable information. The cited media inspire more confidence than the Army (63%), the newspapers (61%), and the President (53%). According to the same survey, in cases of controversial or conflicting information people trust above all the Bulgarian National Television (46%). The Bulgarian National Radio comes second (14%), and the newspapers boast only 8% of confidence. Some 59% of the respondents agree with the statement that mass communications influence political life in the country (Media credibility, 1994).

Another sociological survey, carried out by *BBSS Gallup International* in November and December of 1994, during the campaign, on the confidence of the population in the electronic media, showed 56% and 60% for Bulgarian National Television and 66% and 65% for Bulgarian National Radio (Political and Economic Index, 1994). A similar survey conducted again by *BBSS Gallup International* in April of 1995 deals with the confidence Bulgarians have in various institutions. The Bulgarian National Radio ranks first with 68%, followed by Bulgarian National Television (Political and Economic Index, 1995).

As the economic and political situation in Bulgaria continues to evolve, it is clear that the mass media retain an important position in the public confidence. Consequently, the electronic media in particular provide great potential for influencing both electoral outcomes and the conduct of and success of elected governments.

REFERENCES

An Act for Members of Parliament, Municipality Counsellors and Mayors' Elections (1991). Sofia: Official Gazette.

Archive of the Central Electoral Commission.

Archive of the Council of Ministers.

The Constitution of Republic of Bulgaria (1991). Sofia: Official Gazette, No 56.

Decision of the Central Electoral Commission. (1997).

A Decision of the Grand National Assembly on the access to the National Electronic Media during Pre-Election Campaigns (1991). Sofia: Official Gazette, No 71.

An Election Act for Grand National Assembly. (1990). Sofia: Official Gazette, No 28.

A Local Elections Act (1995). Sofia: Official Gazette, No 68.

Mass Media Behavior in "Elections' 90. (1990). A Sociological Survey conducted by the School of Journalism and Mass Communication of the St. Kliment Ohridsky Sofia University.

Media Credibility and Journalistic Ethics. (1994). Sofia: NOEMA Co. Ltd. Social Studies and Marketing.

National Statistical Institute Reports. (1995). Sofia.

Ordinance No 1 of the Committee for Postal Services and Telecommunications. (June 18, 1992). Sofia: State Newspaper: 43.

Pachkova, P. (1996). *The elite in the lime light of elections.* Sofia: M-8-M.

Pesheva, M. (1992). *Television, the political machine.* Sofia: Hercule Publishing House.

Petev, T. (1995). Transitive democratization of the Bulgarian press: Postponed victories. In N. Genov (Ed.), *Sociology in a society in transition.* Sofia: Bulgarian Academy of Sciences.

Political and Economic Index. (1994). Sofia: BBSS Gallup International. Report 8994.

Political and Economic Index. (1995). Sofia: BBSS Gallup International. Report 2595.

A Local Elections Act. (1995). Sofia: Official Gazette, No 68.

A Presidential Elections Act. (1991). Sofia: Official Gazette, No 82.

A Radio and Television Act. (1996). Sofia: Official Gazette, No 77.

Raycheva, L. (1995). The impact of new information technologies on the Bulgarian mass media system. In *Drustvo I Tehnologija' 95.* Rijeka: Gradevinski Fakultet Sveucilista u Rijeci.

Raykov, Z. (1990). *Elections and mass communications.* Sofia: Bulgarski Journalist Magazine, No 11.

Report of the Commission for Control of the Incomes, Expenditures and Property of the Political Parties with the National Assembly. (1995).

Report of the Committee for Postal Services and Telecommunications. (1995). Sofia: Parliamentary Commission for Radio and Television.

Sociological Survey conducted by "ASSA-M". (1994).

Sociological Survey conducted by "Delphis". (1997).

Velikova, M. (1997). *Elections' 97 and their coverage on the TV screen.* M.A. thesis, University for National and World Economics, Sofia, Bulgaria.

Chapter 6

ROMANIAN ELECTIONS AND THE EVOLUTION OF POLITICAL TELEVISION

Dorina Miron, Valentina Marinescu, and Lori Melton McKinnon

The role of the media in political elections in Central and Eastern Europe after the fall of Communism has undoubtedly changed. Two contextual factors make the topic interesting: the emergence of private media and the fierce fight for power between incumbents and opposition. This study attempts to analyze the media and political processes that resulted in the 1996 defeat of the new political structure that took control of Romania following the ouster of Communism in 1989.

Romania, a culture of Roman origin that is geographically isolated in a region of mostly Slavic populations, has shown a strong resistance to Communism. This helps explain the initial support Ceausescu gained from his people as well as from foreign governments as a dissident within the Eastern Block. That support paved the way for Ceausescu's dictatorship, which was one of the most extreme in Eastern Europe.

After the 1989 revolution in Romania, political power remained in the hands of a center-left group which was initially organized as the National Salvation Front and that ultimately became the Party of Social Democracy in Romania (PDSR). The PDSR won the 1990 and 1992 elections. Its leader, Ion Iliescu, had been a dissident under Ceausescu's dictatorship, and Iliescu's center-left policy was expected to ensure maximum social protection during a gradual transition toward a market economy. PDSR temporarily relied on support from extreme left and nationalistic groups that by and large deserted PDSR in 1996.

The opposition that developed in Romania to this government had a wide spectrum, but it managed to establish a center-right coalition led by the National-Peasant-Christian-and-Democratic Party (PNTCD) whose presidential candidate was Emil Constantinescu. The coalition, called the Democratic Convention of Romania (CDR), won the 1996 parliamentary and presidential elections. Their victory against a leftist party that seemed to be in control of Romanian national radio and television was rather unexpected and deserves close scrutiny. Our research examines the forces, particularly in the media, that may explain this unusual outcome in the 1996 Romanian presidential election.

ROMANIAN MASS MEDIA

Overview of Media Development and Structure

The first newspaper in Romania was published in 1829, and the press grew quickly to 1090 publications in 1922 and 2300 (118 dailies) in 1936. The first news agency was established in 1889. The first radio station went on the air in 1928, television was introduced in 1956 (about 600 hours of programming), and the first small-scale illegal cable operations appeared in the late 1980s.

Under Communism, all mass media operations became public property. Their output was drastically reduced to make a strict control by the party possible. The number of media outlets shrank from 56 dailies and 47 radio stations in 1975 to 36 dailies and 9 national and local radio stations by the late 1980s. The two-channel television station, that broadcast 4,642 hours of programming in 1975, was limited in 1985 to 22 hours a week on a single channel that reached 90% of the country (Gross, 1996, pp. 11, 13; Marinescu, 1995, p.91).

The dramatic events of December 1989 (i.e., street violence and clashes with police in western Romania, the state of emergency decreed by Ceausescu on December 22, his flight from the enraged masses and the unleashed dissenting forces supported by top military officers, followed by the execution of Ceausescu and his wife on December 25) produced mass excitement, fear, and uncertainty. This exacerbated people's need for information and increased demand for all forms of media. The National Salvation Front used the national television station as its headquarters and launched appeals to the population to come and defend it. The self-proclaimed Free Romanian Television provided round-the-clock news service and "became a veritable experiment in community broadcasting" (Gross, 1996, p. 35). The subsequent fight for power among the mushrooming political parties maintained a high level of news interest from the first election of May, 1990, until the second election of September, 1992.

Following the 1989 revolution, newspaper circulation increased dramatically, and television broadcasting increased substantially. While print media became and have remained private, broadcast media have emerged as a dual system of public and private entities. This creates a much more difficult situation for broadcasting than for print, from a political standpoint. Private broadcasting theoretically enjoys the same degree of freedom as print in terms of its right to communicate, but it is more restricted as the airwaves broadcasters use are public property. Therefore, stations must reflect the interests and opinions of the public as a whole, which pragmatically limits broadcasters' rights to communicate. No such conflict occurs in public broadcasting, which is fully regulated, both in terms of public property management and communication content.

Thus, structural and ownership characteristics of the mass media industry in Romania resulted in a differentiated relationship of the three major types of media (print, private broadcasting, and public broadcasting) within the law. From a political perspective, this situation creates different opportunities in the three types of media for democratization through minority access, issue and viewpoint diversity, citizen participation, and expression of criticism. From an electoral perspective, the situation makes the national public radio and television instruments of the government. It leaves the private media for opposition groups to use as a field for their political maneuvers. Since newspaper readership is decreasing, and magazine circulation is comparatively small, print media has less potential for political persuasion than broadcasting.

The role of the news media was also complicated following the fall of Communism by the fact that all journalists trained under the earlier system were subject to the need for loyalty to the party in power. Journalistic style was intellectual and French, i.e., "highly subjective, polemical and partisan" (Gross, 1996, p. 6). Consequently, the population had little respect for and confidence in journalists when the wave of revolution sweeping Eastern Europe finally hit Romania in December, 1989. The journalistic profession in post-revolutionary Romania had to rebuild its status and power starting from negative values.

By 1996, the plummeting standard of living sobered the population from the revolution scare and reactivated its self-interest. Aggressive private media seized the opportunity to take the lead in the power game. They did this by playing the opposition against the incumbents and defying existing legislation and regulations that required media impartiality. The population lived a cathartic moment of self-assertion occasioned by the elections, but practically endorsed the pro-opposition choice already made by the private media.

It is important to understand how the social and political situation in Romania may have affected the public's opinions about both politicians and the role of the media at this crucial point in evolution of democracy in Romania. According to Gross (1996, p. xi), "Only 10-15% of Romania's population of 23 million could be considered middle class. Ten and a half million today live below the official poverty level, and nearly 12 million more are daily concerned with the possibility of joining the former." Thus, a critical question that arises is to what extent the relationship between the impoverished Romanian population and the politicians was mediated by the press. The answer involves two aspects: (1) media's potential to exert an influence on the electorate (which depends on such factors as media consumption, incentives for the media to get involved in politics, legislative and regulatory restrictions against manipulations by the media, law enforcement, population manipulability), and (2) the extent to which that potential for manipulation was actualized, i.e., what manipulative acts occurred (if any), and with what results.

Media consumption registered considerable fluctuations in Romania. Right before the revolution, the audience was tired of Communist propaganda. Consequently, the audience had turned away from public television and controlled newspapers and received a great deal of information from anti-Communist foreign radio (Gross, 1996). During the revolution most Romanians stopped working and media consumption became an addiction. However, after a few years, poverty, political disappointment, and boredom with the stereotypical media fare brought the situation back to some level of normality. This may be one explanation for the decisive role played by private television stations in the 1996 elections.

The Public Opinion Barometer (CURS, 1996, Oct.) showed that Romanians' reliance on various media for political information presented a rather stable pattern between March, 1995, and October, 1996. During this time, television ranked first, slightly growing in importance from 61% to 64%; radio was a distant second, in decline from 20% to 15%; newspapers ranked third at a low and stable 7% level. Only 7 to 8% of the population declared lack of interest in politics in 1995-1996, and another 6% relied on private conversations for political information.

Regulations on Media in Political and Election Contexts

The Constitution of Romania adopted on November, 1991, has two (out of 152) articles that affect the mass media. Article 30 defines freedom of expression, and Article 31 refers to the right to information. Both articles are filled with contradictions. For example, Article 30 Paragraph 1 says that, "freedom to express thoughts, opinions or beliefs" in all manner of public communication is "inviolable." Paragraph 2 of the Constitution forbids "censorship of any kind," Paragraph 6 restricts media content to expressions that do not prejudice anyone's "dignity, honor, and privacy," and Paragraph 7 makes it unlawful to "defame the country and the nation, to instigate war, national, racial, class or religious hatred, discrimination, territorial separatism or public violence, as well as obscene acts contrary to good morals," etc.

Many yardsticks can be applied by Parliament, depending on the situation. The "electoral importance," for example, was determined in 1996 using the percentage of seats in Parliament as a criterion. This led to a proportional distribution of campaign air time that made it possible for the major political parties to undemocratically silence the small nonparliamentary groups. The procedure ultimately resulted in pressure on small parties to join larger ones, which converted small parties into a clientele for manipulation during the elections. Gross (1996, p. 76) believes that "the flexibility of interpretation built into the Romanian constitution, or rather its vagueness, is not necessarily intrinsically dangerous to freedom of the press and of expression," but he endorses Middleton's (1993, p. 405) opinion that the danger is associated with the ministry of justice, that is still politicized and lacks independence. Unfortunately, Romanian politics are still plagued by the experience-reinforced "wisdom" that "laws are for the underdog."

The Law of Broadcasting (May 1992) was inspired from French, American, Italian, German, and British models, and it includes 45 articles. Article 11 mandates the establishment of the National Audio-Visual Council (NAVC) which Article 34 puts under direct control of Parliament. The NAVC staff cannot include members of political organizations. NAVC's primary duty is to issue broadcasting licenses (the frequencies are established by the Ministry of Communication). The second major function of NAVC is to elaborate regulations for the broadcasting industry. For example, criteria for broadcast commercials, or guidelines for the involvement of both public and private media in election campaigns. NAVC can also establish mandatory norms for public radio and television (Marinescu, 1995, p.88).

The Law of Public Radio and Television (June, 1994) has 54 articles. Article 2 puts public radio and television under direct control of Parliament, and Article 52 requires the two administrative councils to report annually or "whenever Parliament decides." Article 5 requires both public and private services to reserve air time for the political parties represented in Parliament in direct proportion with the number of seats held by each party. Article 8 guarantees editorial autonomy and independence, and program protection from any interference or pressure from public authorities or any other social, political, or commercial organization or pressure group. Finally, Article 9 requires public radio and television to give priority to the free transmission of all communication of public interest received from Parliament, the President, the Supreme Council of National Defense, or the Government. Additional regulations embodied in the Penal Code apply to coverage of security issues, punishing defamation and libel, and other such concerns.

Additional regulatory details specifically for the 1996 elections were issued by the National Audio-Visual Council, upon consultation with Parliament, to which it is directly responsible, and with the political parties represented in Parliament. The 1996 elections were organized in compliance with Law 68/1992 for Parliamentary Elections, Law 69/1992 for Presidential Elections, and Law 27/1996 for Political Parties. At the same time, the election campaigns were under the jurisdiction of the Constitution, the Law of Broadcasting, the Law of Public Radio and Television, the Penal Code, and the Government Decision 578/1996 that set the election schedule. Campaigns were also required to comply with the NAVC Decision 88/1996 that established conditions for candidates' access to broadcast media; regulated the structure, schedule, format, and content of programming related to the elections; and specified limits for campaign advertising. NAVC required stations to keep recordings of their election programs and make them available to NAVC upon request.

NAVC also forbade the presence and coverage of candidates in non-election programming (news, entertainment etc.) during the elections but made an exception for candidates currently in office, which created a potential advantage for power holders, including the incumbent president. This did not prevent NAVC from emphasizing in its regulations equal treatment of the candidates.

NAVC Decision 88 required all stations to inform the audience in advance about their electoral programs and to carry special programming about the election system and the voting procedures. The Decision recapitulated the legal framework of the elections and the responsibilities of candidates and media organizations and employees. NAVC went as far as labeling various categories of programming and setting guidelines for behavior and etiquette.

The distribution of air time on public radio and television was made by a special Parliamentary Commission for Air Time Allocation, that shared the "pie" according to the proportion of seats in Parliament. Private broadcasters were allowed to sell air time "without discrimination," but they had to follow the same pattern of allocation set by the parliamentary commission for public stations. This system has a crucial built-in bias, conducive to a "reproduction" through the elections of the same power structure. Young nonparliamentary parties were automatically excluded from this allocation, and they were unable to buy air time even on private television.

Interestingly, in spite of all these strict and detailed regulations and many specific regulations that tended to favor incumbent office-holders, media performance in the 1996 election campaigns exhibited an overall media bias, not in support of the incumbent, but against him. Most media defied the legislation with impunity because the opposition they supported won, and the population did not protest.

MEASURING THE MEDIA EFFECTS IN THE 1996 CAMPAIGN

The findings we report here are based on two types of data. The first was a series of experiments and focus groups carried out during the 1996 election, using a design outlined by Kaid (Kaid, 1997) and used in other Western democracies (Holtz-Bacha & Kaid, 1990; Kaid & Holtz-Bacha, 1995). The experiments and focus groups were conducted between the first and second ballot of the 1996 presidential election (November 4-12) in two cities (the capital, Bucharest, and Sibiu, a city in central Romania).

The Romanian subject sample included 125 participants, 66 from Bucharest and 59 from Sibiu (40 males and 85 females, ranging in age from 17 to 73 years, with a mean age slightly above 30 years). Convenience samples were used in both locations. They included mostly students at the Academy of Economic Studies (ASE) and the Graduate School of Communication (SNSPA) in Bucharest, and at the University of Sibiu.[1] Both the non-randomness and the small size of the sample call for caution in extrapolating the findings of this study to the entire population.

To compensate for this problem in generalizing the results, we used a second type of data, the results of survey research studies conducted by other researchers in Romania who used national samples. These secondary sources included (1) a public opinion panel study on over 1500 subjects (surveyed four times a year since 1994) that was conducted by Centrul de Sociologie Urbana si Regionala (the Center for Urban and Regional Sociology)/CURS (1996) in cooperation with Institutul de Marketing si Analize Sociale (the Institute of Marketing and Social Analysis)/IMAS and Institutul de Cercetari pentru Calitatea Vietii (the Research Institute for the Quality of Life)/ICCV and (2) a panel study on the electoral preferences and behavior of over 1000 subjects conducted during the election campaign (October-November) by the Institutul de Sociologie al Academiei Romane (the Institute of Sociology of the Romanian Academy)/ISAR (1996). We also used the content analysis data derived from monitoring the prime-time coverage of political issues by the four major television stations in Romania (public television on Channel 1, and three private stations: Tele7abc, Antena1, and ProTV) conducted in September, October, and November, 1996, by Centrul Independent de Studii Sociale si Sondaje (the Independent Center for Social Studies and Polling)/ISSS (1996).

The experimental sessions involved administration of pretest questionnaires to measure reactions to the candidates and other political and demographic items. Subjects then watched a selection of television spots from the major candidates and filled out a posttest questionnaire. Following the experimental sessions, subject participated in focus group discussions. The analysis of the secondary data involved summarizing and calculating central tendencies.

MEDIA EFFECTS IN THE 1996 PRESIDENTIAL CAMPAIGN

The Socio-Political Context and the Media as Players

The negative vote, empty promises, and media's appetite for drama. Dobrescu (1997) has labeled the massive vote against the incumbents in 1996 as a "protest vote" and a "despair vote" (p. 20). According to a 3-wave panel study conducted by ISAR (Institutul de Sociologie al Academiei Romane 1996), at the beginning of the 1996 election campaign, 46% of Romania's voting citizens felt hopeless and only 36% felt hopeful. Most people cast their vote with the idea of opposition in mind (22%), rather then in support of any specific party or group within the opposition alliance (18%). The victory of the opposition was attributed by 37% of the population to the general disappointment with the PDSR government and only by 16% to the quality of the program put forward by the opposition coalition, CDR. Opinion polls between 1994 and 1996 had generally confirmed that citizens felt their lives were worsening, and few were satisfied with the pace of changes in the countries economic and social conditions (Centrul de Sociologie Urbana si Rurala, 1996). CURS panel data (from 11 waves between 1994 and 1996) indicate that 49% of Romanians believed that things in Romania were going in the wrong direction. The unprecedented economic hardships also explain the hierarchy of reasons why Romanians watched the election campaign. Of Romanians, 32% wanted to see how the candidates proposed to solve the problems, and considerably fewer were interested in politicians' behavior (15%) or their (parties') programs (13%).

Despite the fact that the declining standard of living had decreased expectations, the 1996 election campaign effected a spectacular resurgence of optimism, perhaps as a result of the promises made by candidates during the campaign and of a heightened sense of self efficacy, confirmed by the primary data we collected. According to our data, 92% of our subjects expressed partial or total disagreement with the statement "My vote does not matter," and 91% disagreed with the statement "People like me have no voice and no impact on politics and government." Interestingly, Romanians' strong internal locus of control and willingness to participate in the electoral process were not affected by their distrust of politicians. This was reflected by our subjects' 96 to 98% agreement to statements about politicians' unreliability, empty promises, self interest, dissimulation, and lack of transparency. Dobrescu (1997) again speculates that "When people are poor, promises are a psychological remedy," and "Poverty depletes patience and defeats reason into accepting and believing what is being promised" (pp. 181-182). Dobrescu concludes that one reason why the opposition and Constantinescu won was that they made liberal use of promises, and unhesitatingly applied the principle "First you promise, and then you see what you can do" (p. 181), while Iliescu refused to play the electoral game and applied his own moral rule "I cannot make promises that have no basis," which reflected pragmatism and a long-term perspective (p. 181).

The margin of manipulability and media as manipulators. If the population has some susceptibility to be manipulated, through a willingness to believe promises, did this characteristic vary by region in the country and what role or responsibility did the media have in this situation?

One objection that may be raised in connection with our research is that the sample included urban and mostly young intellectual subjects. If these populations have a more "tuned-in" view of what is going on in Romania, then urban intellectuals should have had a decisive role in the elections, and our data may be close to representative for the whole constituency. On the other hand, the rural population may not be aware of changing realities, imbedded as they are in their old routines and with fewer reasons to distrust politicians. The different dynamics of manipulability between cities and the countryside can account for the "wisdom" traditionally attributed to peasants, their lower margin of manipulability being paradoxically due to misplaced confidence in politicians. An important factor to consider in relation with manipulation is the percentage of undecided voters, which in Romania, between October 5 and 15, 1996, was as high as 29% at the parliamentary elections, and 26% at the presidential elections (Institutul de Sociologie al Academiei Romane, 1996). And according to ISAR data, 13% of Romanians watched the campaign to make up their minds for whom to cast their vote.

To what media were these manipulable voters attending? According to the Public Opinion Barometer (Centrul de Sociologie Urbana si Regionala, 1996), between March, 1995, and October, 1996, the population that subscribed to newspapers in Romania oscillated between 21% and 13%, with a mean of 16%. In 1996, subscriptions declined sharply from the maximum 21% in March to a minimum 13% in October. The ISAR data (Institutul de Sociologie al Academiei Romane, 1996) show that the two most widely read newspapers in Romania in October, 1996 were the leading opposition champions Evenimentul Zilei (274 mentions) and Romania Libera (144 mentions) followed by the "independent" anti-establishment Adevarul (126 mentions), totaling 544 mentions. Meanwhile, the pro-establishment Cronica Romana (19 mentions), Vocea Romaniei (9 mentions), and Dimineata (6 mentions) totaled only 34 mentions. So, if newspapers had an overall impact on the electorate, that could only be a pro-opposition influence.

The CURS Barometer shows that the audience of the national radio dropped from 71% in March, 1994, to 54% in October, 1996 (losing 17 percentage points), while the audience of private local radio stations rose from 10 to 29% of the population over the same period. A similar switch from national to private local stations occurred with television viewers. The TVR1 audience decreased from 85% in March, 1994 to 74% in October, 1996 (lower loss than the national radio, only 11%), while private local stations jumped from 8% in March, 1994, to 28% in December 1995, and soared in the election year 1996, to 41% in December and 48% in October (Institutul de Sociologie al

Academiei Romane, 1996). The ISAR data indicate that television, especially private local stations, had the potential to be the major opinion leader in the 1996 campaign.

Our own research data also reflect Romanians' preference for television as the major source of news (60% of our respondents watched news every day), much more popular than newspapers (only 15% of respondents read newspapers daily, and 51% read newspapers between 2 and 4 days a week). Both the CURS public opinion barometer and the ISAR panel confirm that the population perceived television to be the most informative source of political and campaign information (Table 6.1).

Table 6.1 - CURS and ISAR Data about the Relative Importance Political Information Sources

Sources	CURS (preferred source)	ISAR (multiple sources)
Television	64%	42%
Radio	15%	25%
Newspapers	7%	18%
Discussions with other people	6%	20%
Opinion polls		7%
Posters		4%
Brochures, fliers		3%
Personal contact with candidates		1%
Public meetings with candidates		1%

The ISAR panel on electoral behavior (Institutul de Sociologie al Academiei Romane, 1996) shows that at the end of October, 1996, 24% of Romanians perceived television to exert a strong influence on the public's political opinions, while only 16% of the population gave that credit to the radio, and as little as 11% appreciated newspapers as a strong source of influence. Table 6.2 summarizes ISAR data on news sources used on a regular basis in October, 1996 (percentage of mentions per total number of participants). Although the ISAR question allowed for multiple sources and the percentages overlap, the data suggest that in television the private stations had the upper hand, while in radio the national and regional public stations dominated the news market. According to ISAR, national television slightly increased its audience as the presidential elections approached, while the private stations began to lose ground, which signals the audience's discontent with their coverage. The trend in radio was in the opposite direction, with people's attention shifting toward private local stations.

Table 6.2 - Sources of News During the 1996 Election Campaign

Sources	Oct.5-15	Oct.21-31
TVR1 (national public television)	37%	39%
ProTV (private TV station)	24%	24%
Antena1 (private TV station)	15%	14%
Tele7abc (private TV station)	5%	4%
Local private TV station	4%	5%
Radio Romania News (national)	25%	25%
Regional public radio	8%	7%
Local private radio	8%	9%

What could have caused viewers' discontent? In order to answer this question, political content of television programming must be examined. CIS (Centrul Independent de Studii Sociale si Sondaje, 1996) monitored prime time coverage of politics on national television (i.e., TVR1) and on the three leading private stations ProTV, Antena1, and Tele7abc, whose newscasts were watched daily by 24%, 14%, and 4% of the population, respectively. The study was subsidized by the European Union PHARE Program for Democracy and by the Soros Foundation for an Open Society, and it consisted in a content analysis of 6 o'clock to 11 o'clock p.m. socio-political programming and news. The study included three waves, September 9 to 15, September 30 to October 6, and November 12 to 18. CIS researchers assessed the frequency of news about incumbents, opposition, and others. They also examined the distribution of air time (as coverage frequency and duration) among incumbents, opposition, and others among parties and political alliances, and among political leaders.

The findings from this study of news content during the 1996 presidential campaign are somewhat surprising. First, in terms of frequency, prime-time news surprisingly favored the opposition over the incumbents on national television by a 2.13 ratio, more than the private station Tele7abc (1.80 ratio), while the private stations ProTV and Antena1 gave equal attention to power holders and incumbents. Only when news is expanded to include social and political programming did the incumbents have a strong advantage over the opposition. And, looking at the power/opposition balance in terms of frequency of coverage of the major parties and alliances and of the top three presidential candidates, the pattern is different. The national television favored the governing party (i.e., PDSR) and the president in office (i.e., Iliescu), while all three major private stations favored the opposition. This difference in pattern is due to the fact that news and overall coverage of power vs. opposition included the government as a major actor. Once government is taken out of the picture, the pro-opposition bias of the private stations in terms of frequency of coverage becomes apparent.

Beyond frequency of coverage, it is also significant to assess the evaluations of parties and candidates by the national television and the three leading private stations in Romania. TVR1 had a laudatory/critical ratio of 28:1 for the governing party, and of 5:2

for the challenging alliance. The TVR1 laudatory/critical ratios for the top three presidential candidates again favored the incumbent (20:0) over his main challenger (3:1 for Constantinescu). The private station with the largest audience, ProTV, abstained from any criticism but gave more positive coverage to the opposition than to incumbents (i.e., 4:1 at the party level, and 5:1 at the level of presidential candidates). The next top-ranking private stations, Antena1 and Tele7abc, obviously favored the opposition, their respective laudatory/critical ratios were 3:24 and 2:7 for the governing party, and 21:0 and 9:1 for the opposition parties. The laudatory/critical ratios at the presidential candidate level were 0:4 for the incumbent at both stations, and 9:0 and 2:0 respectively for the opposition leader, Constantinescu.

Qualitative data from the Sibiu focus group revealed the fact that Romanians did perceive media biases. Simona pointed out that "there is no middle-of-the-road press," Olimpianu agreed that "there is no such thing as 'independent press,'" and Marcel indignantly observed that "everybody knows that the national television is subordinated to the power." Iliescu's counselor for press relations filled in the picture, "Indeed, the [national] television allotted more air-time to information about the power, that is true. But it is also true that the cultural programming and the political debates were dominated by opposition representatives" (Dobrescu 1997, p. 141). Monica (Sibiu focus group) noticed that the partisan media tended to distort the truth more than the independent press, "I think that to a large extent they disinform the public, especially those that support the Convention [i.e., CDR] or PDSR." As to the impact of the media, opinions were divergent. Some participants believed that "everybody's opinion is influenced somehow by television, ...by what we read, by discussions with friends, because we cannot form an opinion without these elements" (Nae, Sibiu focus group). Others believed in limited and peripheral effects. According to Doina (Sibiu focus group), "the mass media have influenced the constituency very little, but flared up people's passions," and according to Flavius (Sibiu focus group) "the mass media had a relatively big influence on the turnout."

A key issue in connection with media bias is the population's tolerance for this phenomenon, that determines the degree of public pressure to correct the problem. According to our mid-November data, collected after the first presidential ballot, Romanians were rather distrustful of politicians, and 74.4% of our respondents scored higher than midpoint on our cynicism scale. The ISAR panel data (Institutul de Sociologie al Academiei Romane, 1996) from the second wave (October 21-31) show that 36% of the population was rather displeased with the campaigns (compared to 31% who declared overall satisfaction), and 35% said the campaigns had weakened their confidence in politicians (compared to 33% who expressed the opposite view). But the participants in our Sibiu focus group (e.g., Simona and Olimpianu quoted above) indicated that media biases were considered inherent to the press, and people were rather resigned to the problem.

"The small brick overturns the big cart." This Romanian proverb accurately illustrates the 1996 presidential elections in Romania. The quantitative and qualitative pro-opposition biases of the private television stations were reflected in the public opinion trends during the election year. The CURS data (Centrul de Sociologie Urbana si

Regionala, 1996), reveal that at the beginning of 1996 the percentage of population that had a positive opinion about the incumbent president was higher than the 1994-1995 average (63% compared to 55%). Constantinescu started his campaign approximately just under a 50% level of positive support. In March 1996, before the beginning of the campaign, Iliescu enjoyed a higher percentage of positive views from the public (63% vs. 49% for Constantinescu). During the campaign, positive opinion about Iliescu regressed to 55% without dropping lower, while opinions about Constantinescu improved to put him on a par with Iliescu, also at 55%. The CURS data (Centrul de Sociologie Urbana si Regionala, 1996) show that in July Constantinescu was still behind Iliescu in terms of positive public opinion. The data indicate that Iliescu's campaign had negative effects, annihilating his 1995 gain in positive public appreciation. Constantinescu's campaign pushed him up seven percentage points until July, after which it took a downward turn, resulting in a loss of a single percentage point. The best campaign was that of the second challenger, Roman, whose efforts gained him thirteen percentage points by July, and kept gaining ground until the end of the campaign. Given the Iliescu-Constantinescu tie (reflected rather well by their respective 32% and 28% shares of the votes in the first ballot), Roman's exceptionally effective campaign and the resulting increase in his popularity explains why his support of Constantinescu in the second presidential ballot was decisive for Constantinescu's victory (75% out of Roman's 17% share of the electorate in the first ballot followed his example and voted for Constantinescu in the second ballot).

All sorts of misconceptions. So far we have discussed the campaign at a macro level, in an effort to identify the general dynamics that contributed to the rather unexpected victory of the opposition in Romania in 1996. What follows is a close-up of our experimental findings, with the purpose of explaining the effects of demographics (at pretest, and at posttest in conjunction with spot viewing) on candidate evaluations and also the media and the campaign effects. The discussion in the following three sections will be organized around popular beliefs about the factors that contributed to the challenger's victory.

Is Transylvania different from the rest of Romania? Was it Transylvania that got Constantinescu elected? After the 1996 elections, Dobrescu (1997, p. 254) looked at a map of Romania showing electoral preferences that had favored Iliescu in the southern and eastern counties and Constantinescu in the central and western regions. That newspaper picture reminded Dobrescu of Samuel Huntington's (1993) thesis of cultural conflict between Eastern and Western Europe, and the American politologist's belief that the borderline between East and West crossed Romania, separating Transylvania from the southern and eastern part of the country. According to Huntington, Transylvania belonged to the Western civilization, while the rest of Romania, including the territories occupied by Slavic populations, belonged to the East.

This theory may be interesting, but the primary data do not provide much support for it. A reminder is in place here, our sample was relatively small and non-random, it included 66 subjects (53%) from Bucharest, the capital situated in southern Romania, and 59 subjects (47%) from Sibiu, a city in Transylvania. Consequently, caution must be exercised in extrapolating our findings, and justify further research on the issue, using a nationally representative sample.

Our arguments against a "clash of civilizations" in Romania are that (1) from an "electoral culture" perspective, geographic location had few main effects on our campaign-relevant variables, and (2) the patterns of interaction between location and the other variables under study differed between the two candidates, which means that they were candidate-specific rather than location-specific. Overall, geographic location affected Constantinescu more than the incumbent Iliescu, who was better known by everybody, and therefore evaluations of him and his campaign were more homogeneous across the country.

Our results indicate absolutely no significant main effects differentiating Bucharest (i.e., the capital situated in southern Romania) from Sibiu (situated in Transylvania) in terms of candidate thermometers[2] and Likability Indices. Whatever impact geographic location had on those variables was indirect, through interactions with other variables.

In Iliescu's case, the change from pre- to posttest in people's liking of him by location (means: -2.82 in Bucharest, and .29 in Sibiu) came close to reaching statistical significance ($p = .06$). Iliescu's spots increased very little his liking in Sibiu (i.e., in Transylvania, far away from the capital), but strongly disappointed people in the capital. One more finding concerning Iliescu's campaign may help explain the mechanism of disappointment. An almost significant interaction occurred between location and campaign watching ($p = .06$) as independent variables of information acquisition from Iliescu's spots. The information-acquisition means of location-by-campaign-watching (Bucharest: 3, 4.72, 4.07 on a 0 to 12 scale; Sibiu: 5, 4.28, 5.67) indicate that more watching raised Iliescu's perceived-information-acquisition scores in Bucharest relative to little watching (by people who did not rely much on the campaign for information), but intensive watching diminished the perceived information gain. In Sibiu, more watching was associated with lower information acquisition scores that little watching, and intensive campaign watching produced a 2.39-point increase on a 0 to 12 scale. This shows that in Bucharest more campaign watching was associated with an impression of decreasing information gain from Iliescu's campaign, but in Sibiu it produced an impression of increased information gain. People's attitude towards the campaign as a source of information seemed to be different in the capital and outside the capital, or in southern Romania and in Transylvania. Our results suggest that people in Sibiu may have paid more attention to the campaign and learned more from it than Bucharest dwellers did.

In Constantinescu's case, 2-way ANOVA results show that location interacted with age as independent variables of his thermometer (i.e., people's liking of him). The interaction was close to significant at pretest ($p = .07$) and became highly significant at posttest ($p=.02$). The interaction effect was a polarization of the 51+ age group, with capital dwellers liking Constantinescu about twice as much as Transylvanians in Sibiu (corresponding means: 82 and 41.67 on a 0 to 100 scale), whereas Constantinescu's liking means in the other age groups ranged between 63.36 and 75.82). Location-age interactions also occurred when the two variables were considered as possible factors of Constantinescu's thermometer change ($p = .02$), and of the emotional impact of his spots

(p = .01). Those interactions had the same polarizing effect with the 51+ age group, resulting in a 10.4 difference in thermometer change (on a 0 to 100 scale), and a 2.70 difference in emotional impact (on a 0 to 18 scale). Interestingly, location interacted with campaign watching as independent variables of Constantinescu's posttest thermometer (p = .05) and of the emotional impact of his spots (p = .01). Again, the interaction effects were somewhat similar to that of the location-age interaction: high levels of campaign watching tended to polarize liking and emotional impact in the capital and in Transylvania with people aged 51+, being associated in Bucharest with higher scores, and in Sibiu with lower scores.

Our findings indicate that the relevance of location to the 1996 presidential campaigns in Romania was, in Iliescu's case, mostly in terms of information acquisition and mediated by campaign watching. Whereas location in Constantinescu's case was mostly in emotional terms and mediated by age more than by campaign watching.

As an alternative to Huntington's cultural conflict between East and West, we hypothesize the level of urbanization as a source of the differences found between Transylvania and the southern part of Romania in terms of politically relevant variables and their relationships. The urban population tends to be more active politically and more manipulable (as shown in our discussion on the margin of manipulability), while peasants are less likely to participate in the political process and more conservative. The fact that Transylvania, the central-western part of Romania has more larger towns and cities, i.e., is more urbanized, may account for Transylvanians' preference for "western" Constantinescu in the 1996 presidential election. We could not test our hypothesis using the data we collected for this study because our sample did not include the rural population. But the very shortcomings of our research generated some support for our hypothesis. Our sample had a pro-opposition bias revealed by the pretest 66-degree average liking of Constantinescu vs. 28-degree average liking of Iliescu, i.e., a 2.36 ratio, much higher than the 1.2 preference for Constantinescu over Iliescu in the second ballot. That bias was probably caused by the fact that all our respondents were city dwellers and was aggravated by an age bias (mean: 30.37, mode: 19). Since rural areas in Romania have an older population, our sample tended to reflect urban trends.

In addition to these observations, the election analysis published in *Evenimentul Zilei* (November 19, 1996), provides two stronger arguments in support of our untested hypothesis, along the same lines. First, 79% of the peasants cast their votes for the incumbent. Secondly, 66% of persons aged thirty-four or younger preferred Constantinescu over Iliescu.

Did the students get Constantinescu elected? The fact that Constantinescu was a university professor, and the widespread belief that students constitute the political avant-garde, made Romanians credit youth with Constantinescu's victory (Dobrescu 1997, p. 22). We assessed the relevance of age to the 1996 presidential campaign in Romania based on 2-way ANOVA results.

The data we collected showed that age had a significant effect on Iliescu's thermometer (p values between .02 and .04) both at pre- and posttest--the older the subjects, the stronger their liking of Iliescu (average ratings: 24.68 with people up to 30, 31.1 with people aged 31-50, and 42.12 with people aged 51+). The tendency for age to interact with campaign watching at pretest ($p = .05$) disappeared at posttest, when the influence of campaign watching in general was overpowered by the effect of viewing the experimental spots. In Iliescu's case, the effects of age were also found with pretest/posttest thermometer change and emotional impact as dependent variables ($p < .05$). When information acquisition from Iliescu's spots was considered, interactions were found between age and gender ($p = .03$) and between age and political preference ($p = .01$) as independent variables. Information acquisition with people up to 30 was about the same for males and females (corresponding averages: 4.19 and 4.34 on a 0 to 12 scale), and then it differentiated strongly with people aged 31-50 (means: 3.1 for males and 6.0 for females), and reversed the balance with people over 51 (means: 6.22 for males and 5.13 for females). The age-political-preference interaction had the following effects: similar levels of perceived information acquisition with people up to 30 (means between 4.13 and 4.51 on a 0 to 12 scale), then a strong differentiation between 31 and 50 among leftists (mean: 3.0), supporters of the right (mean: 6.33), and independents and others (mean: 5.2). Within the over 51 age group, leftists declared higher information acquisition than conservatives (mean: 6.5), supporters of the right scored lowest (mean: 3.2), and independents scored highest (mean: 8.0). With independents, perceived information acquisition increased steadily with age, with leftists it ebbed between 31 and 50, and rose with people over 51. With conservatives it improved between 31 and 50, and declined after that age.

In Constantinescu's case, age had an effect on candidate liking only at pretest ($p < .05$), when people aged over 51 tended to like Constantinescu significantly less (means: 68.68 up to 30, 68.35 between 31 and 50, and 50.47 for over 51). Age interacted significantly with location as independent variables predicting the level of posttest liking ($p = .02$), of thermometer change ($p = .02$), and of the emotional impact of the spots we presented in the experiment ($p = .01$). These interaction effects were reported and discussed in detail in connection with location.

In Iliescu's case, age had a stronger direct influence on our respondents' perceptions of the candidate and his spots, and its impact was to some extent mediated by personal variables (i.e., gender and political preference) and by a media-related variable (i.e., campaign watching). In Constantinescu's case the direct effects of age were weaker, and its impact tended to be mediated by geographic location, which is an impersonal factor. Means reveal an overall tendency toward uniformity with people up to 30, and more differentiation after that age, with a tendency to reverse gender and left-right polarizations from adulthood (31-50) to old age (over 51).

According to our thermometer data (Table 6.3), growing older made people like Iliescu more (absolute difference in pretest liking means between the youngest and the oldest age groups: 17.44) and Constantinescu less (absolute difference: 18.21). Based on this finding, it would be correct to say that Constantinescu is a president of the younger people. But on the other hand, the 2-way ANOVA cell means discussed above indicate that young people tended to be less responsive to the election campaign, and the effectiveness of the campaign was mediated by age mostly with people over 31. If we compute the pretest/posttest differences in liking per age group, we find -1.45 for Iliescu and +1.32 for Constantinescu with people up to 30, -4.75 for Iliescu and -1.75 for

Constantinescu with the 31 to 50 age group, and +3.17 for Iliescu and +3.06 for Constantinescu with people aged over 51. These numbers suggest (1) a low but discriminative change with the younger people, who were enthusiastic about Constantinescu and critical of Iliescu; (2) a totally negative response of the 31 to 50 group to the television spots of both candidates-indicative of critical viewing-with a more intense disappointment with Iliescu's spots; and (3) a strong and totally positive response of the over 51 group-indicative of benevolent viewing-with almost equal increases in the liking of both candidates. According to the means presented in Table 6.3, Constantinescu won because of an overall preference for him. What the campaign contributed to the victory were attitude changes with people up to 50, i.e., a 3-point differentiation in candidate liking within the 31-50 group, and a 2.77-point differentiation with the younger voters up to 30.

Table 6.3 - Candidate Liking by Age Group: Cell Means and Probability Values from One-Way ANOVAs)

Candidate	Test	Liking Means by Age			Significance
		Up to 30	31-50	Above 50	
Iliescu	Pretest	24.68	31.10	42.12	.06
	Posttest	**23.23**	**26.35**	45.29	.02
Constantinescu	Pretest	68.68	68.35	50.47	.06
	Posttest	70.00	**66.60**	53.53	.14

According to the significance levels shown in Table 6.3, the relevance of age to candidate liking was higher overall and increasing from pre- to posttest in Iliescu's case, whereas in Constantinescu's case age was close to significant at pretest but became insignificant at posttest. This indicates the possibility that Iliescu's spots may have carried messages more specifically addressed to certain age groups, or messages that triggered divergent reactions from different age groups. Constantinescu's spots, however, seem to have de-emphasized age differences.

Did women fall for good-looking and younger Constantinescu? This question was triggered by the fact that 52% of women expressed an anti-Iliescu preference (*Evenimentul Zilei*, November 19, 1996). But the 58% male preference for Constantinescu is always ignored, or said to reflect a deeper male understanding of politics.

Two-way ANOVAs showed that gender did not have any main effects on the liking of candidates at pre- and posttest. But it did impact Iliescu's thermometer change in our experiment ($p = .01$). As a result of viewing the spots, male participants registered a significant decrease in their liking of Iliescu (-5.20 on a 0 to 100 scale), whereas female participants did not change their preference significantly (.46 positive change on the same scale).

One possible explanation for the gender-specific change in Iliescu's thermometer may be the gender-sensitive information acquisition from his campaign, revealed by the interaction we found in his case between age and gender as independent variables of information gain ($p = .03$). According to our data, information gain from Iliescu's campaign was not significantly different between genders with people up to 30. It tended to decrease with males aged 31-50, and to increase sharply toward old age (means for males: 4.19, 3.1, 6.22 on a 0 to 12 scale). With females, information acquisition from Iliescu's campaign tended to increase between 31 and 50, and then to decrease slowly toward old age (means: 4.43, 6, 5.13). This finding suggests an indirect influence of gender on people's liking of Iliescu, mediated by information acquisition, which was affected by gender in interaction with age.

Another significant finding was the interaction between gender and political preference as independent variables in Iliescu's Likability Index ($p = .02$). The disappointment of males vis-a-vis Iliescu was lower with self-declared democrats than with conservatives, and it was highest with independents and others, while the most disappointed women were in the leftist group. The interaction suggests that males' assessment of Iliescu was mediated by their political preference, leftist supporters being less disappointed than conservative opponents. The criteria used by females to evaluate Iliescu seem to have been their own expectations, therefore the most disappointed women were democrats who felt betrayed by the center-left incumbent. Our empirical findings indicate that Romanian women were not naive, but pragmatic, while men tended to be driven mostly by ideology.

Our political Cynicism Index was sensitive to gender. In addition, a significant direct effect of gender on general media consumption was present, indicating that political preference, political cynicism, and general media consumption are related, and have a gender-colored impact on the changes in overall candidate evaluations and feature-by-feature evaluations, as well as on information acquisition from the campaign.

Did the media get Constantinescu elected? Iliescu's campaign team kept complaining about the "extraordinary importance of the press" (Dobrescu 1997, p. 138), which in their view had become "the first estate." They justified Iliescu's defeat by arguing that "in any battle between the power and the press, the press will win"(Dobrescu 1997, p. 6). This media fright was assiduously and self-interestedly cultivated by Romanian journalists. Marius Petrean, from the Curierul National daily warned power holders that "One cannot win the elections having an adversary press" (p. 6). Ion Cristoiu, the editor-in-chief of the largest circulation tabloid *Evenimentul Zilei* bragged that he had directed toward Ion Iliescu his whole journalistic artillery (Dobrescu 1997, p. 149).

In order to assess the role of the media in the 1996 presidential election in Romania, we looked at the impact of campaign watching and of general media consumption on our respondents' evaluation of the candidates (i.e., candidates' thermometers). We also explored the emotional impact of our experimental treatment, and on the information acquisition from the spots we presented.

The statistical procedures we used to examine these two aspects of media effects were ANOVAs and correlations. The relevant independent variable in the ANOVAs was the watching of the campaign on television. Its study revealed the effects of the whole, real campaign. The dependent variables of interest were; (a) each candidate's thermometer change from pre- to posttest (i.e., Liking Index change), (b) each candidate's Likability Index change from pre- to posttest, the tentative Emotional Impact Index, and (d) the tentative Info-Acquisition Index. For each candidate we also ran correlations among general media consumption, the tentative Cynicism Index, the pretest/posttest thermometer change, the pretest/posttest Likability Index change, the tentative Emotional Impact Index, and the tentative Info-Acquisition Index.

The ANOVAs in our experimental data reveal a main effect of campaign watching on the pretest/posttest change in Constantinescu's thermometer ($p < .05$). Respondents who had watched the election campaign on television "very little" tended to like Constantinescu significantly better after viewing our experimental spots (.55 thermometer gain), people who had watched "some" or "almost all" of the campaign on television were not impressed by the spots we presented (which they apparently knew), so their liking scores for Constantinescu at posttest were about the same (only a .05 thermometer gain). Heavy campaign watching seems to have stabilized impressions about the least known candidate, Constantinescu, and/or to have exhausted the capacity of the spots to increase people's liking of him. This finding challenges the belief in "bullet effects" of the media, which is still wide-spread among inexperienced politicians in East-Central Europe.

Another main effect of campaign watching was the emotional impact of Iliescu's spots ($p < .01$). Respondents who had watched the campaign on television "very little" manifested the strongest negative emotional reaction, and those who had watched "almost all" had the strongest positive response (means: -1.45, -.35, 1.91). Heavy campaign watching appears to have created with viewers a positive emotional disposition toward Iliescu. This seems to have been a familiarity-through-mere-exposure effect. Our finding challenges a pernicious prejudice that undermined Iliescu's camp, namely that "overexposure" to the media is detrimental to a leader's public image and may "cause the most perverse and uncontrollable effects" (Dobrescu 1997, p. 143). Nevertheless, Dobrescu realized that what matters is not what the incumbents do, but what the press makes known (p. 138). He consequently deplored the fact that Iliescu and his governments did not care to publicize their achievements, while the opposition made huge efforts to publicize the power holders' shortcomings and mistakes.

Based on the ANOVA findings, we can also speak of generally relevant effects of campaign watching that are not contingent on our experimental treatment. Such effects are the main effect that relates campaign watching to political cynicism, and the interactions between campaign watching and political preference, geographic location, and age as independent variables of candidates' pretest thermometers. It is important to notice that our data showed no main effect of campaign watching on people's pretest liking of either candidate, which means that campaign watching was not a powerful linear factor of candidate liking, but an insidious one, affecting liking through interactions with other variables. However, we can speak of circumstantial and short-lived effects revealed through our experiment. Such effects are involved in the changes produced by our experimental treatment, thermometer changes, emotional impact, and information acquisition.

Table 6.4 - Iliescu: Correlations among Liking and Likability Indices, General Media Consumption, Newspaper Reading, TV News Watching, Information Acquisition, Emotional Impact of Spots, and Cynicism

	Thermom. change	Likability index change	General media consumption	Newspaper reading	TV news watching	Information acquisition	Viewer cynicism	Emotional impact of spots
Therm. Chg	1.0000							
Likability Chg	.2633**	1.0000						
General media use	-.0283	-.0492	1.0000					
Newsp readg	-.0234	.0488	.8637**	1.0000				
TV news	-.0247	-.1412	.8326**	.4399**	1.0000			
Inform gain	.0143	.0114	.1282	.0727	.1485	1.0000		
Spot Emotion Impact	.1768*	.2204*	.0350	.0314	.0279	.2820**	1.0000	
Political cynicism	.1187	.0400	-.2012*	-.1811*	-.1595	-.0441	-.0779	1.0000

* p ≤ .05** p ≤ .01   (2-tailed)

Table 6.5 - Constantinescu: Correlations among Liking and Likability Indices, General Media Consumption, Newspaper Reading, TV News Watching, Information Acquisition, Emotional Impact of Spots, and Cynicism

	Thermom. change	Likability index change	General media consumption	Newspaper reading	TV news watching	Information acquisition	Viewer cynicism	Emotional impact of spots
Thermometer change	1.0000							
Likability index change	.0175	1.0000						
General media consumption	.0115	-.1039	1.0000					
Newspaper reading	-.0002	-.0833	.8637**	1.0000				
TV news watching	.0206	-.0936	.8326**	.4399**	1.0000			
Information acquisition	.1179	-.2229*	.1629	.1538	.1212	1.0000		
Emotional impact of spots	.1617	-.3148**	.1075	.1346	.0436	.4655**	1.0000	
Political cynicism	-.0885	-.0001	-.2012*	-.1811*	-.1595	-.1005	-.2579**	1.0000

* $p \leq .05$ **$p \leq .01$ (2-tailed)

Another variable we examined in order to assess the impact of the media in the 1996 presidential elections in Romania was general media consumption, with its components, i.e., newspaper reading and TV news watching. We looked at their correlations with all the changes triggered by our experimental treatment (thermometer and Likability Index changes, emotional impact, and information acquisition). Since political cynicism was found related to campaign watching, that variable was also included in our correlational study.

Table 6.4 shows high correlations between our general media consumption index and its components, newspaper reading being a better predictor of general media consumption by our respondents than TV news watching ($r = .8637$ vs. $r = .8326, p = .01$).

Similarly to campaign watching, general media consumption was significantly and negatively related to political cynicism, but the correlation was rather low ($r = -.2012, p = .01$). Newspaper reading had an even poorer correlation with political cynicism, also negative ($r = -.1811, p = .05$), but TV news watching was not significantly correlated with political cynicism. Newspaper reading and TV news watching correlated between themselves positively but only moderately ($r = .4399, p = .01$).

Tables 6.4 and 6.5 reveal the fact that neither our general media consumption index nor its components were significantly related to any indicator of change used in our experiment (i.e., thermometer and Likability Index changes, information acquisition from spots, and emotional impact of spots). This shows that general media consumption did not have a significant impact on our subjects' response to the spots we presented, and it may not have affected the responsiveness of Romanians in general to the whole campaign.

Beside showing the unrelatedness of general media consumption to the impact of the spots upon viewers, the correlational study raises another crucial question, that of the consistency in viewers' evaluations of the candidates and of the spots.

"The heart has reasons that reason cannot grasp." This French saying illustrates our findings relative to viewers' judgments. Our correlation results show that the thermometer change correlated positively but in the low range with the Likability Index change in Iliescu's case(Table 6.4), and did not correlate significantly in Constantinescu's case (Table 6.5). This indicates that the feature-by-feature evaluation of candidates had little to do with people's liking of them. Maybe they liked the candidates for other qualities that were not covered by our questionnaire, or for reasons that had nothing to do with the candidates' intrinsic qualities.

As shown in Table 6.4, the emotional impact of the spots we presented in our experiment correlated positively but very low with Iliescu's thermometer change and Likability Index change, and modestly with information acquisition. Information acquisition from Iliescu's spots had no significant correlation with the thermometer change and the Likability Index change. In Constantinescu's case (Table 6.5), information acquisition had a stronger positive correlation with the emotional impact than it had in Iliescu's case. This finding suggests that Constantinescu's spots tended to be more emotionally charged, or they appealed to more feelings than Iliescu's spots did. But it may also mean that people had a more emotional approach to Constantinescu's spots and processed them in a peripheral, impressionistic mode rather than a central (i.e., logically-analytic) mode.

The emotional impact of Constantinescu's spots had a low negative correlation with political cynicism, indicating that only non-cynical people could experience positive emotions as a result of spot viewing. However, Constantinescu's Likability Index change had a somewhat higher negative correlation with the emotional impact of the candidate's spots, and a lower but still significant negative correlation with information acquisition from his spots. This reveals two surprising facts, that the more viewers learned from Constantinescu's spots, the more critical of his features they became, and that the more negative the emotional impact of Constantinescu's spots, the more benevolent viewers became in their feature-by-feature evaluation of him. It appears that in Constantinescu's case information worked toward correcting his sugar-coated electoral image. Negative emotional effects produced a compensatory reaction with viewers, who adjusted their judgments of the candidate to reduce the source of their disappointment. That may have been a situation of emotional dissonance resolved through a cognitive artifice. Nevertheless, Constantinescu's thermometer was neither affected by any feelings induced by the experimental treatment nor by the heightened critical disposition or the information win. The level of liking seems to have been "pre-set," to have been a "must." But this seems to have been the case for both candidates. If we look at the pre- and posttest thermometers and Likability Indices of the two candidates, we notice extremely high correlations between the pre- and posttest thermometers of each candidate.

When the candidates were evaluated feature by feature, the incumbent's Likability Index scores proved stable, probably because he was well known. The challenger's pretest/posttest Likability Indices had a somewhat lower correlation. The thermometer-Likability Index correlations were similar for the two candidates at pretest, positive and rather high ($r > .78$, $p = .01$). At posttest, the coefficients show that people were more consistent in evaluating the incumbent, whose coefficient was higher than at pretest ($r = .81$, $p = .01$), while the challenger's coefficient was lower ($r = .75$, $p = .01$). The spots we presented in the experiment tended to close the gap between the overall and feature-by-feature evaluations of the incumbent, and to increase the gap, i.e., people's confusion vis-a-vis the challenger.

Campaign Effects

Beside this quantitative aspect of media effects in terms of stability/variability, we also looked at the qualitative aspect to see what spins the campaigns covered by the media managed to put on people's perceptions of the candidates. The following two sections will present our findings about campaign effects on people's perceptions of candidate qualities, and on the relevance of spot content to viewers.

Did Iliescu lose because of his aggressive campaign? According to Dobrescu (1997, pp. 178, 180), Iliescu's campaign manager employed American consultants, and that mistake resulted in a negative response from the electorate. Participants in our Sibiu focus group corroborated Dobrescu's judgment. Dumitru observed that after the incumbents lost the parliamentary election, "they started a very unfair attack" against the presidential candidate of the opposition. Nae argued that "Both parties attacked, and we cannot say that one side was better than the other." Letitia explained that the population had not expected aggressive behavior from Iliescu and Constantinescu because they were highly educated people. The electorate was disappointed. Said Flavius, "In this campaign there was no confrontation of ideas among candidates, only personal attacks." Ioan philosophized that "Those who shout do it because they have no arguments." Marcel concluded, "they [i.e., PDSR, Iliescu's party] did influence me, but in a negative way," which practically means that the PDSR and Iliescu's campaigns estranged at least some part of the electorate.

Peacefulness/aggressiveness was one of the twelve candidate features we used in our semantic differential scale administered at both pretest and posttest. When we analyzed the data we paid special attention to that feature because many people in Romania believed it was responsible for the incumbent's failure.

The electoral significance of candidate features derives from their capacity to differentiate competitors and to elicit diverse responses from voters and thus make decisive the balance of opinions about the candidates in terms of the critical features. In order to assess the contrasting power of the twelve candidate features used in our study we ran inter-candidate correlations on Iliescu's and Constantinescu's pretest and posttest feature evaluations. We ranked the features with significant negative correlation coefficients, then we compared the pretest and posttest hierarchies to identify the features associated with the biggest pretest/posttest changes in ranking, which indicated increased or decreased relevance to our respondents. Table 6.6 shows that the three most significant factors of differentiation were correctness, competence, and sincerity, with moderately high correlation coefficients between .5 and .6, and significant at $p = .01$. Aggressiveness ranked third lowest in the pretest, significant at $p = .05$, and became insignificant at posttest, together with activeness.

Our inter-candidate correlation results point to the fact that the single most important likability feature conveyed by the spots that made the greatest impact on candidate differentiation was not peacefulness/aggressiveness but calm/nervousness, which ranked least important in the pretest, but sixth most important in the posttest. This indicates that Iliescu failed because he lost his temper, i.e., he failed psychologically. Interestingly and significantly, calm was followed by successfulness, that jumped from position 7 in the pretest to position 5 in the posttest. This finding about the impact of perceived successfulness on the outcome of the presidential elections supports our thesis that Iliescu's perceived underperformance in the first ballot (29.1% fewer votes than expected) reversed the expectations and preferences for the second ballot.

Table 6.6 - Negative Correlations Between Iliescu's and Constantinescu's Likability Features

Likability features	Pretest		Posttest	
	r	rank	r	rank
Correctness	-.5963**	1	-.5477**	1
Competence	-.5653**	2	-.4574**	3
Sincerity	-.5382**	3	-.5062**	2
Credibility	-.3562**	4	-.3612**	4
Attractiveness	-.3516**	5	-.3291**	7
Activeness	-.2797**	6	**-.1724**	11
Successfulness	-.2704**	7	-.3451**	5
Friendliness	-.2638**	8	-.2008*	9
Powerfulness	-.2532**	9	-.2137*	8
Peacefulness (vs. aggressiveness)	-.2181*	10	**-.0540**	12
Sophistication	-.1777*	11	-.1973*	10
Calm (vs. nervousness)	-.1766*	12	-.3317**	6

* $p \leq .05$ ** $p \leq .01$ (2-tailed)

After identifying the contrasting features that helped our respondents distinguish between the presidential candidates, we examined the pattern of likability features that determined candidate liking. Our purpose was to see whether the two front runners' patterns were similar, and whether they were stable from pretest to posttest. We ran stepwise regressions with the thermometer as dependent variable, looking for the critical, most controversial candidate features that determined voters' preference at the aggregate level. Table 6.7 shows that, in Iliescu's case, correctness and competence were significant both at pretest and posttest, but the perception of power and calm at pretest was replaced by that of aggressiveness at posttest. In addition, the sincerity issue that impacted the electorate only from Constantinescu's side at pretest, gained in importance and was applied to both candidates at posttest, becoming a variable against which the candidates were compared.

In Constantinescu's case (Table 6.7), the correctness criterion, which with Romanians meant fulfillment of their own expectations rather than fulfillment of candidate's promises, was applied only to the incumbent, because Constantinescu had never been in office before.

Our respondents seem to have measured the two candidates with somewhat different yardsticks, and they were more harsh toward the incumbent.

Table 6.7 - Stepwise Regressions on Likability Features with the Thermometer Dependent

Candidates	Significant variables	Beta	Signif. level	R square (cumulative)
Pretest				
Iliescu	correct	.492	.000	.595
	powerful	.146	.015	.651
	competent	.243	.004	.675
	calm	.136	.022	.689
Constantin.	competent	.481	.000	.595
	sincere	.213	.011	.635
	friendly	.194	.010	.656
	sophisticated	-.110	.045	.668
Posttest				
Iliescu	correct	.447	.000	.693
	competent	.213	.002	.727
	peaceful (vs. aggressive)	.144	.009	.744
	sincere	.189	.023	.755
Constantin.	competent	.528	.000	.632
	sincere	.380	.000	.705

As a conclusion to our regression analysis, our findings support the idea that the aggressiveness of Iliescu's spots produced the biggest negative attitudinal change with viewers, and aggravated their dislike of him. That does not make it the cause of Iliescu's failure. The crucial problem was his failure to deliver,in other words, his incapacity to meet people's expectations. Our experimental respondents provided further evidence of this conclusion in their response to free recall questions about the spots they watched for the candidates. Respondents often mentioned the emphasis on the respective candidate's relationship with ordinary people, especially peasants (24 mentions in Iliescu's spots, and 50 mentions in Constantinescu's spots). This was indeed perceived and retained as the dominant motif. Paradoxically, as it was stressed by both candidates, it became irrelevant because it failed to distinguish the competitors. Beyond this, however, the other items retained from the spots were significant. According to our data, the decisive elements respondents retained from Iliescu's spots were mostly negative (i.e., the communist stage direction [17 mentions], and personal attacks [13 mentions]). Nevertheless, a particular scene showing Iliescu overwhelmed with emotion and crying in the village of his mother had a strong positive impact on our respondents (14 mentions). The corresponding single most liked scene in Constantinescu's spots was one featuring a retired woman with an empty shopping bag, bitterly complaining about poverty (12 mentions). Analysis of these comments also shows that the positive-or-neutral vs. negative ratio for spot elements retained by the participants in our experiment was 123:10 in Constantinescu's case, much better than the 74:49 in Iliescu's case. This finding provides additional support to our argument that Constantinescu won because Iliescu lost.

However, the campaign may have had an additional positive outcome for the Romanian people. An interesting question asked in the ISAR questionnaire (Institutul de Sociologie al Academiei Romane, 1996) was, "Has this election campaign strengthened or weakened your confidence in politicians and political parties?" Before the second ballot of the presidential elections, most people said their confidence had been weakened (35%). A few days later, after the opposition's victory in the second ballot, 49% of Romanians said the campaign had strengthened their confidence in politics. Is it really the campaign that can be credited? Or is it rather the victory of the opposition, i.e., the result of the media campaign, that altered people's perception of politicians' trustworthiness. This indirect effect of the media campaign is one more argument that the media played a complex and subtle role in the 1996 elections in Romania.

REFERENCES

Botnariu, M. (1993). *TVR: Prezentare generala*. Unpublished.

Centrul de Sociologie Urbana si Regionala CURS (1996). *Barometrul de opinie publica*. Bucharest: CURS.

Centrul Independent de Studii Sociale si Sondaje (1996). *Monitorizarea reflectarii vietii politice in emisiunile posturilor TV TVR1*, Tele 7abc, Antena 1 si Pro TV. Bucharest: CIS.

Dobrescu, P. (1997). *Iliescu contra Iliescu*. Bucuresti: Diogene.

Gross, P. (1996). *Mass media in revolution and national development: The Romanian laboratory*. Ames, IA: Iowa State University Press.

Herr, P. M., Sherman, S. J., & Fazio, R. H. (1983). On the consequences of priming: Assimilation and contrast effects. *Journal of Experimental and Social Psychology, 19*, 323-340.

Huntington, S. P. (1993). The clash of civilizations. *Foreign Affairs, 72 (3)*, 22-49.

Institutul de Sociologie al Academiei Romane (1996). *Ancheta panel asupra comportamentului electoral: Whom do Romanians vote for and why?* Bucharest:ISAR.

Kaid, L. L. (1997). Effects of the television spots on images of Dole and Clinton. *American Behavioral Scientist, 40*, 1085-1094.

Kaid, L. L., & Holtz-Bacha, C. (1993). Audience reactions to televised political programs: An experimental study of the 1990 German national election. *European Journal of Communication, 8*, 77-99.

Kaid, L. L., & Holtz-Bacha, C., (Eds.). (1995). *Political Advertising in Western Democracies*. Thousand Oaks, CA: Sage.

Law on the Organization and Operation of the Romanian Radio Company and the Romanian Television Company (1994). *Balkan Media, 3(3)*, 50-56.

Marinescu, V. (1995). Romania: Private versus state television. *The Public, 2(3)*, 81-95.

Middleton, K. R. (1993). Applying Europe's "First Amendment" to Romanian libel and access law. In A. Hester & K. White (Eds.), *Creating a free press in Eastern Europe* (pp. 405-430). Athens, GA: James M. Cox, Jr. Center for International Mass Communication Training and Research, University of Georgia.

U.S. Information Agency (1990, June 14). *Romanians confident about future... VOA relied upon before the revolution.* Research memorandum.

NOTES

1. The experiment consisted of the administration of a pretest questionnaire, followed by a screening of a half-hour videotape with spots randomly selected from the campaigns for the two front-runners in the presidential race (i.e., Iliescu and Constantinescu). After viewing the spots, the subjects were requested to complete a posttest questionnaire.

In Bucharest, the experiment was conducted in two locations, at the Academy of Economic Studies and at the Graduate School of Communication. In Transylvania, the experiment was replicated in one location only, at the University of Sibiu. Immediately after the experiment, focus groups where conducted when possible. One focus group was conducted in Bucharest at the Graduate School of Communication, and another was held at the University of Sibiu. The focus group samples included twenty participants in each location. They were pre-selected from the respective experiment samples in order to ensure a large demographic representation.

The material for the Romanian experiment consisted of a 30-minute videotape, for which the experimenters randomly selected three spots from Iliescu's campaign (totaling 15 minutes) and three spots from Constantinescu's campaign (totaling 15 minutes). The selection was made from an almost exhaustive collection of spots covering the entire 1996 presidential campaign. The order of spots was random for each candidate, but the experimenters presented alternatively one spot of a candidate followed by a spot of the other candidate.

Both the experiment questionnaires and the focus group guidelines were provided by the Political Communication Center. They followed a standard format and were translated for use in all countries that participated in the project. To better explain the Romanian data, several questionnaire items were collapsed, allowing researchers to develop cumulative indices concerning media consumption (Media Index), voter cynicism (Cynicism Index), candidate preference and personal attributes (Likability Index), impact of spots for each candidate (Emotional Impact Index), and voter learning (Info-Acquisition Index). Moreover, in addition to standard focus group questions, several issues emerged during our discussions. These issues included, expertise of campaign and media professionals (Bucharest) and foreign policy models and influences (Sibiu).

2. The thermometer scales consisted of ratings scales where respondents were asked to rate their feelings toward the candidates from 0 (cool) to 100 (warm).

Chapter 7

PARTY BROADCASTS AND EFFECTS ON HUNGARIAN ELECTIONS SINCE 1990

Jolán Róka

"Before the late 1980s, media policy throughout East Europe was rather simple. State responsibility for print and broadcast media was legitimized in terms of the political, educational, and cultural importance of the media to society (and, of course, to the state). Because of their educational and propaganda functions, the media represented a means of transmission (similar to other educational institutions) for an authoritative definition of reality. Broadcasting was severely limited by state restrictions and control." (Splichal, 1994, p. 27)

This authoritarian, state and one-party dominated model had characterized the entire East European media system (with Yugoslavia the only exception) until the mid-1980s when the international political landscape began to change profoundly and rapidly. In Hungary the inner crisis became apparent in 1987 (though the first signs of crisis became visible in the spring of 1985, at the 13th Congress of the Hungarian Socialist Workers' Party) due to the withering economy and the growing inflation which resulted in declining standards of living especially for the middle class. Hungarian society started facing a complex challenge for political and media democracy.

The democratization of the institutional political system had evolved between 1987 and 1989 as a result of which a multiplier system came into being, and the state power gained a totally new legal frame of operation. The government also started the process of abolition of the centrally planned economy and the development of a new market-based economy. The Hungarian political arena was being shaped by the symbols of Europe, democracy and market economy. The collapse of the Socialist system was a fact in Hungary when in 1988 János Kádár, whose government had been ruling for 32 years, was ousted; and in 1989 Hungary became the escape route for East Germans to the West.

Mihály Bihari considers the change of the power structure of the political system between 1987 and 1989 as having revolutionary importance which led to a change of regime in 1990. "In 1989-1990 in Hungary, the change of power extended to the personal, institutional, organizational, structural and decision-making (enforcement of will) dimensions alike in the power system. The transformation of the power structure accelerated the change in the entire political system and through this that of the entire social system" (Bihari, 1991). According to Bihari, the change of regime had been the result of several factors including strengthening of opposition and reform movements and changes in governmental structure culminating in the 1990 Parliamentary elections that resulted in changes on a mass scale (Bihari, 1991).

THE HUNGARIAN POLITICAL SYSTEM

The year 1990, when the first free elections were held, is considered to be a turning point in Hungarian political history. In the spring of that year a multiparty Parliament was elected (six parties entered Parliament: Hungarian Democratic Forum, Independent Smallholders' Party, Christian Democratic People's Party, Alliance of Free Democrats, Alliance of Young Democrats, and Hungarian Socialist Party; and a coalition government came into power. The Hungarian Democratic Forum built a coalition government led by Prime Minister József Antall with the Independent Smallholders' Party and the Christian Democratic People's Party having a 59% majority in Parliament. The coalition government represented the national-conservative, Christian Democratic political center in opposition with the social-liberal and social democratic centers. The Christian Democratic political center during its four-year governing period carried along a debt burden of over $20 billion dollars, the highest per capita in Eastern Europe combined with the economic disaster the government led the country to. "In summary, it can be said that, besides the inherited crisis and the transition crisis, new crisis elements and factors also made the economic situation worse between 1990 and 1994. The depth of economic catastrophe could be equally illustrated by absolute or relative figures. For example, agriculture production decreased by 50%, and it went down close to the 1938 production level" (Bihari, 1995, pp. 31-33). Among the new crisis elements Bihari mentions the government controlled bureaucracy, the weakness of the government necessary to make democracy really work, a one-person governmental structure, the lack of inter-party talks among coalition parties, abuses of power, economic scandals, and corruption. "All these reasons made it obvious that after the founding democratic elections the first real elections with concrete alternatives would bring governmental changes with them in 1994" (Bihari, 1995, p. 35). In spring 1994 the Hungarian Socialist Party won an absolute majority which meant a 54% electoral victory, and as a result a new coalition government was formed with the participation of the Hungarian Socialist Party and the Alliance of Free Democrats.

POLITICAL AND REGULATORY SYSTEM RELATED TO POLITICAL ADVERTISING

Political System

Parliamentary elections both in 1990 and 1994 were based on the "Act No. XXXIV of 1989 on the Election of Members of Parliament." This law represents a complicated mixed electoral system: a combination of single-member or direct constituencies and proportional representation or list system with a share of 176 single-member mandates and 210 list mandates (i.e., 152 regional list mandates and 58 national list mandates). The 386 seats in Parliament with six political parties remained unchanged in 1994. The country was divided into 176 constituencies (i.e., 176 members out of 386 could be elected as Members of Parliament from single-member local constituencies either winning the absolute majority of votes in the first round or the relative majority in the second round). "But voters were handed two voting slips at the polling station; 152 seats were to be elected on a proportional basis from 20 multi-member county and metropolitan electoral districts. The district magnitude varied from 4 to 28, with an average magnitude of 7.6. The requirement of a turnout of over 50 per cent for a valid election in the first round, and similarly of 25 per cent in the second round, also applied to each of these regional districts. The parties submitted their regional lists of candidates in order of preference. The voters could only vote for a party, not for a candidate" (Pridham & Vanhanen, 1994). Bihari (1995) points out that as a consequence of the Hungarian electoral system there was a high disproportionality (i.e., an overrepresentation of the winning parties by 1.5 (according to share of votes and mandates) and an underrepresentation of the smaller parties in Parliament.

The Hungarian election campaigns in 1990 and 1994 were structured very much alike. In 1994 the campaign started officially on February 8, when the President (Árpád Göncz) announced the exact date of the first round of the parliamentary elections, which was being held on May 8, and the second round on May 26. As was stated above, in Hungary the parliamentary elections have a bipolar structure, meaning that the citizens are supposed to vote on the national list for a certain party and on the regional list for a Member of Parliament. In order to get on the regional list the candidates had to collect from the potential voters not less than 750 recommendation coupons. The deadline was April 9. The total number of candidates was approximately 2000, out of which more than 100 belonged to the category of independent candidates representing a certain party but without any party membership. Out of 130 parties only 20 managed to set up a regional list, and only 15 could fulfil the requirements necessary for setting up a national list. However, only 8 were able to set up the regional list everywhere, in 20 different regions. (In 1990 out of 65 parties only 19 could set up a regional list and only 12 the national list.)

The situation was rather embarrassing as there were too many parties coming forward without clearly outlined political programs and/or with clear overlaps in their platforms. The recommendation coupons should have served as a screen between the candidates in the regions, but due to the dearth of candidates the final clearance could take place only in the second round. Even more disturbing were the violent, often rude and negative campaigns waged against each other, which would surely render the formation of a coalition government more difficult after the elections. It also meant that the political culture had undergone a fundamental change since 1990, the time of the first multiparty elections. In 1990 almost all the different parties formed an ideological unity against the former communist ideology. In 1994 there was no really threatening power after the collapse of communism, but there were a lot of different parties competing for the voters' support. This, of course, led to an increase in negative campaigning and to a bigger role for political extremists. Instead of the party image, the politician's image received greater attention. On the whole, the political culture became more corrupt. That was the reason why the number of voters with uncertain party preference increased (approximately 2 million inhabitants or 40% of the electorate). According to the public opinion polls the majority of the citizens were sure only about their opposition to the government of that time because of the high unemployment rate, the drastic economic situation, the worsening public safety, etc.

It is a obvious that the more parties, the more divided the political agenda; and it also means that it is more difficult to win the elections, because the votes are distributed among several parties. However, 1994 seemed to be a turning point, as none of the parties had a real chance for victory, so they were forced to form coalitions. In Hungary before the elections, four coalitions existed: (1) the middle-class or liberal coalition (Alliance of Young Democrats, Alliance of Free Democrats in cooperation with the Agricultural Alliance and the Party of Entrepreneurs), (2) the left-wing coalition (Hungarian Socialist Party with the National Alliance of the Hungarian Trade Unions), (3) the national conservative coalition (Hungarian Democratic Forum, Christian Democratic People's Party, United Small Holders Party -- the governing coalition), and (4) the right-wing radicals (Hungarian Party of Life and Justice and some others).

The final results of the party election campaign in 1994 were as follows: all the six parliamentary parties, in addition to 9 non-parliamentary parties (Workers' Party, Agricultural Alliance, Republic Party, Hungarian Party of Life and Justice, Party of Entrepreneurs, National Democratic Alliance, Hungarian Social Democratic Party, United Small Holders Party, Hungarian Green Party) were able to set up a national list. The first and second round produced the results below:

	% Votes	% Votes
	1st Round	2nd Round
1. Hungarian Socialist Party	32.99	54.14
2. Alliance of Free Democrats	19.74	17.87
3. Hungarian Democratic Forum	11.74	9.84
4. Independent Smallholder' Party	8.82	6.74
5. Christian Democratic People' Party	7.03	5.70
6. Alliance of Young Democrats	7.02	5.18

Regulatory System

The "Act No. XXXIV of 1989 on the Election of Members of Parliament" (Enacted by Parliament on 20 October 1989) contained the regulations concerning suffrage, the electoral system (Members of Parliament, nomination, determination of election results)), and electoral procedures (electoral campaign, polling, electoral bodies, polling wards, registration of voters, publicity of electoral procedures, legal remedies, by-elections, final provisions). Chapter IV (Electoral Campaign), Article 11, briefly defines the media presentation of the campaign:

(1) Until the day preceding election at the latest, the Hungarian Telegraph Agency, Hungarian Radio and Hungarian Television shall carry on an equal footing the electoral calls of parties putting forward candidates at least once free of charge. This same duty shall devolve upon the local studios in their respective area of broadcast with regard to the electoral programs of candidates. Other advertisements that go toward making a party or any of its candidates more popular can only be broadcast with a clear message declaring such publicity as "Paid Electoral Advertising."

(2) During 30 days preceding election the Hungarian Radio and the Hungarian Television shall cover the parties presenting national lists--in their news of electoral events-- on an equal footing and--in their electoral reports--in proportion to the candidates nominated.

(3) On the last day of electoral campaigns the Hungarian Radio and the Hungarian Television shall--under equal program conditions for parties, for equal lengths of time and without comments--broadcast the electoral summary reports prepared by parties presenting national lists. (Act No XXXIV, 1994, p. 25)

The key words of the act are equality and proportionality in media presentation of the parties and the candidates. These principles guide the application of the regulatory system to campaigning.

ASPECTS OF MEDIA SYSTEM STRUCTURES AND REGULATIONS

In any election campaigns there are at least four different channels for influencing the citizens' political beliefs and party preferences: TV, radio, print media, and street posters. In Hungary manipulation through these channels started to operate almost simultaneously both in 1990 and 1994. The main form of discourse of the parties' media appearance became political advertisements. In political ads the skirmishes and internal disputes between the parties, which had rarely been made public in the past, now became external; and they started to function as a basis for their public evaluations. As political ads offer equal opportunities for all the parties, this means of poli4tical struggle seemed somehow democratic.

It is a world-wide phenomenon that in election campaigns TV possesses the widest range of visual and verbal possibilities of persuasion. In Western democracies, especially in the USA, TV not only broadcasts the elections, but it is the most important "performer" in the campaign. This means the voters believe mainly in the ideas and propositions that have a media voice. But it is also true that any medium can maintain its manipulative and influential role if it is verbally and visually authentic, and politically neutral. The increased role of TV in political campaigns may result in misleading consequences, namely that the political debates will be dominated more by symbols, slogans, and personalities than by logical arguments. That is why TV is not really adequate for changing or modifying the ideological views of the different social groups, for shaping the parties identities, or for the in-depth explanation of their political programs. On the other hand, TV is efficient for constructing the visual image of political leaders, for increasing their popularity rapidly or ruining it immediately.

According to the results of public opinion polls in Hungary, the media election campaigns had a great impact on the voters' decisions, but it did not bring about any major restructuring. Three-quarters of those interviewed admitted that the election campaign had some kind of influence on their beliefs. The media impact might have affected 90% of the eligible people to vote. It also turned out that, though the media campaign may have made it more difficult to make a decision, it largely contributed to stabilizing the existing political attitudes especially for those potential voters who were lacking a clearly outlined party preference. However, it is also true that the huge mass of the campaign information may have diverted the so called "politically passive" voters from the intention to vote.

A survey carried out by the Hungarian Public Opinion Research Institute clarified the issues that had the largest impact on the voters' decision making attitudes in 1990 by asking the question: "When you elect a party how much will you consider the following issues?" The survey was carried out
March 1-16, 1990, with a sample size of 1000. The answers given by those interviewed are displayed in Table 7.1. They indicate that the "party's promises" and "the party's leaders" were the most influential considerations for voters in the survey. The party's popularity and the "party's campaign" also received ratings above the mid-point.

The Hungarian political parties realized the extraordinary importance of the media in the political campaigns as early as the first democratic Hungarian election in 1990, which after all in 1993 led to the media war, i.e. the never-ending disputes about the inconsistency of media independence and neutrality on the one hand and the controlling power of the governing parties on the other. "The sharpest discussions arose around the questions of what is meant by the freedom of press; the social role and responsibility of the media in a transitional period 'from the communist dictatorship to a real democracy'; the privatization or ownership of media, especially the former communist media ownership; the professional, human and political qualities of journalists; the legitimating of the professional federations; the participation of foreign capital in the media; the threat of new monopolies; and above all, around the subject, the forms of media control" (Splichal & Kovats, 1993, p. 36).

Table 7.1 - Sources of Influence on Voting in 1990 Elections

The party's promises

The party leaders

The local party leaders

The party's popularity

The party's campaign

The party's name

The party's posters

Your family members' or

friends' opinion

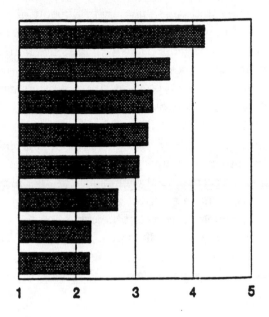

Scale: 1 = definitely not, 5 = very much.
(Országgyülési választások, 1991, p. 572.)

Media, as in the other Eastern European countries, had become a political institution in their own right well before the first free elections. They started to possess a derivative role in political processes as a means of social power. Their significance has clearly been represented in the political, especially election, campaigns. Media (in particular visual media), due to their agenda-setting effects, are able to assign importance to certain issues. In other words: what the media shine a spotlight on or ignore has its own consequences. In the Republic of Hungary--among the media institutions-- TV had attained a crucial importance in shaping the political process as one of the most powerful means for political influence. Its overwhelming importance is due to the fact that, through visual images in appropriate combination with verbal expressions, it can manipulate symbols and meanings to influence the audiences' political orientation). In 1993 the situation became quite dramatic as TV had become the target of the parties' political struggle. In Hungary there was no Media Law officially accepted by the Parliament to regulate the functioning of Hungarian Television until 1996. Hungarian society faced its second democratic elections among these confusing circumstances.

The Parliament finally passed the new Media Bill on December 21, 1995, and it came into force on January 1, 1996. The "Law No. 1" about the radio and television broadcasting defines what advertising is in general: it is an item of program announced as a public information for some counter-value or counter-performance or it is a kind of program time placed at disposal, which contributes to the disposal of the specified or described goods--product, service, property, right and obligation--or to its utilization for some counter-value or to the achievement of the desired effect.

It also defines the meaning of "political advertisement": it is a program item that influences and calls upon a) the support of participation in the elections of a party or political movement, its successful actions, its candidate, its initiative for plebiscite and b) popularizes its name, activity, aims, slogan, emblem, and the image created about it. In the paragraph about the restrictions and bans on advertising, the law decrees:

In election periods political advertisements can be broadcast according to the orders of the laws about the election of Members of Parliament, the local and regional candidates, the mayors. In any other periods political advertisements can only be communicated in connection with a decreed plebiscite. It is prohibited to announce political advertisements in any programs broadcast to foreign countries. The person or institution that sponsors the political advertisement cannot decrease the responsibility and freedom of the broadcaster and cannot have an effect on the content and placement of the program, just the timing. The broadcaster is not responsible for the content of the political advertisement. A political advertisement must be broadcast visually and acoustically separated (with special announcement about its character before and after the broadcast) from other pieces of the program. (See more in detail: Magyar Közlöny, 1996, p.3.)

POLITICAL COMMERCIALS: THEORY OF PERSUASION

"If we consider democracy not just a political system, but as a set of institutions which do aim to make everything available to everybody, it would not be an overstatement to describe advertising as the characteristic rhetoric of democracy" (Boorstin, 1986, p. 37).

Advertising is an essential part of our culture, forming our images of society through the impact of its messages. Advertising--in a broad sense-- means persuasion. Persuasion usually goes with the attempt to provide information, but the giving of information does not necessarily equate with persuasion. The three main aspects of successful persuasion are the total culture in which persuasion operates, the tactics of persuasion, and the direction of persuasion. One has to be well aware of the cultural climate for constructing the operational map of persuasion, especially when the outcome is not clearly foreseen. That is why professional advertisers often use the results of public opinion polls and content-analysis. In any political campaign the success or failure of persuasion depends on the knowledge of the cultural climate in which the advertisements are structured and on the nature of the information the advertisements contain. The nature of information included in advertisements can be positive or negative. Here we have to comment on the similarity of goals in commercial and political ads; they both want to sell some goods or ideas to the public. One important difference is in the testing. In commercial situations there is an opportunity for immediate testing, while in political life testing comes after the effect of persuasion, and it can have dramatic consequences. So it seems that political advertisements, according to their nature, are commercial messages with long-term social effect.

The dilemma of modern democratic life lies in how to manage political culture so that it will not be dominated by any suppressing power, in order to convey the social truth. In the strictly composed structure of political campaigns and elections, ads have their special purpose and public to influence. Political ads are considered to have an impact on those groups of voters who are uncertain in their party preferences and lack precise political ideas. But it is also true that the public needs and seeks orientation through identification with certain types of political personalities and not so much with ideas. One of the greatest advantages of TV is that it is able to propose images simultaneously both verbally and visually. In the special literature on media effects there is a controversial evaluation of Television's sufficiency for political purposes. Some state that TV is not really sufficient for political purposes because TV is primarily a visual means of communication conveying fast movements and quick cuts of vision and politics needs longer presentation and discussion. On the other hand TV is inevitably one of the most powerful social and political institutions, which is able to assign importance to issues and direct the audience's attention to some events and to divert it from others. It is able to support some political personalities and ideas and neglect others or it can play an equalizing role between the competing parties. The role of television as a means of manipulating the receivers' political orientation is primary in the sense that the public's reactions to a political campaign are determined very much by the media presentation of the event. Consequently, TV has become one of the most important social factors in shaping the political process. This of course means the mediatization of politics.

In any election campaign different sets of interests are confronted. The candidates are interested in winning the electorate. For this purpose they try to get as much access to the public as possible in order to manipulate symbols for themselves and against the opponents. TV and other media institutions intend to provide a public service by seeming to be neutral, not promoting any side but serving the candidate on the one hand and the audience on the other. The public is the passive object of the manipulation who is interested in getting objective information. From the audience's point of view there are two main criteria regarding the candidates: likability and credibility. Likability presupposes the existence of the following features: the candidate's image is suitable for identification and for association with positive symbols, and it is also physically acceptable and familiar. Credibility means trustworthiness and expertise. Consequently, there are socially set visual and verbal or ideological requirements concerning the candidates. In a political campaigns these features are over-emphasized by the media, especially on TV. Audience members are in a so called high context cultural relationship with each other through television. Our symbolic world could not have its pseudo-mythical values without TV. That's why TV should not misuse its power and authority. The audience may not draw any distinction between fiction and reality. TV is a homogeneous entity, which absorbs the authentic culture of the spectators as individuals and offers a global culture instead. In the terms of politics it means that through TV politics may possess a long-term effect.

An Overview of Prior Research on Political Advertising

The emergence of political communication (including the study of political advertising) as a distinct domain of publication, a professional endeavor, a teaching area is new in Hungary, going back to 1990. Publications on political advertising, especially on television, are limited. One of the first published studies on Hungarian political advertising was the analysis of values in party programs by Ágnes Kapitány and Gábor Kapitány (1990). They continued their studies of political advertisements during the second democratic elections in 1994 (Kapitány & Kapitány, 1994). The goal of their analysis was mainly to answer some questions that the voters were concerned about and that might have had a decisive effect on the outcome of the elections. One of the basic points of the authors' interest was to find out what kind of values the different parties emphasized (e.g. Europe, nation, property, party image, attitude to the communist past etc.), what the main differences and similarities were among the parties in that respect (the quantity and quality of the mentioned values), and what sort of verbal and nonverbal means of communication they used for representing those values (e.g., the form of the party program, the political candidates as the performers of the programs, the situation, the background music, the style and language usage). As a result of their analysis an "inventory" of the political values used in the election campaign was prepared which led to the conclusion that the political success of a party lies in the shared values between the party and the voters.

In 1994 these same authors performed a similar task in analyzing the sample of the political advertisements. They were interested in the explicit and implicit values the parties emphasized, their frequency, their tendencies in the programs, the influencing and modifying role of the different components of the programs like that of music, background, number of participants, their sex, character and style, the symbolic meaning of the values, and the differences and similarities between the parties according to the analyzed values. The advance in that study was the cluster analysis of the value groups and party groups that shed light on some tendencies which could be categorized as key values for political success: the existence of identical values between the party and the citizens.

The author of the present study came to similar conclusions concerning the success of election campaigns (Róka, 1997). The main objective of the research project has been to elaborate the possible ways of interaction between media agenda and public agenda in political campaigns in cross-cultural perspective and the dynamics of agenda-setting and agenda-building in public opinion formation. The basic theoretical paradigm of the study offered by the essay of Gabriel Tarde (1922) was based on the assumption that the newspapers imposing the majority of their daily topics upon conversation activate, direct, and nourish first individual, then public opinion, thus shaping social relationships and acts. As a result of the analysis of two election systems (American and Hungarian) in three election campaigns (1992 American, 1994 Hungarian, 1996 American), the author found that, due to the technological revolution in media communications and telecommunications, the structure of social interaction has undergone a radical change.

As a consequence, Tarde's original four-element paradigm was simplified to the linear sequence of media--opinion--action. In the social interaction sphere media and telecommunications to a great extent involve conversation as well. As a result of the investigation the difference between the media impact and political communication impact on public opinion formation can also be stated: the strategy of successful media communication has to be based on agenda-building, while in political communication the emphasis is on agenda-setting.

The author has also analyzed the verbal and visual aspects of the Hungarian election campaign in 1994 (Róka, 1994).

Some studies on the Hungarian election campaigns of 1990 and 1994 in their general discussion of the campaign have referred to the televised political advertisements as well. For instance, László Kéri (1994) evaluates the 1994 televised campaign as being a failure from the very beginning. The parties' 5- and 10-minute political programs were broadcast instead of the usual commercials just before the evening news (more precisely, they were intermingled with the commercials in the advertising section). Antal Böhm (1995) expresses his criticism of the 1994 media campaign because of its bitter negative character, not only from the start but preceding the elections and turning into "a dirty campaign of slanders." Some other weak points of the campaign were that it started too early, but having "a boomerang-effect" at the end, its manifested symbolism was monotonous, lacking imagination, though it was more sophisticated and better structured than the 1990 campaign. The 1990 elections were characterized by voting against the old party-state. *Anybody, but them* was the main theme. In 1994, however, there were more opportunities to choose among the party programs. Both the opposition and the government had built their election strategy on two factors: that of promoting their past accomplishments and an attack on the other side.

As Böhm put it, "There is a lot of truth in how the Monitor Group of the Public Opinion Club estimated the campaign: In Hungary, the Government failed because of their own television. Disinforming news aroused mistrust in viewers while ideologically loaded training films scared away people who had had enough of being treated as half-wits.... As regards the Socialist Party, every possible means had been used to achieve the goal, like intentional editing of programs and incredible manipulation of the facts in the programs" (Böhm, 1995, pp. 56-57).

VISUAL AND VERBAL MEANS OF IDEOLOGICAL MANIPULATION IN THE 1994 CAMPAIGN

In 1994 the broadcast campaign started on April 11 and ended on May 6, a day before the first round of party elections. All 15 parties that had managed to set up a national list got equal media voice, i.e. two time segments (the first a 5-minute segment, the second lasting 10 minutes). In 1990 the parties were provided 5 minutes on two occasions for demonstrating their own political programs. The parties also had the opportunity to buy some time (in 60 second segments) for the purposes of paid political advertising. In addition, twice per week the live telecast of the party leaders' debate was transmitted. Consequently, the parties could make use of three audio-visual genres: political declaration commercials, political debate, and political advertisements. The first two genres provided mainly the verbal possibility for clarifying their views, for ideological demarcation, for outlining future perspectives, and for offering solutions for the most urgent social and economic problems in Hungary. The declaration style entailed an over-emphasis on verbal content to the detriment of visual imagery. Even the 5 and 10 minute declaration commercials were mainly composed as a series of stills with little dynamism in the visual clips. This monotonous official manner could hardly catch the viewers' attention, and that is wh it was not able to fulfil its intended purpose: to manipulate and to win the undecided 40%. Robert Angelusz and Robert Tardos (1994) emphasized that this was a significant drawback compared to the number of undecided voters in 1990 which was just 18-20% right before the elections. The cause might be the general distrust of a great number of voters in the political parties and their abstract, often alien style and rhetoric to the citizens.

Consequently, in 1994 three time segments (1-, 5-, and 10-minute) were available for the political parties for the purposes of promoting the party programs and candidates and for formulating appealing party images in the form of commercials. The free time for the 5- and 10-minute commercials was provided by the network; the shorter paid commercials were sponsored by the political parties themselves. Most of the 5- and 10-minute commercials were of mixed formats: combining the features of testimonials, issue statements, and dramatization, but some of the parties also used a documentary format (e.g., the Young Democrats). The paid commercials were produced as video clips encompassing symbolic meaning.

As a result of the Parliamentary Elections in 1994 the total seats in the Parliament were distributed among 6 political parties. In the concrete analysis of the verbal and visual symbols used in the commercials, this analysis focuses attention mainly on the parties above and their agenda-setting strategies in the 5- and 10-minute commercials.

The style and rhetoric of the commercials can be categorized into several groups and subgroups: some of the parties tried to introduce a "new" style and rhetoric which might be characterized as being sophisticated, pathetic and borrowing the ideals from the politicians of the Reform Age in the 19th century (Democratic Forum and seven others). Some other parties used conversational style (Alliance of Young Democrats, Christian Democratic People's Party) sometimes combined with irony (Alliance of Free Democrats).
The Hungarian Socialist Party's rhetoric was considered to be skilful, "objective," emphatic including sophisticated, literary elements if necessary. The didactic and vulgar style was also represented but was not generally characteristic. The most successful parties chose their style and rhetoric with consciousness of the appeal to voters on a higher plane.

As mentioned earlier, the explicit verbal message of many advertisements was ineffective, but the implicit verbal content may have long-term influence on the audience's party preference. The implicit verbal messages included the implied message in the slogans and logos. The hidden meaning provides the variety in their connotation (e.g., Alliance of Free Democrats: "With Heart, Wit, Honesty," "We'll be successful together!"; Hungarian Democratic Forum: "Thanks for the Calmness. For the Power of Patience," "We have future," "Firm Steps, Calm Future"; Christian Democratic Peoples' Party: "We count on Everybody," "Domestic product, domestic place of work"; Hungarian Socialist Party: "Maybe Different! Maybe better! The Reliable Solution"; Alliance of Young Democrats: "The Orange Ripens," "Solidarity").

The symbolism of the slogans was strengthened by the logo (or emblem) symbols: e.g., orange for the Young Democrats, flying dove for the Free Democrats, red/pink for the Socialists, cross for the Christian Democrats, red circle for the Workers' Party. These slogans and logos formulated the parties symbolically demonstrated and visually communicated images together with plenty of other signs and codes. The codes contained implicit and explicit values referring to the characteristics of subcultures, cognitive structures, and ideology. Besides the individual symbols, often global symbols contributed to the understanding of the messages. Among the global symbols there were cars, roads, computers (high technology), undamaged countryside, different social groups (technical intelligentsia is coming forward), children, family (1994 is the year of the family), the building of Parliament, the mesh of modernism and tradition, sport (for emphasizing team spirit). The most important values mentioned in the political programs were: Hungarians, citizenship, enterpreneurism, safety, stability, Christianity, the homeland, expertise, privatization, and unemployment. (In 1990 the order of ideological values was as follows: Hungarians, nation, freedom, Europe, democracy, homeland, Christianity). Consequently, the most important attributives for the voters became human values, leftism and rightism, external or internal political attitude, social transformation and radicalism.

The political parties are also characterized by the manner of persuasion they chose. In persuasion the communicator (i.e., the political party) is supposed to aim at the cognitive abilities of the viewers. It is a psychological fact that if the message contains too much information, the persuasion can turn to the "sideways" -- diverting the coder's attention from the main stream of the issues. Sideways persuasion contains a rich paradigm of guiding techniques with hidden motivations, key words, symbols, emblems, the evocation of tension or desire, and different psychological effects.

In the broadcast campaign of 1994 a broad variety of persuasion techniques and elements were used:

1. *Music*: In the majority of the commercials music was present. The style of the music was in accordance with the general image of the parties: modern (pop, rock) for the Free Democrats and the Young Democrats, classical music (in some cases pathetic, tragic music) for the Democratic Forum, instrumental (signal) music for the Socialist Party, announcing music for the Christian Democratic People's Party, folk music for the Independent Smallholders' Party. In most of the cases the text and music were balanced in the clips.

2. *Attack*: There were two main targets of attack: the past regime (Democratic Forum, Young Democrats, Independent Smallholders' Party) and the past four years (Socialist Party, Young Democrats, Independents Smallholders' Party). The direction of the attack: Socialist Party set itself against the right wing, The Independent Smallholders' Party--the

former communists, Democratic Forum--past regime, Young Democrats--the government and the former communists, Free Democrats--intolerance, the lack of ideological unity. In most of the commercials the attack was directed against ideas, the past, the present government, but not directly against politicians or candidates. (The main forum of negative campaigning was the weekly party debates.) The attacks were mainly done verbally or with negative association.

3. *Setting*: The majority of the parties used the formal indoors (office, the TV studio), 5 parties combined formal indoors with outdoors, 3 used just outdoors. The informal setting was also present but just as an illustration (market, factory, store, church, Parliament, metro, park etc). The Christian Democratic People's Party used the greatest variety of different settings. There was no direct connection (with the exception of just a few parties) between the setting type and the party image.

4. *Objects*: The inanimate objects in the clips served mainly as decorations: flower, statue, painting, wall carpet, technical devices. National colors as having dominant role in the clips were characteristic for the Democratic Forum, Free Democrats, Christian Democratic People's Party, religious symbols for the Christian Democratic People' Party, Democratic Forum, representation of prior symbols (e.g. Soviet soldiers, Statue of Lenin, Marx etc) for the Democratic Forum, playfulness for the Young Democrats. Most of the different symbols were used by the Democratic Forum.

5. *Performers*: The performers in the clips were mostly men. Women were underrepresented with the exception of Free Democrats. Children played a significant role as the means of emotional influence just in the clips of the Socialist Party and one other. The clips showed the candidates positively as the member of a family (Democratic Forum, Free Democrats), having good social relationships (Free Democrats, Democratic Forum, Christian Democratic People's Party) and deep practical experience (Democratic Forum, Free Democrats, Christian Democratic People' Party). The candidates when they talked and declared the party's program usually had eye contact directly with the viewers, they looked serious, sometimes smiling with moderate body movement. But in the illustrations they were shown in different situations: the leaders of Young Democrats taking part in demonstrations, being beaten up, delivering speeches, the Prime Minister (Democratic Forum) fulfilling his duties in the office, the candidate of the Free Democrats was in the restaurant, with his wife, he was playing with a dog, driving a car. He was shown as a man of the future: dynamic, full of energy. The majority of the candidates were formally dressed (Independent Smallholder's Party, Free Democrats, Socialist Party), varied dressing was characteristic for the Young Democrats and some others.

6. *Issues and images*: In the spots importance was attached more to verbal issues than to visual images. In the candidates' verbal statements logical appeal was often combined with emotional appeal. The issue statements directly linked the party and its candidates with certain demographic groups (Hungarian Socialist Party: the young people, the pensioners, the minorities, entrepreneurs; Alliance of Free Democrats: blue-collar workers, middle class, young generation, minorities, people from the country; Hungarian Democratic Forum: proprietors, the poor; Independent Smallholders' Party: employees in the state sector, the poor; Christian Democratic Peoples' Party: entrepreneurs, people

from the country; Alliance of Young Democrats: young generation, pensioners, entrepreneurs, the poor, the capital inhabitants, people from the country.

In accordance with the parties' program and general image there were particular sets of symbols and issues emphasized in the ads:

- Hungarian Socialist Party: symbols: democracy, freedom, Europe, nation, enterpreneurism, economic development, expertise, collaboration, unemployment; issues: increase of expertise and competence, modernization: promoting the development of national economy and entrepreneurism, improvement of living conditions, decrease of unemployment, poverty, and corruption.
- Alliance of Free Democrats: symbols: economic development, knowledge, collaboration; issues: increase of national economy and standard of life, reform of the system of taxation (decrease of taxes), promotion of social dialogue.
- Hungarian Democratic Forum: symbols: economic development, stability, nation; issues: The Prime Minister itself was in the focus of attention with no specially outlined political program.
- Independent Smallholders' Party: symbols: Europe, nation, Christianity; issues: the importance of the party' historical role as one of the most traditional Hungarian parties.
- Christian Democratic People's Party: symbols: privatization, enterpreneurism, nation, unemployment; issues: economic transformation, protection of domestic job possibilities, promotion of entrepreneurism.
- Alliance of Young Democrats: symbols: democracy, collaboration, nation, citizen; issues: relief of government, national union.

7. *General impression*: Most of the parties used different camera angles (straight-on, high, low, movement combination) and types of camera shots (medium, tight, long, movement combination). There was a more significant difference between the parties in the usage of the implicit symbols like montage effects and the general symbolic meaning of the clips. The montage effects created association between the party leaders and Christian martyrs of the past in the clips of Young Democrats, The Democratic Forum used the combination of falling dominoes and stopping the fall by the Democratic Forum. Free Democrats formed the star image of its candidate for Prime Minister in association with some rock concert, in the clips of the Christian Democratic People's Party there was a parallel scene of starting an up-to-date car and the party leaders going to the Parliament.

The general impression that the clips evoked, showed some similarities and differences:

- Hungarian Socialist Party: competence and expertise
- Alliance of Free Democrats: star image of the party leader, competence, unity, individuality.
- Hungarian Democratic Forum: competence, firmness, anti-communism.

- Independent Smallholder's Party: star image of the party leader: party of average people, loyalty.
- Christian Democratic People's Party: competence, unity.
- Alliance of Young Democrats: star image of the party leader, competence, firmness, unity, anti-communism, heroism.

The contrast of light and darkness as a nonverbal means of symbolic expression also contributed to the general impression of some parties' clips. The Socialist Party created the visual image of bright and sunny natural scenes gradually bringing into the focus the Houses of Parliament implying the prosperous future. The Free Democrats on the contrary used the scenes of sunset, dawn as the symbol of satisfaction after the successful daily work or the figure of its candidate for Prime Minister set in the spotlight from darkness. In the center of the Democratic Forum's clips there was the Prime Minister's enlightened figure who was working for the benefit of the nation even at late night hours. The Young Democrats and the Christian Democratic People's Party created a contrast between the present and the past using color and black-and-white shots.

8. *Verbality*: A slight change in the language usage could be observed in comparison to the clips of 1990, which indicated a move from the didactic, pathetic, alien to the citizens' style and rhetoric to a more modern/postmodern, pragmatic, standard language usage. It did not mean at the same time the total disappearance of the high-flown style, it was still present in the spots of Democratic Forum, Christian Democratic People's Party, Socialist Party and the didactic style remained characteristic for the Independent Smallholder's Party, Democratic Forum. In general the applied style and rhetoric became more serious giving less space to humor but emphasizing the closeness of the party and the general public by introducing the rhetoric means of "in medias rest" (9 parties out of 15).

In the spring of 1994 15 political parties were competing for governing position. They had been trying to compose marketable party images for almost two months. Whose image proved to be the most appealing was easily predictable after the first round of the campaign. The Hungarian Socialist Party and the Alliance of Free Democrats were the most successful to identify themselves with the value order of the citizens and develop the most acceptable agenda-building strategies.

The Hungarian Socialist Party built its campaign on the myth of the greater expertise of the last communist government and on the feeling of nostalgia toward past values. Its symbol was the party leader and the smiling face of a child. Its program could be characterized as pragmatic aimed at all the social layers of the society.

The broadcast campaign of the Alliance of Free Democrats was also based on the personality and individual values of the party's first man, whose image had been carefully constructed. He was endued with symbolic values, being the man of the future. He possessed all the necessary physical and mental requirements for becoming the prime minister: a thoughtful, hard-working politician, a good-looking man, husband, one of us, so -- as one of the ads declared--we would desire to have a prime minister like him. The pronounced slogan closely corresponded to the visual image "I trust him!"

The election campaigns of the 1990s have proven that mass media play a global role in shaping and modifying the social reality. They develop a multilateral relationship with the institutions of democracy especially with respect for the formation of public space. Our basic source of information about the political candidates come from mass media, which is able to influence our ideological, political, aesthetical views, concepts, values by their visual and verbal means of manipulation and their agenda-setting possibilities. The public-opinion-formation function of the media is also mainly realized in the political campaigns: the tactics and strategies of the political campaigns that are aimed at the ideological persuasion of the citizens would surely be ineffective without their media presentation. In the democratic state systems the influencing role of the media and the persuasive function of political campaigns differ strategically. Mass media become a decisive social power due to their agenda-setting function, but in political campaigns the clue to success lies in agenda-building, in the ability to influence public opinion.

REFERENCES

Act No. XXXIV of 1989 on the Election of Members of Parliament. (1994). Budapest: National Election Office of the Ministry of the Interior.

Angelusz, R., & Tardos, R. (1994). Bizonytalan választók vagy rejtözködö nem választók. In L. Gábor, A. Levendel, & I. Stumpf (Eds.). *Parlamenti választástok 1994*. Osiris-Századvég.

Bihari, M. (1991). Change of regime and power in Hungary, 1989-1990. In K. Sándor, P. Sándor, & L. Vass (Eds.), *Magyarország politikai évkönyve*. Ökonómia Alapítvány--Economix RT.

Bihari, M. (1995). Parliamentary elections and governmental change in Hungary in 1994. In K. Sándor, P. Sándor, & L. Vass (Eds.), *Magyarország politikai évkönyve*. Demokrácia Kutatások Magyar. Központja Alapítvány.

Böhm, A. (1995). Election behaviour--The political culture of voting. In *Hungarian parliamentary election 1994*. Budapest.

Boorstin, D. J. (1986). The rhetoric of democracy. In R. Atwan, B. Orton & W. Vesterman (Eds.), *American mass media: Industries and issues*. New York: Random House, 1986.

Kapitány, A., & Kapitány, G. (1990). Ertékválasztás. A választási pártmüsorok elemzése [Value choice. The analysis of the programs of party elections]. *Mövelödéskutató Intézet*. Budapest.

Kapitány, A., & Kapitány, G. (1994). Ertékválasztás. A választási és kampánymüsorok szimbolikus és értéküzenetei. [Value choice. The symbolic and value messages of the election campaign programs]. *Societas*, Budapest.

Kéri, L. (1994). Kampány és politikai kultüra '94 tavaszán. In *Parlamenti választások 1994*. Osiris-Századvég.

Magyar Közlöny (1996, January 15). Budapest,, 3, szám).

Országgyülési választások (1991). In K. Sándor, P. Sándor, & L. Vass (Eds.), *Magyarország politikai évkönyve*. Ökonómia Alapítvány--Economix RT.

Pridham, G., & Vanhanen, T. (1994). *Democratization in Eastern Europe: Domestic and international perspectives*. Routledge.

Róka, J. (1994). *Media and elections: The role of visual manipulation in political image-making*. Paper Presented to Turbulent Europe: Conflict Identity and Culture Convention, EFTSC, London.

Róka, J. (1997). *Public space: From rumour through conversation to opinion-formation*. Research Support Scheme of the Central European University. Grant No.: 1013/94.

Splichal, S. (1994). *Media beyond socialism: Theory and practice in East-Central Europe*. Boulder, CO: Westview Press.

Splichal, S., & Kovacs, I., Eds. (1993). *Media in transition: An East-West dialogue*. Budapest: Ljubjana.

Tarde, G. (1922). Opinion and conversation. In *L'Opinion et la foule*. Paris: Alcan.

Chapter 8

ELECTIONS IN THE NEW YUGOSLAVIA: TV COVERAGE AND EQUAL ACCESS

Misha Nedeljkovich

After five decades of suppression of political pluralism, with the fall of Communist regimes in Eastern Europe, pluralization of post-socialist societies is identified with their democratization. Suddenly, civil society, the rule of law, and public opinion became the foundations of a new social order that is today most commonly referred to as the new era, or the liberal-democratic era. In the former Yugoslavia, with its multi-national and multi-religious population, the almost overnight disappearance of the one party regime triggered a chain of democratization reactions. The beginning of "democratization" for Eastern European Socialist countries was also the beginning of the civil war in the former Yugoslavia. By 1987-88, politicians in the republics of Slovenia and Serbia began openly to seek popular support on the basis of nationalism. They asserted their republics' right to national self-determination, to economic resources, and to political control. Whereas the Slovenian goal was anti-federalist, claiming states' rights against federal powers, the Serbian goal was anti-provincial; it reclaimed states' rights against the powers granted by the 1974 constitution to its provinces Vojvodina and Kosovo.

The post-socialist, one-party societies moved toward democratization through the painful process of national identity identification. The changes in the constitution of most of these countries reflected new-born state-promoted nationalisms. National and religious backgrounds became more important than political orientation. The growth of these sentiments provoked fear and insecurity among the minorities who lived within the administrative boundaries of the former federal units. Practically overnight, administrative borders became international borders, and many minorities found themselves living in a new independent nation-state, a country in which they had expressed no desire to live. In the multi-cultural, multi-religious regions of the former Yugoslavia this deepened the crisis, widening the mutual suspicions between different ethnic groups within these newly created nation-states. This, combined with several other factors, propelled the peoples of the former Yugoslavia into a bloody and vicious civil war.

The disintegration of the existing structure, Federal Yugoslavia, and its unified media system created space for the foundation of new, purely national and nationalistic media systems, television and radio networks. Public information, as it had previously been under the Socialist state, became an instrument of the actual legitimization of the new nationalistic political power. The institutional skeleton of political pluralism created in 1990 was very much influenced by its former one-party political culture. In fact, one of the most famous concepts of Bolshevism, unity of the nation and the party, became an integral part of the programs of every one of the political parties registered in 1990 in the former Yugoslavia.

In the dilemma between analytical-synthetic (in its essence sociological) and normativistic concepts of political pluralism the second is the social reality (about political pluralism please see Goti, 1989; Izazovi Pluralizma, 1989; Pecujlic & Milic, 1990; Popovic, 1988; Smiljkovic, 1991; Stranke i Udruzenja, 1990; Stranke u Jugoslaviji, 1990). Within the post-socialist societies this dilemma is reduced to the bare conflict of organized interest groups epitomized within political parties and movements. Unfortunately, the previous Bolshevik repression of its subjects (citizens) is still maintained. It appeared for a while as if the one-party system and its alienation from the people was a question of the past. However, this is not so. The main indicators for this condition are: weak opposition to a strong central party, an electoral system which as a consequence has a one-party majority in the parliament, the absence of a social-democratic party (which is usually the party of the center within Western parliamentary democracies), as well as the absence of autonomous public opinion. However, the intermediary type of political representation (utilizing political parties as specific mediators of the interest) is slowly bringing about a very important component, public opinion, as the third constituent of the civil society. In this triangle, citizens-political parties-state, public opinion slowly arises as a form of control with potential force that one day may limit the power of the state. However, the political sphere that was, because of the long domination of one party and its ideology, mystifying and inaccessible to the ordinary citizen, continues with its silent obstruction of this progress.

Most of the political party programs in Serbia equate public information with citizens' principal freedoms and rights. In the previous one-party regime, the press was also an important instrument of ideological legitimization of the system. At times, it appeared almost as pure ideological propaganda. However, it must be noted, without any intention to establish the correlation between the two, that since 1990, this trend has continued during the establishment and registration of new political parties. These different groups and political parties have different approaches to the concept of public information. So, the notion of public information for ideological political parties differs between religious, ethnic, class, ecological, or professional parties. Therefore, the pluralism of a multi-party system established after 1990 is the pluralism where the process of transformation of instruments of communication from ideological apparatus into instruments of public information for the formation of democratic awareness is evident. The multi-party systems of the former Yugoslavia are pseudo-democratic because of the absolute domination of one party in the parliament. Very similar governmental systems are present in the political party structure of Slovenia, Croatia, and Macedonia.

THE LAW AND REGULATION: THE CHANGE IN THE INFORMATION SYSTEM

The Law of Public Information that was published in the *Official Gazette* (Sluzbeni Glasnik RS no. 19, 29, March, 1991) did not bring about many changes. The emphasis on freedom of the press existed in the previous law as well, and it seems as if the democratic opposition did not influence the government to bring about significant changes in this new law. The new law still allows the ruling party (presently the Socialist Party) to have absolute control over the information system. This, of course, means that all future ruling parties will qualify for the right to establish control over the media. The basis for this initial domination arises from appointment rights. The ruling party reserves the right to appoint directors, editors-in-chief, and gate-keepers of all the major media.[1] These rights, automatically acquired after the elections, give the ruling party primary control over public information. Under previous law the Program Council or Publishing Council formally approved the media gate-keepers' nominations. In reality, this council rubber-stamped the prior decisions of the ruling party. Although it did not have the authority and competence to influence appointments, the council's formal approval was a part of the procedure where, at the very least, discussions about the appointees were certain.

The new law circumvents this procedure, and no other has replaced it. This circumvention allows the ruling party to appoint their members to key media gate-keeping positions without any outside consultation. In spite of various economic and political changes, in essence, the condition of public media organizations has not changed very much. In fact, for many, the situation has worsened. At first, the main problem was still the monopoly of the ruling party over the public information organizations, even after the first multi-party elections. The new party in power strengthened government control over the major media in each country. In Serbia, in fact, the major media are reduced almost to the level of a bulletin news release apparatus of the ruling SPS party.

The expectations that the emergence of privately owned and independent media, as well as legalization of existing semi-legal television stations and newspapers, would significantly affect the ruling party monopoly over public information were not realized. There were several reasons for this: the lack of financial resources, small circulation (in the case of the printed press), and small area coverage (in the case of new over-the-air TV stations). All of these elements contribute to a local, as opposed to national, character. Major newspapers operate distribution networks and printing facilities that contribute to the domination of the ruling party monopoly over the print media. The situation is almost identical in the area of broadcasting. The print and broadcasting "monopoly" are often referred to as "the official media," and they still, beyond doubt, create and shape public opinion.

The complex and unresolved question of ownership in the media is yet another problem that contributes to the overall confusion. In this new society, the transformation of ownership for each type of medium develops entirely different sets of issues and problems to be solved. In the area of radio and television broadcasting, ownership issues of systems such as communication hardware (transmitters, relay stations, etc.) that belonged to the formerly state owned and operated broadcasting network became critical questions of monopoly and control. Emerging independent and privately-owned broadcasting stations, together with the political opposition, are protesting, claiming that the present situation is nothing but monopolistic behavior and unfair competition. For example, RTS (Radio TV Serbia) is both the producer of TV and radio programs and the owner of the network of transmitters and relay stations that transmit signals to the entire country. Despite this problem, the major controversy regarding RTS appears to be its recent foundation. The Parliament decided to merge three major TV stations: RTB (Radio-Television-Belgrade), RTNVS (Radio Television Novi Sad), and RTP (Radio Television Pristina).[2] This act created RTS (Radio-Television-Serbia) by converting its ownership from public property into a communal property and naming it an enterprise.[3]

RTS continued to be financed mainly from subscription, as it had been under the previous government.[4] However, as the overall economic situation in the country worsened, the enterprise was faced with massive unwillingness of the population to pay the subscription fees. Therefore, the RTS Research Center did some initial studies and came up with several recommendations. The final decision was to attach the subscription fee to the electric power bill. Households, therefore, have no choice. If they refuse to pay the subscription, they face a power cut-off.[5] Two problems arose after this transformation, those of ownership and monopoly. The RTS inherited all transmission, production, and post-production equipment that had belonged to three separate television centers (RTB, RTNS, and RTP). All transmitters, relay stations, and antennas, as well as production and post-production equipment (including remote cars and studios) as well as all accompanying television technology, became the part of the one system (RTS). Any newly formed television stations must develop their own transmitter network, and they cannot use transmitters that belong to RTS. Initially, therefore, they are financially and technically incapable of quickly becoming serious competitors to RTS.

Despite the reformation of the technical and physical resources in the development of RTS television, the policies regarding employees have remained relatively unchanged. Hiring procedures, as well as personnel policies, have not changed very much except for employee retention. Under the old system, all positions were considered permanent, but, under the new guidelines, lay-off procedures have been introduced. However, appointments of key positions within this giant enterprise are still directly controlled by the government's ruling party.

TV STATIONS: THEIR PROGRAMS AND RANGE OF COVERAGE

Recently, a number of independent TV stations have appeared, and at present there are five television stations that broadcast programs in the city of Belgrade: RTS with its Program 1, Program 2, and Channel 3 (3K); TV Politika (TVP); NTV Studio B (Nezavisna Televizija, Studio B -- Independent Television Studio B); TV Palma; and Art Kanal (Art Channel). In addition to these, TV KBM is another TV station waiting for permission to air programs.

RTS airs its programs using six transmitters which, with the network of its transmitters and relay stations, practically covers the entire country.

RTS is at present the largest TV and Radio program producer and distributor in the country. It broadcasts a variety of educational, news, entertainment, and sports programs. RTS is commonly referred to as "The State Television," and it has been frequently accused of favoring Serbian Socialist Party (Socijalisticka Partija Srbije - SPS), the ruling party and not giving enough coverage to the opposition during the pre-election campaigns. The consistent pressure of the opposition brought a number of changes regarding election and campaign coverage as well as some personnel changes in RTS (formerly RTB - Radio Television Belgrade).[6]

Independent TV Studio B (Nezavisna TV Studio B - NTV Studio B) was the first independent commercial TV station in Serbia. It has permission to broadcast its programs using four transmitters and a relay station. It can be seen within a perimeter of approximately 100 km., and it broadcasts a variety of entertainment and news programs. The station is well known as a loyal supporter of the opposition.

TV Politika was founded four years ago by then-directors of Politika, the daily newspaper, and TV Belgrade. It was conceptualized as a commercial TV station in the city of Belgrade and basically established as a competitive commercial response to the appearance of the explicitly independent TV station, Independent TV Studio B (NTV B). The station can be seen in a perimeter of approximately 50 km., and it has permission to broadcast from its three transmitters. Program orientation presents a variety of news, information, and entertainment. The competition (especially RTS officials) accuses TV Politika of illegal and unfair business practices and of broadcasting pirated foreign films and programs. TV Politika considers itself politically neutral.[7]

TV Palma and Art Kanal TV are both private commercial television stations. TV Palma with only one transmitter can barely be seen in all parts of Belgrade. TV Palma's program orientation is predominantly music and entertainment; it does not air information or news programs. Art Kanal TV is a television station with an art and entertainment program orientation, and it carries only entertainment news programming. This station broadcasts from two transmitters in the city of Belgrade and, very much like TV Palma, can barely be seen in all parts of the city. Although this television station does not have permission to broadcast its programs, it has been on the air for more than two years. It is unclear why officials continue to tolerate its illegal operations. Initially, the government gave temporary permission to this station only to test its equipment. However, after the test, the station started broadcasting its programming, and its operation was never officially shut down, even though the competition accuses it of broadcasting pirated programs.

Almost two years ago, KBM TV and its founder[8] were temporarily given permission for three months to test the equipment for the new television station. With its transmitter atop the former Communist Party Central Committee building, KBM TV continues to broadcast its test on channel 36 even after the expiration of its temporary permission. The test signal from this transmitter interferes with home VCR's in the city. However, it is again unclear why officials do not shut down this illegal broadcast.

Elections 1993: RTS, NTV B, TVP and Equal Access

Within the past several years, mass media (especially television)have been constant sources of political tension in Serbia. The opposition strongly believes that RTS supports and favors the ruling Socialist Party and that it is exceptionally negative when it reports about the opposition. According to this opinion the new commercial television stations are more likely to favor the opposition parties. This is especially important during elections and is one of the reasons why television programming has been considered a major factor in the politics of Serbia.

RTS is financially superior. It also has program, technological, and political superiority as well as a near monopoly. Because of these factors it represents an almost unbeatable competitor. Despite this monopoly power, and despite the painful start-ups of small independent TV stations, the public voice of these small stations, united with political opposition, at one point contributed to the crisis that forced the government and RTS to make major concessions in the form of leadership changes.

The resolution of this conflict also brought the adoption of a number of media ordinances prior to the Parliamentary Elections in December 1992. The regulations adopted then were kept and carried over into the next election year. Election rules required that RTS significantly change its programs. That meant political parties' equal access to the major media (mainly RTS) and equal airing time for parties' promotional programs on RTS prime time news programs. The agreement included three different program time slots: prime time evening news programs, a specially designed electoral chronicle, and a slot for electoral political commercials.

Three of the TV stations have regular evening informative programs. According to the pre-election media agreement only RTS was required to include a special segment ("Election Chronicle") in its evening prime time TV news program. This segment was visually divided from the rest of the program with a specially designed logo "Elections '93." In this segment all the parties could present their own activities (according to their own selections) for no longer than three minutes. The number of segments per party was proportional to the number of submitted electoral lists. Since NTV Studio B, and TV Politika are commercial television stations they were not required to abide by the same regulations. Their informative programs just reflected the editorial politics of their TV stations.

The agreement also called for the establishment of a special political commercial program segment. The number of political commercials and the frequency of their appearance on the air was significantly smaller than those aired during the campaign of 1992. The agreement again bound only RTS. The airing of the political commercials started twenty days before the elections, 5 December 1993, in pre-election political advertisement time-slots. The commercials were separated from the regular TV programming by the same, specially designed logo, "Elections '93," and were aired only during normal program intermissions (Milivojevic, 1993).

The total time reserved for political commercials was limited to 65 minutes. The first six days political commercials were aired in the segments before and after RTS' prime-time, evening news program, "Dnevnik 2" (7:30 PM). During the next three days, commercials were aired immediately prior to or after the news program. The final three days before the elections were reserved for a political advertisement blackout. The number of commercials within the reserved commercial segment was from 9 to 30 (on average 15). All together, the December 1993 election campaign incorporated fifteen political advertising segments with an average length of 4 minutes and 20 seconds. During the pre-election campaign only 10 parties came up with political commercials (322 commercials were aired).[9]

The Election Media regulations gave the other smaller parties a chance to present themselves to the public as well. In the pre-election TV campaign 53 commercials from smaller parties and "groups of citizens" were also presented. There were 184 news stories (on average 13 per program) about parties, but only twenty parties had more than three news stories within the last 14 days before the election. Eight parties had a maximum number of news stories (total of 75 stories) on average 9.4. Twelve parties had on average 5.4 stories (65 stories total) and 33 remaining parties got 44 stories (on average 1.33) (Milivojevic, 1993). Some of the parties whose significance was marginal were given large amounts of air time, even though their actual influence was irrelevant.

The relationship between the time allocated to the party in the "Election Chronicle" and the time dedicated to the other party activities in the news stories is the best indicator of unequal coverage for different parties. Outside the agreed upon election program structure content of RTS TV, programming was the product of the editorial politics of this station. For example, SPS and UL got much more publicity within the presentation of their "other party activities" than any other party. SPS got seven times more air time, and UL 1.4 times more than any other party. The other parties' promotions were limited to the agreed upon media coverage (the "Election Chronicle" program). For some, that was their only appearance in the media (RTS). For example, the stories that featured the SPS and UL party members were not directly related to their party activities. They simply got a space and time to elaborate on their opinions regarding certain political questions and problems. Therefore, the lack of balance within the total amount of the time designated for the political parties' coverage indicates an unequal treatment of the different parties (Milivojevic, 1993).

Media Coverage during the Federal and Local Elections in 1996

The first round of elections (both for federal parliament and local government) took place on November 2, 1996. The main political participants were:

1. *The United Left* (UL) was comprised of the ruling Socialist Party of Serbia (SPS) (S. Milosevic, leader), The Jugoslav Left (JUL) (M. Markovic, wife of S.M., leader), and The New Democratic Party (ND) (D. Mihajlovic, leader) and was officially registered under the name Coalition SPS-JUL-ND-"Slobodan Milosevic."

2. *Zajedno*, UL direct political rival, was the coalition formed of The Serbian Renewal Movement (SPO) (V. Draskovic, leader), The Democratic Party (DS) (Z. Djindjic, leader), The Civil Alliance of Serbia (GSS) (V. Pesic, leader), and The Association of the Free and Independent Worker's Union (ASNS). Officially, the coalition was registered as "Zajedno--Dragoslav Avramovic." During the early stages of the campaign, Mr. Avramovic decided to withdraw citing health reasons. The coalition was court-ordered to remove the name of Mr. Avramovic from its title and participated in the election under the name Zajedno. (This was an important issue, since Mr. Avramovic has had an almost charismatic status in the country and a large following due to his successful tackling of the record breaking inflation of 1993. The bitter court battle went so far as to include arguments about whether the dash in the officially registered title "Zajedno--Dragoslav Avramovic" could remain).

3. *The Serbian Radical Party* (SRS) (V. Seselj, leader), was an ultra national party and one-time unofficial partner of the ruling SPS.

In the first round of elections (November 2, 1996), the UL coalition was the winner by a landslide, securing almost all the federal seats. The runoffs for the local government had to be held for a number of cities throughout Serbia. These runoff elections were held on November 17, 1996. The preliminary results suggested that the coalition Zajedno had won a majority in the 13 largest towns in Serbia and in nine counties of Belgrade, including a majority in Belgrade's parliament. This was an unexpected result. The ruling SPS Party, which had held local power in almost all Serbian towns, and a majority in the Belgrade parliament, even conceded the defeat in semi-official statements by its spokesman (I.Dacic). However, in the days before the official election results were released, local voting officials submitted a huge number of complaints regarding violation of standard voting procedure. The Election Committee, after considering the complaints overturned the preliminary results, and practically robbed the coalition Zajedno of their victory. The President of the Election Committee was B. Govedarica.

This action by the Committee caused a large popular protest. Tens of thousands took to the streets in outrage. The protests gained wide support from the international community. Pressure from the US, Europe, and OESC (The European Organization for Security and Cooperation) escalated. Eventually, the matter was resolved in a court which ruled in favor of the ruling party. After all legal procedures had been exhausted, President Milosevic decided to invite an independent international committee@ to assess the situation and suggest a resolution. The OESC Committee, led by F. Gonzales, examined the evidence and on December 27 ruled in favor of the Zajedno victory. At the same time, the OESC Report called for the liberation of the media and for democratic election procedures. The Report even mentioned that The Federal Republic of Yugoslavia could not expect to become an equal partner with Europe without changing its laws regarding freedom of speech. After much maneuvering on the part of the ruling party, the matter was finally resolved by President Milosevic who invoked "Lex Specialis" to give victory to the opposition. This law came into effect on February 17 by a decision of The Serbian Parliament.

The coverage of the campaign process, including the elections and their aftermath, by the media was a central issue of the popular protests. The media's coverage of the election was given a prominent place in the OECS Report. On several occasions, the Committee for Protection of Journalists (CPJ) had called President Milosevic's attention to violations of democratic freedom of the media. During the 88 days of protest, Ms. Katty Morton of the CPJ vilified Belgrade and spoke to Mr. Milosevic regarding the events with Radio B92. This radio sation was much in the news during this period, since what happened to it is characteristic of many opposition media.

In an attempt to control the media, the ruling party has intentionally left the law regulating the distribution of frequencies and broadcasting licensing completely disorganized. In fact, much of the law regulating this matter is from the era of the former Socialist Federal Republic. The new law is in the preparatory stages and is in parliamentary procedure as of June, 1997. The parliamentary versions of this law circulated publicly for a few months in the Spring of 1997. Many critics consider the proposed new law the "blueprint for media control." The official reaction of the United States was critical, particularly regarding the coverage range. The new law under the pretext of "limiting the monopoly" in the broadcasting space, while it should allow for the complete freedom of different stations and open competition for public attention.

Radio B92, founded in 1992 and the most important source of information during the protests, was disconnected on December 2, 1996, after a history of having its broadcasting repeatedly interrupted. Following public outcry and international pressure (President Clinton had even mentioned the case of B92 on two occasions, and *The New York Times*, CNN, and other news agencies had widely reported the incident), Radio B92 was back on the air on December 5. The interruption of its program was officially explained as "technical problem" which had been corrected. In actuality, state television, Radio Television of Serbia (RTS), has a monopoly on broadcasting frequencies and technical support. Radio B92 uses one of RTS's transmitters to broadcast but has no technical access to the transmitter or control over its functioning. The media coverage of the protests was practically nonexistent on the part of the official main institutions (RTS, daily "Politika," TANJUG news agency, etc.), and the only stations covering daily events were B92 and Radio Index (student radio).

Other radio institutions, like Radio Boom93 from Pozarevac and Radio Smederevo, which has a rebroadcast program in Serbian from Deutche Welle and Radio Free Europe, had been shut down. The official reason given was noncompliance with federal broadcasting regulations and no broadcasting license. The lack of regulation in the domain of broadcasting frequencies and licensing has opened the way to practically limitless possibilities in the manipulation of the media by the state government. However, a similar situation also exists with non-government controlled stations such as TV "4 Channel" in Bajina Basta and TV Nis. The main coverage of the election was provided by Channel 1 of the RTS, which broadcasts over Serbia with its 7:30 p.m. evening news, "Dnevnik 2", simultaneously broadcast in Montenegro. It is considered the most important and most influential daily news service in the country.

New elections in Serbia, both parliamentary and presidential, took place in the Fall of 1997. The law regulating media coverage and broadcasting licensing is still in parliamentary procedure, to be verified in spite of many of its critics. The President of the Election V-Committee is once again B. Govedarica. The coalition Zajedno has dissolved and no longer exists as a political entity.

FREQUENCY ALLOCATION

One of the changes in the new Law of Public Information was in the area of frequency allocation. The Ministry of Information is responsible every year for organizing an open competition to distribute free radio and TV frequencies. This law has been in effect since March, 1991. In 1993, the Ministry did not allocate any frequencies and failed to abide by the regulations. The political opposition was furious. It raised this issue after the elections, citing the Ministry=s failure to provide these frequencies as the main reason why the opposition did not do well in the elections. The area which RTS covers versus independent TV stations' area coverage is overwhelmingly in favor of the RTS. The December, 1993 elections came and went, and the opposition lost again. Finally, on February 6, 1994, the government announced an open competition for the frequencies allocation. However, the deadline to file an application was reduced from 30 to 15 days with no right to file an appeal, although legal charges against the committee's decision could be brought to the Supreme Court within 30 days after the disclosure of the committee's decision.

After the competition was completed, it was announced that there were 23 applicants for TV frequencies and 50 for the new radio frequencies. However, only five TV frequencies and thirteen radio frequencies were awarded (Dodeljene frekvencije, 1994). Among those not selected were TV and radio stations that have been broadcasting their programs without permission for the past several years, although their applications were also in the competition (TV ART Kanal, TV KBM, and Radio B 92). Also, no new frequencies were given to TV Palma and TV Politika.[10] Disappointed contenders brought up several charges and announced that they would collectively file a lawsuit against the frequency allocation committee with the Supreme Court (Hoci li, 1994). Their first two objections were the committee members' nomination process and the committee's composition. It has been suggested that the committee consisted of a group of people directly interested in the outcome of the frequency allocation. Its membership included two directors from a competing TV station (RTS), government appointees, and members of the ruling party (the Minister of Information and his six associates).[11] Furthermore, the outgoing government ratified this committee's decision on its last meeting on March 14,

1994 before adjournment so no action could be taken against the members of the committee, no doubt because they were also a part of the departing government. Therefore, the decisions of this committee should be revoked, and a new nonpartisan committee formed and a new frequency competition open.[12]

Despite the biased composition of the committee, members maintained that they strictly followed the operating procedure that was approved and published in the *Official Gazette*, and several guidelines within the procedure were rigorously followed. Most of the contenders were unable to fulfill the basic requirements, and therefore were excluded from the contest, while some were only partially able to meet the required standards. The committee endorsed only the candidates with complete adherence to the prescribed principles. These principles included: technical requirements, financial responsibility, and program orientation. An advantage was given to the competitors from the areas with small or no program diversity.

The main technical requirement was a proof of ownership of authorized professional equipment for program production and broadcasting. The second criterion included a proof of financial potential to support the proposed program requirements. Also, this principle included the assurance that all internationally recognized broadcasting intellectual property rights would be respected and guaranteed and that all broadcast program records would be available for inspection in the case of copyright inquiries. The financial backer was required to provide documents that would certify its reputation as well as its capability to support the broadcast. The third criterion is related to the broadcasting concept; it notes that only program proposals that will contribute to the telecast diversity and enrichment of the present media milieu will be taken in consideration.

Meanwhile, RTS officials also complained about unfair competition exercised by the small independent TV stations. RTS's first complaint was that many of these stations started their operations with temporary technical permission. Once they got on the air, they gained popularity primarily by broadcasting first class foreign movies and television programs. Unfortunately, most of these films and programs were not legally purchased. Therefore, according to RTS, not only did these stations represent unfair competition, but they could also be practically labeled as "pirate TV stations."[13] Because of popular support for this first class programming any government action directed toward closing these stations is routinely referred to as "freedom of the press restriction."

The officials who run these stations claim that they are incapable of meeting all financial requirements with the foreign partners, considering the current economic blockade and especially the trade embargo. So, in this way they justify their illegal actions. However, some other voices in the opposition are considering the governmental conspiracy behind all of this "TV Farce" in Serbia. The fact is that recently government did close down one of the popular TV stations. But that station was not only broadcasting pirated foreign movies, it was also one of the small private TV stations in Sandzak that was run by Serbian ethnic Muslims. Therefore, the opposition claims, as long as the little Belgrade TV stations stay little, and as long as they remain semi-legal, with short-term, experimental and technical permissions to broadcast, and as long as half of their transmitters and relay stations are only semi-legal as well, and considering the obscure origin of their programs, these stations will have to behave or else!

CONCLUSION

The fact is that the process of democratization is working. The small TV stations are becoming bigger and their influence is growing every day, in fact, every minute. It is to be hoped that with some time and under better economic circumstances they will terminate their "pirate" habits. They must come to understand that nothing can be done overnight; as they grow, their audiences will grow, as, too, will their responsibilities toward their viewers. On the other hand, the RTS must learn to live with competition and understand that the days of the monopoly are finished. This is the era of healthy competition where the only thing that matters is the viewer share, and in order to win viewers back, they will have to learn how to serve them better. Whichever party runs the parliament in the future and subsequently appoints its people to the gate-keeping positions in the biggest TV station in the country will also have to learn that, yes, television is very powerful, but it also has its limits.

It may take some time for everyone to learn how to "behave" in a social system where government is under constant scrutiny and the watchful eye of the "free press," but, once this point is reached, it will be an easy and gratifying experience to work in an atmosphere where everybody knows the "rules of the game." Therefore, strict adherence to the broadcasting laws, once they are recognized and accepted by everyone and become firmly established, may well be the only way out of the present Serbian "TV Farce."

Finally, it is necessary to qualify any analysis of what has gone before by pointing out that it is not yet possible to judge what the aftermath of the 1999 NATO bombings will bring. Belgrade's television facilities were severely damaged in the bombings, and rebuilding may also bring restructuring. Political observers, in fact, have suggested that as the international community seeks to ensure a lasting peace in the region, serious attention must be given to media as well as political reform. As a reporter for the *London Times* recently suggested: "Whoever administers the peace in Kosovo will need to hold sufficient authority to guarantee free and fair access to the airwaves and editorial independence for broadcasters and newspapers. Anything less will retard democratic development..." (Haselock, 1999, p. 43).

REFERENCES

Dodeljene frekvencije za teeleviziju i radio (1994, March 18). *Politika*.

Goati, V. (1989). Smisao Jugoslovneskog Pluralistickog Soka, *Knizevne Novine*. Beograd.

Haselock, S. (1999, June 18). Freeing media is as vital as clearing mines. *London Times*, p. 43.

Hoce li se ici na Sud: Najavljene Zalbe (1994, March 22). *Politika*.

Izazovi Pluralizma (1989). (zbornik) Zagreb.

Milivojevic, S. (1993). *Istrazivacki Izvestaj: TV Prezentacija Ucesnika na Vanrednim Parlamentarnim Izborima u Srbiji 1993* [TV Presentation of political parties, irregular parliamentary elections in Serbi in 1993]. Gradjanski Savez Beograd, 17 December.

Pecujlic, M., & Milic, V. (1990). *Politicke Stranke u Jugoslaviji*. Beograd: Naucna Knjiga.

Popovic, M. (1988). *Dileme Politickog Pluralizma*. Niksic: Univerzitetska Rijec.

Smiljkovic, R. (1991). Pluralizam i Politicka Apatija. *Privredni Pregled*, Beograd.

Stranke i Udruzenja u Hrvatskoj i Sloveniji (1990). *Nase Teme*, br 3-4, Zagreb.

Stranke u Jugoslaviji (1990). *Novinska Agencija TANJUG*, Beograd.

NOTES

1. In the previous law, The Socialist Alliance of Working People (Socijalisticki Savez) the founder held those rights. This right was later transferred to the Parliament, the Parliament gave this right to the government and within the government all powers were given to the President or the appointed minister.

2. RTNS covers the northern Autonomous Province Vojvodina with its headquarters in the capital city of that Province Novi Sad. RTP covers the regions of Southern Autonomous Province of Kosovo with its headquarters in the capital city of that Province Pristina.

3. Serbian Parliament adopted the new Radio and TV Law on 1 July 1991 effective 13 August 1991. The new enterprise started its operations 1 January 1993.

4. The income from subscription amounted to 72%, Commercials 12%, 2% amounted to public income, and 13% other (undisclosed). Source: *Izvestaji i Studije*, RTS Istrazivanja, br.3, IX 1993.

5. According to the information published in "Izvestaji i Studije," RTS Istrazivacki Centar, Mart 1993, ("Reports and Studies," RTS Research Center, March 1993), the

overall TV population (over 10 years of age) in Serbia (excluding province of Kosovo) was 5,800,000.

6. The opposition called several demonstrations to protest the RTS program bias and finally succeeded (March 9, 1991 demonstrations) in forcing the government to replace four people who were in the leading positions in RTV Belgrade. RTB General Director - Dusan Mitevic, TV Belgrade Director - Sergej Sestakov, Slavko Budihna - Editor in Chief of News Documentary and Special Features Program (Informativni Program) and Ivan Krivec - Editor in Chief of the 3K (TV Belgrade's newly formed Channel 3).

7. Interview, editor in chief Aleksandar Tijanic, 21 April 1994.

8. Dusan Mitevic, former TV Belgrade's News Documentary and Special Features Program (Informativni Program) Editor in Chief (1971-1981) and former TV Belgrade's Director (forced to resign after demonstrations in March 1991).

9. SPS (Serbian Socialist Party), DSS (Democratic Party of Serbia), DEPOS (Serbian Democratic Movement), SRS (Serbian Radical Party), DS (Democratic Party), SSJ (Serbian Unity Party), UL (United Left), SNO (Serbian People's Defense) SDS (Serbian Democratic Party), and SDP. The number of times the commercials aired were different SPS, (70 times or 31.5 of the total), DSS 41 times (18.3%), DEPOS 20 times (13%), SRS 25 times (11.3%) DS 21 times (9.4%), SSJ 15 times (6.8%), UL 12 times (5.4%), SNO 7 times (3.1%), SDS one time (0.45%) and SDP one time (0.45%).

10. Permission to start TV broadcasting was given to the following 5 new TV stations: Belgrade--BK Telekom was given two frequencies one in the city of Belgrade for channel 12 and the other for the city of Novi Sad for channel 46; SO Trstenik-- Trstenik TV (for channel 37); Kragujevac--TV K9 (for channel 9) and Cacak--TV Studio Spectrum (for channel 40).

11. The members of this committee have been appointed by the government and their nomination has been announced in

Sluzbeni Glasnik (Official Gazette), No. 110 of 22 December 1993. They are: Chairman of the committee, Stanoje Andjelkovic then Vice-President of the Government of Republic of Serbia; Members of the committee: Milivoje Pavlovic, the Minister of Information; Zarko Katic, the Minister of Transportation and Communications; Natasa Curcic-Damnjanovic Vice-Minister for Information; Vladimir Mladenovic, Vice Minister for Transportation and Communications; Dr. Milan Topalovic, Technical Director RTS; Milan Lucic, Vice-Minister of Information; Dragomir Jerkovic, Director TV Beograd; Damir Cop, Business Association of Broadcasting Organizations and Bratislava Topalovic, Adviser to the Minister of Information.
Sluzbeni Glasnik (Official Gazette), No. 110 of 22 December 1993. They are: Chairman of the committee, Stanoje Andjelkovic then Vice-President of the Government of

Republic of Serbia; Members of the committee: Milivoje Pavlovic, the Minister of Information; Zarko Katic, the Minister of Transportation and Communications; Natasa Curcic-Damnjanovic Vice-Minister for Information; Vladimir Mladenovic, Vice Minister for Transportation and Communications; Dr. Milan Topalovic, Technical Director RTS; Milan Lucic, Vice-Minister of Information; Dragomir Jerkovic, Director TV Beograd; Damir Cop, Business Association of Broadcasting Organizations and Bratislava Topalovic, Adviser to the Minister of Information.

Sluzbeni Glasnik (Official Gazette), No. 110 of 22 December 1993. They are: Chairman of the committee, Stanoje Andjelkovic then Vice-President of the Government of Republic of Serbia; Members of the committee: Milivoje Pavlovic, the Minister of Information; Zarko Katic, the Minister of Transportation and Communications; Natasa Curcic-Damnjanovic Vice-Minister for Information; Vladimir Mladenovic, Vice Minister for Transportation and Communications; Dr. Milan Topalovic, Technical Director RTS; Milan Lucic, Vice-Minister of Information; Dragomir Jerkovic, Director TV Beograd; Damir Cop, Business Association of Broadcasting Organizations and Bratislava Topalovic, Adviser to the Minister of Information.

12. In an April 21, 1994 interview given to the author Dr. Milan Topalovic, Technical Director of RTS, said that ten members of this committee made all their decisions final in a democratic way, by voting, one decision one person one vote. Also, according to his testimony there was not one case in which the committee members had to repeat the voting procedure because of a tie; in all cases they reached an overwhelming majority.

13. TV Politika, TV Palma, and TV ART Kanal in Belgrade regularly broadcast pirated films and TV programs. Some other illegal TV stations in Nis and other smaller Serbian cities also do the same.

Chapter 9

RUSSIAN TELEVISION, POLITICAL ADVERTISING, AND THE DEVELOPMENT OF A NEW DEMOCRACY[1]

Sarah Oates

Russian television struggles with both the chaotic politics of a new democracy and a Soviet legacy of heavy-handed broadcast propaganda. While the government has passed progressive laws to give the public access to political information, especially during campaigns, problems remain in terms of fair television coverage. In particular, television displayed a strong bias toward incumbent president Boris Yeltsin during the 1996 presidential elections. In addition, there is worrying evidence that financial pressures, harassment and even violence against journalists are not uncommon. Despite its flaws, however, it can be argued that Russian television has played a key role in the development of democratic institutions in the country. This chapter provides a brief outline of television in the late Soviet period, the development of political advertising since the collapse of the Soviet Union in 1991, the important laws regarding political advertising, and how both journalists and the public have reacted to the massive challenge of assimilating a huge volume of political information in a short time span. The focus is on the 1995 parliamentary and 1996 presidential campaigns in Russia, using surveys of Russians to discuss the interaction between voters and television during campaigns in this new democracy.

A BRIEF HISTORY OF TELEVISION IN RUSSIA

Television dominates the media market in Russia, in particular because the broadcast medium was developed quite aggressively as a propaganda tool by the Soviet regime (Mickiewicz, 1988; Mickiewicz, 1997). By the end of 1995, television was available to 98.8% of Russian households (RSE, 1996), an amazing feat in a country in which less than 87% of the homes had running water and less than 40% had telephones by the same year (UZNR, 1996). In addition, the economic and infrastructure problems after the collapse of the Soviet Union meant many newspapers and magazines either went out of business, became too expensive for most readers, or failed to reach subscribers, making television even more dominant in the media market.

There are hundreds of state and private TV stations in Russia, but the market is dominated by a handful that have national reach. Cable channels (including Cable News Network International) are available in some areas, but their penetration is so far limited. During the Soviet regime, the state directly owned all television networks. Currently, the ownership of the networks is mixed (see Table 9.1). The channels that broadcast nationwide in Russia include Russian Public Television (ORT), which is 51% state-owned and shown on Channel 1; Russian TV and Radio (RTR), which is wholly state-owned and broadcast on Channel 2; and the commercial network NTV, controlled by the Most financial group and broadcast on Channel 4. Channel 3, which used to be the Moscow channel, became TV-Center in 1997 and carries programming by Moscow authorities and others. According to figures from Reino Paasilinna (1995), there were 438 hours of daily transmission in 1994. Channel 1 reached 99% of the country. Channel 2 reached 96%, while Channel 3 reached 50% in 1994. By the beginning of 1995, Channel 4's privately-owned NTV reported that it could reach a potential audience of 70 million viewers--although the audience could be tapped only with better receiving technology (Mickiewicz, 1997, p. 223). Virtually everyone watches ORT and RTR, according to a survey by Russian organizations at the end of 1997, and NTV is now watched in about three-quarters of households in Central Russia (McCormack, 1999).

Table 9.1 - TV Channels in Russia

No.	Name	Chan.	Ownership
1	Russian Public Television	ORT	51 percent owned by state, rest owned by mix of public, private corporations, including banks and natural resource companies. Advertising permitted.
2	Russian Television and Radio	RTR	State-owned. Advertising permitted.
3	TV-Center		Private, with 67% of shares owned by the Mayor of Moscow. Advertising permitted.
4	Independent Television	NTV	Private; major investor is MOST Bank. Advertising permitted.
5	Culture		State cultural channel created by presidential decree in 1997. Programming concentrates on cultural events, educational and training programs, feature films, plays, and classical music. No advertising permitted. Former St. Petersburg channel.
6	TV-6	TV-6	Privately-owned. Advertising permitted.

Source: McCormack. 1999.

While Russian television has developed some excellent news and discussion programs, it lags in the entertainment area. In addition, a lack of money at state-controlled networks often prevents the purchase of high-quality programming from abroad. This problem was exacerbated by the Russian financial crisis in August, 1998, in which the ruble devalued sharply, and the country's banking system almost completely collapsed. Meanwhile, the state-financed networks struggle to receive adequate funding from the government to supplement their advertising revenue, which was hit hard by the financial crisis. In December, 1998, even the massive ORT was forced to curtail its news program one evening after bailiffs had seized equipment. Television stations have faced curs and layoffs to deal with the fiscal shortfalls. The situation is worse for broadcasters outside main cities, who must rely almost entirely on the capricious state funding system, as there is little advertising revenue in the Russian hinterlands.

As a result of tight funding, Russian broadcasters offer a hodge-podge of inexpensive imports, including a wildly popular Mexican soap opera called *The Rich Also Cry*. Other offerings in recent years have included the American evening soap opera, *Santa Barbara*, and *Dr. Quinn: Medicine Woman*. While intellectuals complain of the lack of a native film industry to produce high-quality Russian drama, many of the Western imports are extremely popular. While the shows may have little social relevance for Russian viewers (such as a show about an American doctor in the Wild West), they do keep Russians tuned into television in general.

The Soviet Legacy

Soviet leaders were quick to identify the potential of television to educate the public about Communism and to encourage support of the government. In addition to the direct control through censorship and direction from party officials, the Soviet regime fostered a journalistic culture that encouraged support of the party. In order to get and keep jobs in the media, journalists had to prove their ability to produce stories and broadcasts that were supportive of the party line. This development of an "internal censor" was quite effective in screening out dissident elements in television reporting. If journalists chose to work in the extremely visible sphere of broadcast journalism, it was necessary for them to toe the party line.

Yet even under the heavy control of the Soviet period, the propaganda model did not provide a full explanation of the relationship between state television and the viewer (Mickiewicz, 1988). The state could not merely broadcast positive messages about Communism and expect the public to absorb the information uncritically. Rather, messages generated by the central Soviet state were destined to be interpreted in differing ways by Soviet citizens.

By the time Soviet leader Mikhail Gorbachev started to usher in sweeping changes in 1985, Soviet television was both immensely powerful in terms of its ability to reach the population and extraordinarily well controlled by the norms of Soviet journalism. The introduction of *glasnost* in 1985 prompted change at an exponential rate in the Soviet media. While journalists were at first suspicious of any encouragement to question Communist Party policies, television coverage of the Afghanistan war became much more realistic, no doubt feeding the waves of protest against the war. Television documentaries started to explore some of the most sensitive issues in the Soviet regime, such as conditions in mental hospitals and prisons. In its eagerness to make up for decades of bland, feel-good coverage, Soviet television began to produce almost relentless images of the failures of the Communist regime.

As Gorbachev tried to continue to use television as a propaganda tool, he found he had lost control of its immense power to expose the public to powerful positive images. For example, he pushed for the live broadcast of the first session of the new Soviet parliament in 1989 and, instead of reinforcing his role as leader, exposed the country to the depth of the debate about Communism. Short of a return to a much stricter authoritarian regime, it would have been difficult for Gorbachev and his supporters to re-establish control after the live broadcast of the parliament in the spring of 1989. The reactionary coup plotters tried to take control of central television in their abortive attempt to seize power in 1991, but even their armed forces could not stop the journalists from opposing their control--at first in small ways by failing to edit out the trembling hands of the coup plotters during a press conference and finally through direct defiance in reporting on the resistance at the barricades in Moscow (Mickiewicz, 1997).

In a brief honeymoon period after the unsuccessful coup of 1991, most of the media were unanimous in their praise of the new Yeltsin government and the destruction of the old regime. However, as the problems of a new democracy began to emerge, most notably the rampant inflation that came with the collapse of the Communist economy, the Russian press quickly reverted to the trend of the *perestroika* era, unafraid to report on the myriad problems in the new society. Many of the problems--the spectacular rise in crime, the new poverty of the working class, the financial scandals of the elite--made for exciting and dynamic reporting. In addition, it made for a great deal of anger on the part of the new government, whose leaders felt that they had to endure a relentless barrage of negative media coverage that did not make allowances for the difficult situation they had inherited from the Soviet administration.

In addition, broadcasters quickly found themselves limited by the constraints of the new market economy. Unable to support themselves economically and dependent on the government for both salary and facilities, most Russian broadcasters found themselves still linked closely with the state. For example, ORT on Channel 1 has been controlled closely by the Yeltsin administration.[2] However, the presence of the private NTV network on Channel 4 as well as numerous radio shows and periodicals representing a broad range of political views has meant that even ORT cannot escape from fairly complete reporting on events. This was particularly apparent during the recent war in Chechnya, in which ORT was forced into more complete coverage of the unpopular conflict after NTV featured many daring, in-depth reports from the war zone (Mickiewicz, 1997).

Although there is still a diverse and lively media in Russia, there is increasing evidence that is geared less toward provided unbiased coverage for the viewer than protecting the interests of the owners and controllers of the television stations themselves.

As a result, viewers may receive a range of views but will find that state-controlled television on the two primary channels provide relatively unabashed support for the Yeltsin administration. While there is some pressure from competing networks to provide a realistic amount of information on the problems confronting the regime or political contenders to Yeltsin, it tends to be dictated by the needs of the owners/controllers. For example, it is expected that TV-Center, controlled by powerful Moscow mayor Yuri Luzhkov, will support Luzhkov's bid for presidency in the upcoming Russian elections. As a result, Russian voters can flip through channels to be exposed to different views but cannot expect disinterested reporting.

This trend is exacerbated by a consolidation of television control and ownership in Russia in recent years. While state bodies still own 51% of ORT and all of the second channel (RTR), a small group of businessmen and enterprises, including many banks and natural resource companies, hold the remaining shares in ORT and own other media outlets. Thus, the construction of media "empires" is well under way in Russia.

In an even more worrying development, analysts have noted growing violence against journalists in Russia. Part of this was due to the Chechen war, which technically has now ended although the region in southern Russia remains extremely hazardous for journalists and others. At times, mafia-style violence spills over into television, apparently because of the financial *and political* power it can wield. For example, ORT director-general Vladimir Listyev was shot in an execution-type killing in 1995, shortly after he announced a reorganization of the advertising practices and suspended all advertising on the channel.

Television and Law

Despite the temptation to control television, the new Russian state has passed a number of laws designed to protect the media against undue influence from the government or other groups. Freedom of speech is guaranteed under Article 29 of the 1993 Russian constitution. However, there are limits--the same article of the constitution forbids the dissemination of propaganda that spreads social, religious, or national hatred. In addition, one cannot publish government secrets. The final part of Article 29 guarantees the "freedom of mass information" and specifically forbids censorship. This constitution was ratified by the voters after being heavily promoted by the Yeltsin government.[3] A new law on the mass media, which establishes norms for owning and operating a media outlet, came into effect in 1992 in Russia. Despite intense debate on the matter, there is still no up-to-date law to regulate television broadcasting in Russia, mostly because the Yeltsin administration is reluctant to grant powers such as licensing, to the legislative branch. Because there is no law on the electronic media, the government and the president use decrees and instructions for broadcasting • including to appoint the heads of the main state-controlled channels (ORT and RTR) as well as establish financing for state television (McCormack, 1999). However, the law on advertising that came into effect in the beginning of 1996 bans tobacco and alcohol advertising on television.

While there may still be no law to regulate broadcasting, the new Russian civil code has affected all media companies. The new code, which came into force in the beginning of 1997, makes media outlets responsible for any dissemination of information that is untrue or defames citizens. Thus, media outlets now must prove the accuracy and authenticity of their information, rather than being presumed innocent. An analysis of court cases show that politicians, businessmen and others often sue media outlets over stories (McCormack, 1999).

By the 1995 elections, the government had developed more detailed laws to regulate the media during elections. On September 20, 1995, the Russian Central Electoral Commission adopted a law covering elections and the media, although it applied only to state-owned media (including the massive Channels 1 and 2). The law requires that media outlets refrain from bias in their news coverage. All parties and candidates are given free time under the law. For example, in the month before the 1995 parliamentary elections, the national television and radio networks had to provide one hour of free time each day to be shared by the 43 parties in the elections. Parties and candidates could buy additional free time.

Parties could spend up to about $2.4 million U.S. (10.9 billion rubles in the fall of 1995), a quite modest amount considering that television advertising time (depending on the time of day) cost between $10,000 and $30,000 a minute at that time. The law required that television networks advertise their rates and charge all parties the same amount. In addition, political advertising had to be easily identified as distinct from editorial coverage. The networks monitored for a project on Russian campaigns did a good job in keeping short political advertisements distinct from political coverage during the 1995 parliamentary elections. ORT even went as far to introduce its nightly series of ads with the logo "This is political advertising" on a black background.[4] While this all might seem quite fair, studies still showed that both coverage and paid advertising tended to favor a chosen few parties or, as in the case of the presidential elections, overwhelmingly favor President Yeltsin. For example, the party "Our Home is Russia" bought more than seven hours of television advertising, about a quarter of the total advertising time in the election, which would have cost about $4 million at the advertised rate. This means the bill for their television advertising time alone would have exceeded the maximum allowable expenditures for the entire campaign by about $1.6 million, making it quite clear that the party was not following the law. On a more troubling note, a review of the editorial coverage during the 1995 parliamentary elections and the 1996 presidential elections show that pro-government groups and the incumbent president received a biased amount of positive coverage (Lange, 1996a; Lange, 1996b; Oates & Helvey, 1997). Other problems have emerged with coverage on NTV, the only major privately-owned television station in the country. While the station provided relatively unbiased coverage of parties in the 1995 Duma elections, the station was so heavily focused on its coverage of the Chechen war that viewers received relatively little information about parties, candidates, or their programs (Oates and Helvey 1997). By the time of the presidential elections in 1996, a top NTV executive was openly working on the Yeltsin campaign and the network's coverage became clearly biased toward Yeltsin and against communist contender Gennadi Zyuganov (Helvey & Oates, 1998).

The Russian Central Electoral Commission is charged with monitoring compliance with the elections and media law but has done little but support the government. For example, it did not investigate the discrepancy of the heavy use of television and official limit on campaign spending for Yeltsin's party in 1995. The commission found in favor of the government when the Communist Party complained of favoritism toward Yeltsin in the presidential campaign, although the Communists had provided content analysis to bolster their point (Lange, 1996b). In addition, the charges of pro-Yeltsin bias levied by the Communists were supported by an independent report by the European Institute for the Media (Lange, 1996b).

The current changes on Channel 3 are an interesting illustration of some of the dynamics of television and politics in Russia (Price, 1997). On June 9, 1997, a new channel called TV-Center was launched on Channel 3 (formerly used by both Moscow TV and a relatively small commercial channel called 2x2). Nicknamed "Luzhkov's Television" after powerful Moscow Mayor Yuri Luzhkov, it is expected that the city authorities will use this station to support the political ambitions of the Moscow bureaucrats (Price, 1997). According to the BBC World Broadcast Analysis, Moscow city officials involved in the project said that one of the aims of the new channel should be "to separate the image of Moscow from that of the Kremlin and the federal authorities," who are associated with corruption and inefficiency, according to political observers in Russia.

As the investment of the Moscow city authorities shows, Russian television is still seen as a tool to be used by those who can seize control of the medium--through financial or political methods--rather than as a public institution to provide dispassionate or unbiased reporting. A report by Radio Free Europe/Radio Liberty on the television industry in Russia found that major financial and industrial groups wanted to buy media outlets as political, rather than financial, investments: "Media magnates often say they are not looking for immediate financial gains, since few Russian broadcasting stations and newspapers are profitable. Rather, they value media branches as conduits for self-promotion and political influence" (Fossato & Kachkaeva, 1997).

As long as television channels are viewed as political or economic "fiefdoms" for information control, it will be difficult for the media to develop as an independent political player in Russia. However, as the Soviets learned and Russian politicians must have come to realize, control of television networks does not necessarily lead to greater support on the part of the viewers. As the type of owners and number of dissenting voices on the airwaves increase, viewers are presented with a range of opinions and images about their young democracy.

RUSSIAN TELEVISION AND POLITICAL CAMPAIGNS

There have been several major elections in Russia since the collapse of the Soviet Union, including the parliamentary elections of 1993, the parliamentary elections of 1995 and the presidential elections in 1996 (see Table 9.2).[5] While the Yeltsin government and Western analysts expected pro-market groups to sweep the parliamentary elections in 1993, both nationalists and Communists had relatively strong showings. Communists increased their strength in the 1995 elections, but Yeltsin managed to beat Communist presidential candidate Gennadi Zyuganov in a hard-fought contest in 1996. A study of campaign news coverage, advertising and free-time political spots shows that political marketing has evolved very quickly in Russia, as candidates and parties have learned to present their messages more effectively to voters.

Table 9.2 - Russian Elections, 1993-1996

Election	Date	Rules	Winners
Duma (lower house of parliament)	December 1993	Half of 450 Duma members elected through party lists, other half through single-member districts. Only parties winning 5% or more get seats in Duma. This Duma elected for 2 years only.	Party list winners: Lib-Democrat Party of Russia (23%), Russia's Choice (16%), Communist (12%), Yabloko (8%), 4 others passed 5%.
Duma	December 1995	Same as above, except this Duma and subsequent Dumas are elected for four-year term (unless dissolved by the president).	Party-list winners: Communist (22%), Lib.-Democratic Party (11%), Our Home is Russia (10%), Yabloko (7%)
Presidential race, primary	June 1996	Winner must have majority, or runoff between top two	Yeltsin--35%; Zyuganov-- 32%
Presidential race, general	July 1996	Winner needs plurality only.	Yeltsin -- 54% Zyuganov -- 40%

Sources: *Byulletin' tsentral'noi izbiratel'noi komissii Rossiiskoi Federatsii*, No. 12 (1994); *Vestnik tsentral'noi izbiratel'noi komissii Rossiiskoi Federatsii*, No. 1 (21), 1996; *Rossiiskaya gazeta*, June 22, 1996; *Rossiiskaya gazeta*, July 10, 1996.

The 1993 Parliamentary Campaign

In 1993, President Boris Yeltsin dissolved the Russian parliament after a reactionary faction tried to seize control of the government by force. He called for elections less than two months after the worst street fighting in Moscow since the Russian revolution. Voters had to choose the members of the Duma, the lower house of the Russian parliament, by picking both one candidate from their district and casting a vote for their favorite party. Half of the 450 members of the Duma would be elected in single-member districts and half would be granted seats from party lists, if their parties garnered more than 5 percent of the popular vote.[6]

Despite some censorship of the pro-parliamentary media, the government introduced liberal laws for equal access of political parties to the media during the election (these laws were modified for the 1995 elections). All parties were to be granted an equal amount of free time on Channels 1 and 2. Political parties were allowed to buy advertising time on television and were given free television broadcast time, which was about an hour on Channels 1 and 2 for all 13 of the parties that eventually registered for the election. The formal campaigning was limited to about a month before the elections, as it is in all Russian elections, with the end of the campaign called two days before polling. Eight parties were successful in crossing the 5% barrier to get party-list seats in the Duma in 1993, including the nationalist Liberal-Democratic Party of Russia (LDPR) with 23% of the vote, the pro-government Russia's Choice (16%), the Communists (12%) and pro-market Yabloko (8%).

It is clear that these laws were sponsored by the Yeltsin government and his pro-reform supporters with a sense of confidence that viewers would be swayed by their messages and ignore the ideas presented by the nationalists and the Communists. However, it was the nationalistic LDPR, led by the flamboyant and controversial Vladimir Zhirinovsky, that waged the most aggressive television campaign in 1993. While the pro-reform and pro-government parties, including Russia's Choice and Yabloko, offered somewhat bland speeches during their free time, Zhirinovsky was unafraid to make extravagant promises in his fast-paced, energetic spots. In addition to clever use of his free time, Zhirinovsky's party bought a large amount of advertising time.

A review of free-time programming in the 1993 elections on *The Voter's Hour* on Channel 1 showed that the LDPR used its free time to advance somewhat extreme, yet concrete policy suggestions.[7] Zhirinovsky spoke for the bulk of the program and suggested closing off Russia's borders to the "criminal element" from the Caucasian area, giving school children free lunches and restoring all former Soviet territories to Russia. At the same time, other major parties in the elections--pro-government Russia's Choice, pro-market Yabloko and the Communist Party of the Russian Federation--were not very successful at making recognizable policy statements during their free-time programming on *The Voter's Hour*. For example, although Russia's Choice argued for a market economy in its electoral platform, party leader Yegor Gaidar failed to take any meaningful position or state any policy about the market on this segment of the free-time programming. His only comment on the economy was a remark that inflation must be brought under control. In addition, his comments on social-welfare guarantees were also vague. Well-known market economist and leader of Yabloko, Grigory Yavlinsky, also failed to discuss concrete policies during his appearance for Yabloko. Both Yabloko and the Communists used much of their time on *The Voter's Hour* to campaign against the proposed constitution, which detracted from informing voters about their parties.

Even in this first election, it was clear that candidates and parties would use their free time in ways that the government had not envisioned when designing the law to provide television access. It was not uncommon in 1993 for parties to spend more time attacking the government and the plans to rush through a new constitution than on their own party policies (Oates, 1993). In late November, Yeltsin Press Secretary Vyacheslav Kostikov complained that the "democratic offer by the president and the Central Electoral Commission [for free television time] is being used by a number of electoral blocs and candidates not to present their programs, but to make flagrant attacks on the President, the government and the blocs' opponents ... Streams of lies, garbled facts, social demagoguery and pure invective have been hurled at potential voters from television screens" (Izvestia, 1993, p. 1). But by the same token, government officials have not been shy about using television for their own ends. In one mild example, government officials have been featured prominently on television in all the elections from 1993 to 1996 urging higher voter turnouts, which analysts have predicted would help pro-government candidates, parties, and the constitutional referendum.

Parties spent large sums buying advertising time on television as well in 1993. According to a report in the Russian newspaper *Izvestiya*, Russia's Choice spent 224 million rubles (about $224,000 at 1993 exchange rates) for air time, more than any other party in the campaign. LDPR was third, spending 154 million rubles, while other parties, including the Communists, did not buy any television air time at all. While Zhirinovsky favored personal appeals in his ads, Russia's Choice used slicker graphics and a softer sell to market the party. Survey results suggested that Zhirinovsky's strategy was very successful in increasing his party's share of the vote during the campaign (Wyman, White, Miller & Heywood, 1995).

The 1995 Parliamentary Campaign

By the 1995 elections, many observers expected that the number of parties would shrink and that voters would be left with fewer, but more predictable choices. Instead, a record 43 parties successfully registered for the elections. Under Russian media law, they were all granted equal time-- from the now powerful Communist Party of the Russian Federation to the tiny, but spirited Beer Lovers Party. Although there were more parties in the race, only four managed to cross the 5% barrier to win party-list seats in the Duma. The Communist Party of the Russian Federation dominated in the party-list contest, garnering 22% of the party-list vote. The other winners were the LDPR (11%), the pro-government Our Home is Russia (10%), and Yabloko (7%) (see Table 9.2).

In 1995 parties were given free time in shorter, but more frequent spots than the long twenty-minute spots in the 1993 campaign. Russian parties were given several spots of $7^{1/2}$ minutes, adding up to equal time for each group on both Channels 1 and 2. Sadly, most of the parties had little to say to fill up that time.[7] Some chose to show films, generally heavy on the image of Russian nationalism and industry. Others had party leaders make speeches. The presentations ranged from mostly dull to downright bizarre. For example, the green party (called KEDR or "Cedar" in Russia) chose to show a radioactive tomato on screen and display to viewers an array of contaminated products found for sale in Russian shops. Very few parties were able to articulate any type of party platform. When television journalists tried to force parties into having debates on issues, parties refused and won the fight by citing Russian electoral guidelines that left the parties free to determine the content of their spots.

Despite the elaborate law mandating equal amounts of free time and fair election coverage, studies have shown that some parties were more equal than others. The European Institute for the Media monitored the five major Russian networks during the campaign to measure the minutes of both paid advertising and editorial time for parties during the election. As Table 9.3 shows, the institute found that the pro-government and pro-reform parties received an unusually high amount of exposure. For example, pro-government Our Home is Russia[8] used almost a quarter of all paid political time and received close to a quarter of the editorial time as well. It was clear that Our Home is Russia violated the overall spending limit of $2.4 million U.S. (10.9 billion rubles) because it bought so much television time. No other party received as much coverage, although the relatively small, pro-reform Russia's Democratic Choice had the second-highest amount of editorial coverage (12.7%), despite being a relatively unimportant party in the 1995 elections and failing to win any party-list seats. The nationalist Congress of Russian Communities, the LDPR and the small pro-government party called Ivan Rybkin's Bloc all had relatively high amounts of advertising time. By contrast, the institute's study found that the highly successful Communist Party of the Russian Federation had virtually no paid advertising on television and a surprisingly small editorial presence given its popularity.

From a more detailed study of the main nightly news on Channel 1 during the campaign, it also is clear that Our Home is Russia enjoyed unusually large amounts of coverage on *Vremya* (*Time*). Coding of most of the news programs during the election found that Our Home is Russia garnered more mentions than any other party (Oates & Helvey, 1997). While *Vremya* devoted an average of about nine minutes a night to the campaign, discussions of the parties themselves were relatively rare, as the news tended to focus on the rules of the campaign, the media in the campaign, and survey results. As a result, there was little transmission of party images in general during this main nightly news program. Thus, not only was there a bias toward pro-government groups, but Russian viewers were not getting much information on the main television news about party politics, ideologies, leaders and other details to make an informed decision among 43 parties.

Table 9.3 - Television Advertising and Editorial Time for Political Parties in the 1995 Russian Duma Election

Party	Minutes TV advert.	Percent of total	Minutes TV edit. time	Percent of total
Our Home is Russia	431	23.4	670	24.6
Congress of Russian Communities	215	11.7	109	4.0
Liberal-Democratic Party of Russia	176	9.6	200	7.3
Ivan Rybkin's Bloc	151	8.2	199	7.3
My Fatherland	137	7.4	34	1.2
Democratic Russia's Choice	103	5.6	346	12.7
Yabloko	43	2.3	88	3.2
Women of Russia	36	2.0	63	2.3
Forward, Russia!	32	1.7	137	5.0
Communist Party	10	.5	160	5.9
Total for all parties	1840	100	2722	100

Notes on the data: Paid and editorial time on Russian channels ORT, RTR, NTV, MTK and TV-6 from November 19 to December 16, 1995; does not include the free time allocated equally to each political party in the Duma race.
Source: Lange, 1996a.

The pro-government Our Home is Russia party benefited from the enormous exposure of party leader and Russian prime minister Viktor Chernomyrdin, who dominated the news as head of government, especially when Yeltsin was ill for long periods before his heart surgery. Chernomyrdin, a solid, broad-shouldered man with a growl in his voice and the mien of a craggy patrician, displayed talent for mingling with crowds of workers, speaking from podiums at meetings, and striding authoritatively through manufacturing plants. In addition, the party recruited several other prominent Russians for its party ballot, including famous filmmaker Nikita Mikhailkov and General Lev Rokhin.[9] Chernomyrdin was used consistently throughout the campaign, both as rationalization for news coverage (he remained in his post of prime minister throughout the campaign) and as a firm, yet likable image as a political figurehead. Posters showed Chernomyrdin cuddling a rooster under the slogan "Don't Sleep Through Your Future" and making a reassuring gesture by bringing the tips of his hands together to form a roof as a symbol of protection.

Chernomyrdin's television appearances were a bit less creative than the campaign posters. In the main spot for the party that was run constantly throughout late November and early December, Chernomyrdin is shown meeting with a crowd and saying some reassuring words about the party from behind a desk. The images are careful and staged, yet groomed to look appealing and natural. Aside from Chernomyrdin, the main spot for the party showed sparks flying in a metal works, a rocket launch, an airplane that had been rescued from hijackers, children marching off to their first day of school as they clutched flowers, and a family group voting. The woman glances up at her husband for reassurance and slips the vote into the ballot box, then the image of a broad-based triangle with the red, white and blue colors of the Russian flag appears on the screen. Throughout the commercial, there is the insidiously catchy Our Home is Russia theme song about the importance of voting for "Our Home" to protect "your home." The broad-based triangle was supposed to represent a roof, but that symbol was not emphasized by the party after the amusement at the double meaning of "roof" as Mafia protection in the new Russian slang.[10]

The use of free time for Our Home is Russia was less well-polished. During the ORT free time, the party featured its leaders talking about the need for their party, yet little was said about definite policy or promises.[11] In the same segment, there is a tape as well, showing Chernomyrdin at a plant, some industrial shots of an assembly line and tree logging. In addition, there are some shots of soldiers leaping into tanks and action shots of the military hardware. At the end of the segment, there are "man-in-the-street" type statements, as people briefly say that they are going to vote for Our Home is Russia. In another free-time segment, an unidentified party official talked about how successful the party organization has been in recruiting people, but he failed to address the party's ideology or planned policies.

Meanwhile, Zhirinovsky repeated his charismatic performance from the 1993 elections to create rather more interesting free-time spots for the LDPR. Zhirinovsky, a balding man with hooded eyes, is perhaps best known for his oft-repeated pro-Slavic and racist views. In his 1995 party platform, Zhirinovsky wrote of support for Russians over other ethnic groups, a return to a state-supported economy, and a more hawklike policy toward the West and other countries.[12] In his free-time segments, Zhirinovsky eschewed the avuncular image of the armchair politician and delivered his messages standing up, staring aggressively at the camera with his arms clasped behind his back. Just as he avoided relaxed poses, he also rejected timid statements. In his rumpled suits, Zhirinovsky assured voters that LDPR was the only honest party --and the only party with the guts to tame the Yeltsin administration.[13] He was quick to assign blame, particularly to former prime minister Yegor Gaidar, the Yeltsin administration and the Communists. Zhirinovsky especially excelled at making sweeping statements to the voters, claiming: "There will be not one hungry person, not one poor person, not one homeless person if LDPR receives a majority of the votes."[14] In three segments, Zhirinovsky assured his viewers that others were "deceiving" them, causing the terrible problems in Russian society.[15] Zhirinovsky warned the viewers on December 6, 1995, "if you don't put LDPR in power, no one will return anything to you." Thus, Zhirinovsky excelled at whipping his audience into anger at the alleged "deceptions" of their politicians, then promising his party was the only to fix the problems. While some Western observers have been quick to dismiss Zhirinovsky as a clownish boor, he clearly touches a chord in the Russian public. Zhirinovsky has relied on his considerable talents as a showman and charismatic politician to create an enduring image for his party.

If the images that best represent the LDPR are not varied, at least they could never be called dull. In one of his more restrained political advertisements in the 1995 campaign, Zhirinovsky is seen visiting a local market, waving around imported packs of frozen chicken parts and complaining about expensive imported food. Other LDPR advertisements featured the leader in more lurid surroundings. In some ads, Russian female figures including Natasha Volkonsky from *War and Peace* and a housewife offered to "do anything" for him. Zhirinovsky clearly thrived on being seen in nightclubs, preferably with topless Italian porn stars or other women in various states of undress. According to the European Media Institute report, Zhirinovsky's party bought the third-largest amount of advertising time (176 minutes or 9.6% of the total) and he garnered 7.3% of the editorial time on television in the 1995 campaign.

While the free time spots for Yabloko were somewhat uninspired speeches by party leader Yavlinsky--as they had been in 1993--this pro-market party made several clever and interesting paid commercials. These included advertisements that played on the party name, formed from the founder's initials and meaning "apple" in Russian. In one ad, an apple falls on the head of a slumped Isaac Newton who then looks joyfully inspired while the announcer quotes Lord Byron. In another, a country lad eats apples while his girlfriend sulkily complains that "you love apples more than me." But no, he insists, he "loves them both." In another ad, a couple plays with their boy, then colorful graphics throw up a slogan on the screen for the support of the party, saying that the party will protect the "hearth" ("Ochag" in Russian). Interestingly, Yavlinsky does not appear in the ads, while he dominates the free-time spots.

The Communist Party of the Russian Federation had virtually no paid advertising on television in the 1995 elections. However, it could be argued that the party's use of free time was somewhat better than most, with an attempt to inform viewers about policies rather than merely introduce leaders or engage in boring, content-free speeches. Nor did the Communists choose flashy music or images in its free-time segments. Rather, they typically featured party leaders talking about the past mistakes of the Communist Party, including labor camps, while stressing the positive aspects of the Communist Party achievements in both Russia and the Soviet Union. Unlike the Our Home Is Russia segments, in which Chernomyrdin sometimes took a hectoring tone, the Communist leaders seemed to find a moderate, conciliatory tone. In its free-time segment on November 28, the Communists did use a brief film at the end of the segment, which showed traditional Soviet images of one of the massive Stalinesque skyscrapers in Moscow, the harvest, a street march complete with a hammer-and-sickle flag, shots of

Zyuganov with a crowd, a rocket liftoff, and films of factory production as some light martial music played. As the film ran, a voice said "For the honest and worthy support of the Russian great power" (in Russian: "Za chest' i dostoistvo russkuyu derzhavy"). In an odd twist, the film also showed scenes of Soviet-era voting. The shots of Zyuganov looked much like the shots of Chernomyrdin in the Our Home Is Russia advertising.

In the end, however, television presence did not seem to be correlated with campaign success. If the results from a poll of 1,601 Russians conducted just before the start of the campaign are compared with the election results, it appears that the LDPR, Our Home Is Russia and the Communist Party all significantly increased their vote share over the course of the campaign, according to Table 9.4. Meanwhile, Yabloko appears to have lost support during the campaign. According to a survey of 1,568 Russians immediately after the elections, supporters of various parties relied on campaign cues from television in differing ways (see Table 9.5). For example, Our Home Is Russia found campaign film clips far more important in influencing their vote choice than Communist supporters.

Table 9.4 - Campaign Success of Parties in the 1995 Russian Duma Elections

Party	Support prior to elections (percent)[1]	Party list elections results (percent[2]	Increase or decrease in support
Communist Party of the Russian Federation	15.7	22.30	+42 %
Yabloko	8.3	6.89	-17 %
Our Home is Russia	7.5	10.13	+35 %
Liberal-Democratic Party of Russia	3.4	11.18	+229% [3]

[1] Survey of 1,601 people across Russia by the All-Russian Center for the Study of Public Opinion conducted in early November 1995.

[2] Central Electoral Commission report on the final results of the 1995 Duma elections, *Rossiiskaya Gazeta*, January 6, 1996, p. 6.

[3] This increase is skewed as Russian survey respondents tend to under-report their support for the nationalist LDPR in pre-election surveys. This syndrome has been noted by many Russian public opinion experts, including those at the All-Russian Center for the Study of Public Opinion in Moscow.

Table 9.5 - Influences on the Electorate in the 1995 Russian Duma Elections

Survey question: What was most effective in influencing your vote for a party?

Response	Communist Party	Our Home is Russia	Liberal-Dem. Party	Yabloko	Over all
See leaders on TV	41.8	45.8	54.8	56.2	45.5
Campaign clips (free and paid)	8.7	18.3	11.9	19.2	14.3
Advice of people close to me	11.7	11.5	13.3	10.8	11.9
Comments/famous people & journ.	9.4	8.4	5.2	14.6	10.1
Direct mail	7.4	9.2	7.4	5.4	7.1
Personal meeting with leaders	4.7	3.1	9.6	3.1	4.6
Campaign posters	5.4	8.4	3.7	3.8	4.3
Talk with campaign workers	3.3	2.3	2.2	2.3	2.2
Campaign flyers	2.0	3.1	0.7	3.1	2.2
Ads on public transport	1.0	0.8	1.5	0.0	0.9
None of the above	27.4	19.1	21.5	18.5	22.5

Source: Survey by the All-Russian Center for the Study of Public Opinion of 1,568 people across Russia from December 20 to December 26, 1995. Percentages are for 1,161 who said they voted. The percentages add up to more than 100 because people were allowed to pick more than one response.[21]

The 1996 Presidential Campaign

The 1996 presidential campaign presented a different type of contest for Russian voters. First, the number of candidates was far smaller than the number of parties in the 1995 Duma elections. There were 11 candidates in the primary elections.[16] Although there were several well-known Russian political figures in the contest, including former Soviet leader Mikhail Gorbachev and populist General Aleksandr Lebed, the real contest was between Yeltsin and Zyuganov. After the Communist Party's success in the parliamentary elections and Yeltsin's waning popularity, Russians expected a close contest.

But from the beginning of the campaign, it was clear that broadcasters were biased toward Yeltsin in a way that far exceeded the partiality of television for the Yeltsin administration during the parliamentary campaigns. In addition, the Yeltsin administration was quite clear about the high level of support and cooperation it expected from state-controlled television, sacking the head of state television just before the campaign to replace him with a man who openly supported the need for television to campaign for Yeltsin. In a review of the news coverage during the primary and general election campaigns, the European Institute for the Media found that news shows not only devoted a disproportionately large amount of time to Yeltsin, but that their coverage of him was far more positive than that of other candidates (Lange, 1996b). In a specific content analysis of the Vremya news program during the campaigns, it was found that coverage of Yeltsin was both more prominent and more detailed than coverage of other candidates (Oates & Helvey, 1997). Even the privately-owned NTV, which was relatively unbiased in its political coverage during the 1995 parliamentary elections, skewed its news coverage to support Yeltsin for president (Helvey & Oates, 1998). Thus, the information passed on to voters was more one-sided than it had been during the parliamentary elections, as even the private NTV network coverage openly favored Yeltsin. In particular, television provided unquestioning coverage of Yeltsin's extravagant--and often unrealistic--promises to voters, as well as failed to probe his failing health.

The Communist campaigners were the only ones to make a formal complaint to authorities about the obvious bias, sending a series of complaints based on content analysis of broadcasts to the Central Electoral Commission (Lange, 1996b). However, the Commission rejected the complaints, saying that the more extensive coverage of Yeltsin was due to need to cover his activities as president. Yet the European Media Institute found that the bias in coverage went far beyond a need to cover the executive activities (Lange, 1996b).

In its spots, the Yeltsin campaign used both well-known actors and ordinary people[17] to talk about support for his leadership. Some of the advertisements used the tagline, "I love, I believe, I hope," while others ended with "Choose with your heart." The advertisements strove to reanimate feelings of gratitude or affection for Yeltsin for playing a key role in the demise of Communism and the attempt to build a new Russia. Yeltsin, so highly visible in much of the television news, did not appear in the free-time spots (Lange, 1996b). Zyuganov did appear in his free-time spots, chatting to the viewers about his family and career. Some well-known artists, such as a former Soviet minster of culture and a prominent filmmaker, expressed their support for Zyuganov in the free-time spots (Lange, 1996b).[18]

As in earlier elections, candidates were allowed to buy air-time as well, up to 30 minutes on the state-controlled networks (including Channels 1 and 2) with no limit on the independent networks. However, the maximum expenditure was not supposed to exceed $2.9 million, with a minute of network time costing between $10,000 and $30,000 (Lange, 1996b). The Yeltsin campaign showed a large number of ads, including testimonials from citizens on the difficulty of life under Communism, endorsements from well-known musicians as well as stories about Yeltsin's childhood and family life. Following earlier Communist strategy in Russia, Zyuganov's campaign did not buy airtime on national television.[19]

The campaign for the presidency presented a much more serious challenge to the tenuous media freedom in Russia than the parliamentary campaigns. While both the 1993 and 1995 parliamentary contests offered a range of choices, the option in the presidential campaign was quite stark. While an examination of policy positions might show that the two candidates were close together on some issues, the underlying difference in ideology between the two was quite marked. Yeltsin represented, if not exactly a democratic alternative, at least a continuation of some attempt to develop Russia into a nation that respects individual freedoms. On the other hand, Zyuganov espoused Communist philosophy, including the need to repress individual rights for the good of the masses. It was not hard for both the Yeltsin campaign and journalists to cast the contest as a choice between the Communist past and a possible democratic future. While Russian voters may have been willing to vote for Communist or nationalist parties in the parliamentary campaigns, they were less willing to hand over the very powerful post of president to a Communist. This is clear from the voting results. While only about 11% of voters chose pro-government parties in the 1995 parliamentary elections, almost 54 percent of the voters chose Yeltsin seven months later.[20]

While the Yeltsin administration controlled television to a large degree during the 1996 presidential elections, there were factors that limited that domination of the airwaves. As Mickiewicz (1997) points out in her analysis of Russian television, three factors had developed by the 1996 election that mitigated against total dominance by one faction. Unlike in Soviet times, free time was given to all candidates. In addition, candidates all could buy time on television. Finally, privately-owned NTV on Channel 4 provided a venue for news that was less under the control of the government, although the network failed to play the role of independent news provider in the presidential elections.

Evidence from Russian elections suggest that the relationship between television and political development is far more complex than a formula equating exposure (generally using Western advertising techniques) with acceptance by voters in the post-Communist state. Although parties such as Our Home is Russia and Yabloko turned in respectable showings in the 1995 parliamentary elections, the Communists garnered the highest amount of votes despite being relatively ignored on the main Channel 1 (ORT) news program and choosing not to pay for national television advertising. The LDPR also had reasonable success in the elections, although far from its spectacular results in 1993. The success of the Communists, despite the failure to capitalize on television coverage or advertising, suggests a complex relationship between Russian voting and Russian television viewing.

RUSSIAN TELEVISION IN A NEW ERA

Russian television has faced a return to a certain set of controls, although the rules of the game are not nearly as clear as they were in the Soviet era before 1985. The most important elements of the Russian media situation are as follows:

1. *There is the understanding that media outlets, even major television channels, take sides in the political battles raging in Russia.* The concept of media as advocate, rather than media as an unbiased purveyor of information to the public, has lingered well

beyond the end of the Soviet regime. Thus, a Russian viewer during the 1995 parliamentary elections would know to watch the 9 p.m. *Vremya* news show on Channel 1 to get the government line and to switch to Channel 4 (NTV) to get a view that was less enchanted with the Yeltsin government on *Sevodnya (Today)*. That being said, the broadcast media overall tends to favor Yeltsin and leaders labelled as "democrats" to protect the existing freedom in the media and this bias became much stronger in the presidential elections of 1996. Other groups, especially the Communists, have made it clear that they would like television to return to a system of very strong, direct state control. Thus, television journalists tend to favor the reformist/democratic groups in the interest of self-preservation.

Both the Russian government and Russian television tend to be based more on individual personalities rather than institutions. While an American viewer will accept that a prominent news show such as *60 Minutes* will go through a succession of correspondents, Russian news and commentary shows are often built around a single personality. Unlike in many Western television systems, prominent journalists are comfortable with showing bias toward a particular political camp. By the same token, journalists with followings among the public are somewhat insulated from the abrupt firings and manipulations carried out from time to time by the Russian government at state-controlled networks.

2. *Competition and privatization of part of the broadcasting sphere has made it much harder for the Yeltsin government to control television through Soviet-style methods.* The greatest threat to a government hegemony on broadcasting is NTV. Backed by the wealthy and influential "Most" banking group, the network has offered viewers a more critical view of the Yeltsin government and new Russian state. Most notably, NTV was much less sympathetic to the government viewpoint in the 1995 parliamentary elections and throughout the Chechen war. It was the bold and courageous coverage of the Chechen war that forced Channel 1 to offer a more truthful version of the events in the breakaway Russian region, although the government was struggling to minimize the flow of distressing images from the region. Channel 1 lost credibility as many viewers could change channels and get a less sanitized version of the war (Mickiewicz, 1997).

This competition has, however, shown its limits. Although NTV appeared to provide a more balanced coverage of the 1995 parliamentary elections and the Chechen war, the channel was overtly supportive of Yeltsin during this successful campaign for re-election in 1996. Immediately after the presidential elections, NTV was granted permission by Yeltsin to broadcast more hours in the day and to increase its range (Lange, 1997). There are still important levers that the government control to have significant influence over the broadcast media. While it is not unusual for a government to control television licensing in democracies, there does not seem to be sufficient protection to prevent fairly direct manipulation in exchange for concessions on coverage.

3. *Russian viewers are sophisticated consumers of broadcast media, not easily swayed by political messages.* It would appear there is a type of "minimal effects" model in operation in Russia, i.e. that citizens virtually ignore television in their voting decision. Actually, survey data and other evidence suggest that media effects in Russia have settled more into a Western pattern by 1995. That means that while television advertising and

media coverage has the ability to affect some of the voters at some periods, underlying voting preferences based on socio-economic variables are generally more important overall in determining vote choice. This makes political advertising a far more sophisticated undertaking in Russia. Although Western analysts have perceived Russian voters as a type of *tabula rasa* ready to absorb political messages without question, they appear, in fact, to be quite sophisticated in their consumption of media messages.

Russian Television: History, Legacy and Future

Russian television points out some of the dilemmas, and much of the excitement, of media systems in developing democracies. While in many ways still reliant on government support for its existence, there is a stubborn and enduring streak of independence in the medium. On the side of constraint, there are several factors, including government control much of the broadcasting infrastructure; considerable pressure to support the Yeltsin government; and that it is normal for journalists to take sides in political struggles. However, there are several elements in the new Russian society that support media autonomy. Prominent television journalists/personalities can circumvent government control by developing personal followings among viewers. In addition, their experiences of fighting censorship and control, especially in the tense moments of the 1991 coup, have left a legacy of bravery and entrepreneurship for many journalists. Finally, it is clear that Russian broadcast journalists are learning that the viewers, rather than government, ultimately hold the key to the influence of television.

On a final note, it is important to consider the role of television in the development of a democratic society. Many studies of Western television have tended to stress the "minimal effects" model, the idea that television has some ability to shape agendas and influence in only limited areas. Yet when television is not balanced by other democratic institutions, such as a stable government and a history of free elections, it takes on a far more critical role in the development of democracy. Especially now that television has so far outstripped other forms of political communication in Russia, it can have enormous power to influence a society just emerging from authoritarian rule. At the same time it would be naive to assume that there is a sort of "maximal effects" model of television in post-authoritarian states. Russian viewers have developed great sensitivity to broadcasting techniques over decades of trying to filter through propaganda and glean news. As a result, overt attempts at manipulation or advertising techniques imported directly from alien cultures are likely to fail, as can be seen to a certain extent in the parliamentary elections. Yet television has played an important role in Russia both in the demise of the Communist regime and the creation of a young democracy.

REFERENCES

Fossato, F., & Kachkaeva, A. (1997, May 20). Russian TV channels as tools of political consolidation. *Radio Free Europe/Radio Liberty Newsline.* http://www.newsline.org/newsline/.

Helvey, L. R., & Oates, S. (1998, September). *What's the story? A comparison of campaign news on state-controlled and commercial television networks in Russia.* Paper presented at the American Political Science Association Annual Meeting, Boston, MA.

Izvestiya, November 26, 1993, p. 1.

Lange, B-P. (1996a). *Monitoring the media coverage of the 1995 Russian parliamentary elections: Final report.* Dusseldorf, Germany: The European Institute for the Media.

Lange, B-P. (1996b). *Monitoring the media coverage of the 1996 Russian presidential elections: Final report.* Dusseldorf, Germany: The European Institute for the Media.

Lange, Y. (1997, October). *"Americanization" of political communication in the former Soviet Union.* Paper presented at the Images of Politics Conference, Amsterdam, The Netherlands.

McCormack, G. (Ed.). (1999). *Media in the CIS* (2nd ed.). Dusseldorf: European Institute for the Media.

Mickiewicz, E. (1997). *Changing channels: Television and the struggle for power in Russia.* New York: Oxford University Press.

Mickiewicz, E. (1998). *Split signals: Television and politics in the Soviet Union.* New York: Oxford University Press.

Oates, S. (1995, January). *The importance of party strategy in developing democracies: Formation and transmission of campaign agendas in the 1993 Russian Duma elections.* Paper presented at Party Politics in the Year 2000 Conference, Manchester, United Kingdom.

Oates, S. (1996, August). *The impact of the campaign on vote choice in the Russian Duma elections of 1995.* Paper presented at the American Political Science Association Annual Meeting, San Francisco, California.

Oates, S. (1997, October). *Parties, television and image in the Russian Parliamentary elections of 1995.* Paper presented at the Image of Politics Conference, Amsterdam, the Netherlands.

Oates, S., & Helvey, L.R. (1997, August). *Russian television's mixed messages: Parties, candidates and control on Vremya, 1995-1996* (Version 1.2). Paper prepared at the 1997 American Political Science Association Annual Meeting, Washington, D.C.

Paasilinna, R. (1995). *Glasnost and Soviet television.* Finnish Broadcasting Company Research Report 5.

Price, M.E. (Ed.). (1997, July 15). *The Post-Soviet Media Law and Policy Newsletter, 38.* http://www.ctr.columbia.edu/vii/monroe/.

(RSE) *Rossiiskii statisticheskii ezhegodnik* (1996). Moscow: Logos.

(UZNR) *Uroven' shizni naseleniya Rossii.* (1996). Moscow: Goskomstat Rossii.

Wyman, M., White, S., Miller, B., & Heywood, P. (1995). Public opinion, parties and voters in the December 1993 Russian elections. *Europe-Asia Studies, 47*, 591-614.

NOTES

1. This chapter was written as part of the Elections and Electoral Change in Russia project, funded by the Leverhulme Trust at the University of Glasgow. Funding for the fieldwork was provided by the Fulbright-Hays Doctoral Dissertation Research Program and the International Research and Exchanges Board.

2. Control of ORT is considered so vital that it came under heavy military attack during the 1993 putsch, when rebel parliamentarians attempted to seize control of Russia from the Yeltsin government.

3. Some analysts argue that the narrow majority that secured the passage of the constitution was due to vote-counting fraud on the part of the Yeltsin administration.

4. Observation from viewing Russian television during the 1995 elections.

5. In addition, there was a referendum on the passage of the new Russian constitution in 1993. This will be addressed in the discussion of the 1993 parliamentary elections, which were held at the same time.

6. In addition, voters had to pick a candidate from their district to serve in the Federation Council, the upper house of the Russian parliament. The elections for the Federation Council were not repeated in 1995 as the government continues to push for an appointed, rather than an elected, upper house. Also, voters had to cast a vote for or against the proposed Russian constitution at the same time. All in all, it was a very complex and confusing election.

7. This chapter uses the following editions of *The Voter's Hour* for analysis: December 7 (Communists, LDPR) and December 8 (Russia's Choice and Yabloko). The programs were recorded from the worldwide satellite broadcast of Channel 1. The parties were granted time on the programs that aired rom 7:45 p.m. to 8:45 p.m. Moscow time and were replayed the following mornings from 7:45 a.m. to 8:45 a.m. The programs were translated and coded by the author. The free-time presentations were watched and taped by the author in Moscow during the elections. The programming on both Channels 1 and 2 was monitored. The tapes were later reviewed by the author. Funding for the taping projects was provided by Prof. Timothy Colton at Harvard University and Prof. William Zimmerman at the University of Michigan. Prof. Laura Helvey of Elon College coordinated the taping projects for the 1993, 1995 and 1996 elections. In addition, the

author would like to thank David L. Cross for his invaluable assistance in taping in Moscow.

8. Our Home is Russia took over the role of the pro-government party from Russia's Choice, which broke with the government over Russia's invasion of Chechnya.
9. After being highly visible during the campaign, however, both Chernomyrdin and Mikhailkov declined take up their party-list seats in the Duma.

10. This was mentioned to me during interviews with Russian political analysts in the fall of 1995 during field work in Moscow.

11. ORT (1995). Free-time political broadcasts from November 22, November 23, December 5, and December 6, 1995.

12. ORT free-time segment, November 16, 1995 (evening); November 30 (morning); and December 6 (morning).

13. ORT free-time segments, November 16, 1995 (morning).

14. ORT free-time segments, November 16, 1995 (morning)

15. ORT free-time segments, November 16, 1995 (morning), also segments on the mornings of November 30 and December 6 on ORT. Zhirinovsky used the verb "obmanuvat" in Russian.

16. One minor Communist candidate dropped out in favor of communist Gennadi Zyuganov late in the race.

18. Although it was not clear whether these were real people or actors portraying real people, as are often used in advertising. The former minister was N. Gubenko; the filmmaker was S. Govorukhin.

19. In theory, Zyuganov relied more on rallies, meetings and Communist publications to drum up support for his campaign, although there has yet to work showing convincing evidence of this activity.

20. The results for Yeltsin were so strong--and the pressure on regional administrators so great to foster support for him--that there have been some questions of falsification of the results.

21. The author would like to thank Stephen White of the University of Glasgow and Matthew Wyman of Keele University for the use of this data.

Chapter 10

TELEVISION AND ELECTORAL SUCCESS IN TURKEY

Baki Can

Turkey has been governed under a republican parliamentary system since 1923. However, even before the republican days, the Turkish nation had some democratic experience. The Turkish people today possess political norms nd values that have evolved as an amalgamate of Ottoman value systems and Western attitudes that have been adopted in the process of Westernization. This current value system, as well as political traditions, influences the perception and evaluation of the political messages in political advertisements and visual propaganda. There is an undeniable role of historically inherited Ottoman value systems present in the Turkish electorate (Can, 1993).

THE POLITICAL SYSTEM BACKGROUND

Between 1923 and 1946 Turkey had a single-party (Republican People's Party) democracy in which voting was open and counting secret. In 1946 the establishment of other political parties in addition to the Republican People's Party (CHP) was allowed, and in the second elections that followed (May 14, 1950) the Democrat Party (DP) won 397 of 487 seats, leaving Mustafa Kemal Atatürk's CHP, the unchallenged ruler for the preceding quarter century, only 90 seats.

Several military interventions have occurred at critical points in Turkey's political history. In all these interventions, the military had raised the same common concern: democracy. For instance, this was expressed by Kenan Evren, the leader of the 1980 coup, in his public radio-television address on the first day of the event, as follows: "The aim of the operation is to... remove the obstacles that have been hindering the democratic process" (Evren, 1980). The military interventions that took place during the republican past of Turkey have all had considerable effects on the political structure, the election system, and the election campaigns as well as on the daily life of the country.

The Democrat Party's (DP) reign continued until the military coup of May 27, 1960. The party was eliminated, its members were jailed, and its leader and prime minister, Adnan Menderes, was sentenced to death, along with two of his ministers. The military created a new Constitution and delivered it to the new parliament assembled according to the new Constitution. The DP was not allowed to reform as a party, and the Justice Party (AP) was consequently established by its followers. The domination of two parties in competitive political systems is a universally established fact, and those two parties in Turkey were DP and CHP from 1950 to 1960, and AP and CHP from 1961 to 1980 (Ergüder, 1980).

Although DP's political life was terminated with the 1960 coup, the party that took its place (AP) became the longest ruling party during the following two decades, until the fall of 1980. On March 12, 1970, the armed forces issued a memorandum that interrupted AP's rule and imposed several readjustments on the system. The 1970 "coup" was followed by a rather lengthy period of coalitions and minority governments in some of which the National Salvation Party (MSP)[1] became a partner.

This period of coalition and minority governments, which was unfamiliar to Turkey, lasted about 10 years, and on September 12, 1980, the nation woke up with another military coup. All political parties were closed and their leaders detained for varying durations (some taken to court) by the military who ruled the country until 1983. The Constitution was modified once again during this period under military supervision. Elections were held in the fall of 1983; however, only three of the newly established parties (Nationalist Democrat Party-MDP, Motherland Party-ANAP, and Populist Party-HP) received the military's approval to compete. ANAP came to power with a safe majority through these elections, collecting 45% of valid votes and winning 211 of 400 seats in the parliament. ANAP's uninterrupted rule survived one more election (1987) and lasted until 1991.

The other two parties in the 1983 elections did not survive for long. MDP, although backed by the military, received the least percentage of votes 23.3% in 1983, and after the 1987 elections it was abolished, having no convincing public support behind it. The runner up of the 1983 elections, HP, united with Social Democrat Party (SODEP) under the name Social Democrat Populist Party (SHP) before the 1987 elections, and the SHP united with the CHP adopting its name shortly before the 1995 elections. During this process, these leftist parties continually lost popularity, their share of votes dropping from 31% in 1983 to 25% in 1987 and to 21% in 1991. The ANAP also lost popularity eventually; the incredible 45% in 1983 was followed by 36% in 1987 and only 24% in 1991, which placed them second after the True Path Party (DYP).

Süleyman Demirel's DYP (established in 1983) was the winner of the 1991 elections with a 27% share of the valid votes. Demirel was a veteran politician, having occupied the premier's chair a number of times with AP governments (alone and in coalition) between 1960 and 1980. DYP formed a coalition with SHP, the third largest party with a vote share of 21%. This coalition ruled the country until the elections of December 24, 1995.

During this period, Süleyman Demirel, leader of DYP and prime minister, was elected president of the country in May, 1993, upon the unexpected demise of Turgut

Özal, who had been occupying the seat since 1989. Demirel was replaced by Tansu Çiller, a former professor of economics and a minister of state (responsible for the economy) in Demirel's cabinet, as the leader of the party. Çiller continued the coalition with SHP, becoming the first female prime minister of Turkey.

When early elections were scheduled in 1995 a DYP-CHP coalition was in office as a successor of the DYP-SHP coalition, although neither party was still headed by their original leaders. While Demirel of DYP was elected president, Erdal Ýnönü of SHP resigned from his chair, and the party (now CHP) was under the leadership of its fourth leader after 1991, Deniz Baykal.

Electoral System

There is no single, well established electoral system in Turkey throughout its democratic history, only a particular system or variation of a system in a particular election or period. The ruling party or parties usually make alterations in the General Election Law to their (expected) advantage shortly before the elections which is clearly illustrated in Table 10.1.

Table 10.1 - Ruling Party and Date of Changing Law

Ruling Party/Parties	Date of Change in Law	Date of Elections
Military	06.10.1983	11.06.1983
ANAP	02.19.1987	05.23.1987
	09.10.1987	11.29.1987
ANAP	09.13.1991	10.20.1991
DYP-CHP Coalition.	10.27.1995	12.24.1995

Those interferences to the law have generally been in the form of alterations in some articles or paragraphs and not radical modifications of the whole law. The main focus of this analysis is on the visual propaganda of the 1995 elections, and thus references made hereafter will be to the latest version (October 27, 1995) of the General Election Law.

Under the Constitution, elections are free with secret ballots and are conducted on the basis of equality, direct suffrage, and open counting and classifying of votes. All Turkish citizens over 18 years of age have the right to vote. The Great National Assembly of Turkey has 550 members (since 1995). Deputies are elected for a five year term through a party-list proportional representation system using the d'Hont method, with restricted options and a double barrier of 10% each at national and local levels. Large provinces are divided into several constituencies according to their populations while smaller ones form a single constituency each. Deputies are identified according to their provinces, yet, by Constitution, they do not represent only their own constituencies but the nation as a whole.

TELEVISION AND VISUAL PROPAGANDA

Utilization of television for political advertisements and visual propaganda in Turkey is very recent, dating back only to the 1991 elections. These elections have a special place in Turkish politics in terms of political communication due to the introduction of fairly new communications media in the campaigns (Can, 1994). Very few studies have addressed these new communications media and strategies, and there have been no previous content analysis of political advertisements or visual propaganda in Turkish television.

Political television advertisements in Turkey have only been possible since the establishment of private television stations. In the 1991 elections, Star 1, Turkey's first (illegal) private television was unchallenged since there existed no other private channel, and the government television (TRT-TV) would not allow political advertisements. The Turkish people were, for the first time, face to face with political advertisements which, in addition to being new, were very interesting. Due to the lack of regulations about private televisions in general and political television advertisements in particular, political parties could broadcast as many advertisements as they could afford, for any duration and at any time during the programs. Star 1 was ANAP biased, which was clearly evident in its programming.

In the following years a large number private television stations have emerged at national, regional, and local levels. These private television stations broadcast many political ads in the following elections, the municipal elections of 1994. Government television TRT-TV continued to prohibit political advertisements or any visual propaganda during these elections.

Before the 1995 general parliamentary elections, some regulations were imposed on the use of both government and private television channels for political campaigns, to be in effect for these elections only. As a result of this, private stations could not broadcast any political advertisements or similar programs. TRT-TV on the other hand, only allowed visual propaganda within the political speeches made on the screen. The difference between visual propaganda and political advertisements is that the former is broadcast free of charge within the period allocated to political parties in government television. Political parties had their visual propaganda prepared by private promotion firms and broadcast them within their allocated propaganda periods. With these regulations, private channels were allowed to transfer the political speeches and visual propaganda broadcast by TRT on their screens, but, there being no financial benefits, it was not a favored format for them.

These regulations also imposed restrictions on the right to visual propaganda, its time, and its duration. Only those political parties who had a "group" in the parliament (minimum 20 Deputies) were allowed visual propaganda on television. The duration of visual propaganda could not be less then two minutes at a time and was limited to a maximum of ten minutes a day. The times of political speeches of different parties had to be pre-scheduled and announced during the news beforehand (Resmi Gazete, 1995).

Contents of Visual Propaganda on Television in 1995 Elections

Since the legislative arrangements referred to in the previous section only allowed political parties with groups in the parliament the right to visual propaganda on television, only 5 of the 12 parties which entered the elections (DYP, ANAP, CHP, RP and DSP) were permitted to benefit from this opportunity. Visual propaganda durations allowed for each party were a fraction of their total time allocations on TV, which differed from one party to another. DYP, the major partner of the coalition at that time, had a total of 50 minutes on screen during the whole election campaign period, whereas CHP, the minor partner, had 45 minutes. ANAP was given 40 minutes, and the other two parties who had groups in the parliament, RP and DSP were given 30 minutes each for visual propaganda on TV. The remaining parties in the parliament with fewer Deputies and those parties outside the parliament (no Deputies) were allocated 20 minutes each for speeches. All propaganda speeches and visual propaganda on TV were broadcast between December 17-23, 1995.

The allocated periods were to be utilized in increments on different days for political addresses by the party leader or someone delegated by the party. Speeches were pre-recorded in the studio by the government television and broadcast at previously announced dates and times, with Turkish national flag and the logo of the particular party displayed in the upper corners of the screen. Visual propaganda material, which was allowed for parties with groups in the parliament, had to be used within the allocated time for each party, but the total time used for visual propaganda could not exceed 50% of total allocated time.

DSP, one of the five parties allowed visual propaganda, did not use this opportunity. DYP broadcast five visual propagandas, all of them for a period of 2 minutes. The leading sixty seconds of these recordings focused on different issues while the remaining time was taken up by the repetition of the same recording with music-on each time. ANAP broadcast four visual propagandas which were a repetition of the same thing; RP used their allowance twice for two and a half minutes each while CHP preferred one visual propaganda period for nine minutes.

All these add up to 37 minutes of visual propaganda in 12 broadcasts. However, ANAP's being a repetition of the same material for four times, the number of visual propaganda materials that can be analyzed individually is nine.

The visual propagandas are coded for the dominant format (eg., documentary, issue presentation, testimonial, candidate statement), for the production format (eg., studio presentation, testimonial, candidate statement), for the production technique (eg., studio presentation, filmed outside, trick film) and for the presence of music and use of special effects, as well as for the overall impression of being professional or not.

Nonverbal dimensions on the code sheet included eye contact, facial expression, body movement, fluency and rate of speech, pitch, and dress; verbal dimensions included appeals (Joslyn, 1980), issues, strategies (Trent & Friedenberg, 1991), characteristics, style, and amount and type of negative visual propaganda.

The visual propagandas were coded by two trained coders; one graduate student and one undergraduate student at the Faculty of Communication, University of Ege in Ýzmir, Turkey. Intercoder reliability was computed using Holsti's (North, Holsti, Zaninovich & Zinnes, 1963) formula, obtaining an average reliability of +.85. The coding instrument was taken from earlier studies which analyzed ads from earlier political elections in the United States, France, and Germany. (Holtz-Bacha & Kaid, 1995; Kaid & Johnston, 1991; Johnston, 1991) Some necessary local changes and adjustments were made.

Results of the Content Analysis

Television time was not bought for visual propaganda for the 1995 elections; however, visual material was prepared at the parties' own expenses. Eight out of nine visual propaganda broadcasts (89%) had durations of two to five minutes; and one (11%) was nine minutes.

Apart from RP, party leaders were generally (78%) in the forefront in these visual propaganda materials. In all of the five broadcasts of the DYP, leader Tansu Çiller's appearances dominated, without her voice. ANAP's material was also dominated with their leader's (Mesut Yýlmaz) appearances; only a few of them with his voice (but without his appearance) and the majority without. Visual propaganda material of CHP, however, featured their current (Deniz Baykal) and past leaders' direct addresses. RP, on the other hand, gave the forefront to images of the works of RP municipalities instead of their leader, Necmettin Erbakan or any candidate.

Eight out of nine visual propaganda materials had music-on, CHP's being the exception. Music used had stimulating text and rhythm and was original in the cases of DYP and ANAP, while DYP's was seemed particularly successful. Visual propaganda of DYP and ANAP were coded as professional; of RP and CHP unprofessional.

As for the rhetorical style adopted in visual propaganda, two styles, exhortive and emotional, come to the fore with equal shares (33%). DYP has adopted the former style in two of their propaganda pieces and RP in one. Emotional style, however, has been adopted by DYP leader Çiller only. During the 1984 presidential elections in the US, in their television debate as candidates for vice president, George Bush had addressed emotions 24 times against Mrs. Ferraro's 42 (Shields & MacDowell, 1987). Çiller's being the only leader to adopt an emotional style in Turkish political campaigns suggests the argument that women in politics favor emotions more than logic. The televised political debates between the Çiller and Yýlmaz were "almost exclusively focused on personal attacks" and deteriorated into emotional insults on both sides (Çarkoglu, 1997, p. 89). In addition, Kaid and Holtz-Bacha (1995) have also found that male candidates in the U.S. and many Western European countries use emotional style in their campaign advertising.

Visual propaganda materials are generally focused on party leaders (67%), while two (22%) are focussed on works of mayors (those of RP) and one (11%) on opponent. Five of these materials (56%) contain negative attacks (two each of DYP and RP and one of

CHP) while four of them (44%) do not. ANAP's material and three of DYP's do not contain any negative attacks.

In terms of production technique, parties have, in general, favored one technique for all of their productions although the favorite technique differs from one party to the other. DYP's materials are typical examples of post-production with digital effects and animations. Rhythm is high, opponents are shown in black and white and are foggy; synchronization is excellent. RP has employed a limited amount of 3D animation and digital effects. Both materials have been individually produced with one by one editing through fixed camera shots in general. Rhythm is high with well synchronized and exciting narration.

CHP's material contains wipe links and zoom-in's; rhythm is low, tight shots dominate; there are no animations. Emphasis has been laid on content and not on appearance, in sheer contrast to ANAP's pieces where the opening is completely 3D animation. Some of the material is post-production while digital metamorphosis has been employed: weapons symbolizing terror fade into factories that symbolize the cure for unemployment; traditional shopping netbag fades into a modern shopping cart. Digital chroma keys and 3D Studio have also been used in several places.

The setting is a combination of different environments in most cases, with an overall ratio of 44%. In four of DYP's visual propaganda materials a rich combination of spaces is observed. In addition to indoor spaces like the parliament, sports halls, meeting halls and the like, various industrial plants and other buildings symbolizing the progress of the country, developments in international trade, and, credibility in international relations are all brought into view with actual shots, mostly with Çiller in the forefront. The medium is sometimes a military environment, sometimes a sports hall, sometimes a press conference, and sometimes the street or an open air meeting with cheerful crowds.

The emphasis is on outdoors in both of RP's visual propaganda materials, but interior shots are also used. Successful works of RP mayors are pictured along with images of historical and cultural buildings that have become symbols of those cities. There are exterior scenes of happy people with their mayors as well as some interior scenes of municipal officials and technicians working on new projects.

ANAP's material centers around 3D animations with limited interior and exterior scenes like class rooms and airports while CHP's setting is indoors throughout. Baykal's and his predecessors' talks are recorded in domestic environments, except for Murat Karayalçýn, who sits at a formal desk.

In eight of the visual propaganda materials (89%) the candidates interact with dominant inanimate objects, CHP's being the exception where no dominant object besides the speaking person is seen. One common object or symbol that all parties have used in their visual propaganda is the Turkish national flag, this being a clear indication of the value attributed by the Turkish people and therefore by the political parties to the country's independence.

All visual propaganda materials of the DYP begin with the Turkish flag covering the whole screen while the music plays the words "... hand in hand, hearts together ..." from the party's theme song. The flag is also used in similar ways by the RP and ANAP. The

RP also refers to faith and faithful people in quite a number of places along with views of mosques.

In DYP's and RP's material narration is provided by an off-screen narrator. In ANAP's some narration in the beginning is recognizable as Mesut Yýlmaz's voice, but later an outside narrator can be heard. Past and present party leaders speak in CHP's visual propaganda material throughout. Party leaders on screen in visual propaganda do not keep eye contact with the viewer, not even those of CHP whose speeches have been particularly made and recorded for that purpose. Çiller and Yýlmaz have limited eye contact while RP's mayors and its leader Erbakan have none.

In visual propaganda materials broadcast on Turkish television, generally party leaders dominate the screen. This reaches a ratio of 78% for the materials used in the 1995 general parliamentary elections. For this reason, body movements were analyzed for party leaders only.

Çiller is generally smiling on the screen, this applies to all five of DYP's visual propaganda materials. Yýlmaz and the leaders of CHP are generally attentive/serious. Overall, 56% of leaders are smiling in the Turkish television programs, 22% are attentive/serious, and the remainder were classified as not seen or not applicable. Frequent body movement was a characteristic particularly of Çiller who was moving frequently in 56% of the spots in which she appeared. Body movements were coded as "moderate" for Yýlmaz and Baykal (22% of the overall movements).

Fluency of speech can only be analyzed for Baykal who performed directly to the camera, and, to a certain extent for Yýlmaz whose voice is played somewhat as a narration of the scenes on the screen. Both leaders are fluent, with moderate speech rates and pitch varieties close to normal. Leaders Yýlmaz, Çiller, and Erbakan, as well as previous leaders of CHP are dressed formally while Baykal wears informal attire.

Only one out of nine visual propaganda materials (CHP's) is recorded in a domestic environment; two of them (those of the RP) are mainly recorded in casual outdoor and indoor environments like parks, construction sites and offices. The DYP and ANAP have both natural appearing and 3D animation. Overall, 67% of the videos used a combination of natural settings with animation, 22% used natural appearing settings, and 11% were all obviously staged settings.

In terms of special effects and production techniques, montages were a dominant production style; 78% used it (seven out nine visual propaganda materials). While ANAP employed computer graphics excessively, RP used stills in one instance.

It is generally believed that positive images generate more sympathy, and therefore more votes, than issues (Rosenberg & McCafferty, 1987). Accordingly, the DYP and CHP laid the emphasis on images of their leaders in visual propaganda (66.7%). ANAP and RP, on the other hand, emphasized issues in all of their materials; RP in particular, devoted both of their visual propaganda materials almost completely to issues with only leader Erbakan appearing briefly in one scene.

DYP preferred emotional appeals, while ANAP and RP relied on logical appeals and CHP on source credibility. Overall, 56% of the television programs relied on emotional appeals, 33% used logical approaches, and 11% relied on source credibility. Fear appeals are used in only one third of the visual propaganda (33%)--by DYP (in two visual propaganda materials) and CHP. While DYP has avoided fear appeals in three of their visual propagandas, ANAP and RP have avoided them completely. The common target of fear appeals was RP. During 1995 elections campaigns RP was the common target not only in visual propaganda but in all other forms and means of propaganda like speeches, newspaper ads, press conferences, interviews, and the like. Parties besides RP identified themselves as "we" and RP as "them" (Bostancý, 1996).

A great majority of the visual propaganda materials contained some mention of primary issues of the country (89%), the only exception being CHP's pieces. Although there are limited references to issues in the material of CHP, leader Baykal placed great emphasis on his personality traits and on the national and international credibility of social democratic thought.

DYP has devoted each one of its visual propaganda materials to a different topic in a determined sequence: the first one handles the aims and the achievements of the preceding four years' coalition period, the second focusses on better education opportunities for the youth and employment strategies, the third is to women's rights and accomplishment in this area, and the fourth one discusses democratic rights. The fifth one deals with several issues from foreign economic and political relations to terrorism.

ANAP illustrated a projected Turkey of 2000: terrorism is finished, industrialization has taken off, a stable economy has replaced inflation, underdevelopment has turned into a steady development, GAP (Southeast Anatolia Development Project) is reactivated, Anatolia has progressed, education has improved, and, in short, the country that everyone had been dreaming of for years is displayed.

RP, in contrast to all other parties, put the emphasis on the accomplishments of its mayors in various large cities around the country, who have taken office only a year and a half ago capturing more than half of the city centers, including Ankara and Istanbul. One visual propaganda material was devoted to these two cities only, the first and second largest cities as well as the capital, while the other covered five other large cities. RP demanded the votes of the people in order to carry its efforts to the central government for similar achievements for the nation as a whole.

In CHP's visual propaganda material, Baykal dwells upon social democracy; he explains the new social democratic approach now dominating in the western world and promotes his party as the representative of this new understanding in Turkey. He also stresses the European Customs Union agreement that he had signed as the Minister of Foreign Affairs during the final months of the coalition, as well as income justice, wage increases, human rights, workers rights, and unemployment. Table 10.2 summarizes the issues referred to by the political parties in their visual propaganda. These data show that the DYP covered a wider range of issues in their videos than the other parties.

Table 10.2 - The Issues Referred to by the Political Parties

ISSUES	DYP	ANAP	RP	CHP
Unemployment	+	-	+	+
Customs Union	+	-	-	+
GAP(Southeast Anatolia Proj.)	+	+	-	-
Education	+	+	-	-
Democratic/Human Rights	+	-	-	+
Terrorism	+	+	-	-
Inflation	-	+	-	+
Industrial Development	-	+	-	-
Bribery	-	-	+	-
Municipal Services	-	-	+	-
Women's Problems	+	-	-	-
Oil Pipeline	+	-	-	-
Housing	-	-	+	-
Water	-	-	+	-
Wages	-	-	-	+
Workers' Rights	-	-	-	+

Only RP, in their visual propaganda, reflected the importance of the office through a short scene where leader Erbakan is seen with a large number of body guards around him. Likewise, only CHP stressed the legitimacy of the prime minister. Parties besides RP have reflected their leaders as competent persons.

Visual propaganda materials that call for change and new ideas are slightly more common that those that do not; the former scores 56% (total of 5) against latter's 44%. These five compose of ANAP's, CHP's, both of RP's and one of DYP's. Four visual propaganda materials of DYP do not contain any messages about change and novelty.

Four visual propaganda materials express optimism for the future despite the current situation of the country. No mention is made of the current situation of the country in any of the five visual propaganda materials of DYP, the major partner of the coalition that had been ruling the country for the past four years. All other parties have referred to this issue including CHP, the minor partner of the same coalition.

All political parties speak of traditional values in their visual propaganda although DYP has done so in only two of their materials. A striking point worth mentioning here is that it is not only conservative RP which adheres to traditional values but all others, too, including social democrat CHP.

In all five of DYP's visual propaganda materials, in several scenes Çiller appears in cordial dialogues with presidents or premiers of developed countries; the aim was to promote Çiller as one of the prominent leaders of the world. No other party had such scenes in their visual propaganda. On the other hand it is only CHP who included people respected by their electorate in their visual propaganda; past leaders of the party as well as those of SHP, which has joined CHP earlier, have all made talks on the screen. This was an attempt to attract more left leaning votes to CHP, which inevitably were to be shared between the two leftist parties, CHP and DSP.

All five visual propaganda materials of DYP and that of CHP emphasize the accomplishments of their parties' leaders while ANAP and RP do not openly consider this point. The latter laid the emphasis on the accomplishments of their mayors in numerous cities, who had taken office a year and a half earlier.

No surrogates were employed for any of the leaders or candidates in any of the nine visual propaganda materials. In CHP's material, however, Erdal Ýnönü , a former leader of SHP but no longer a candidate for the parliament, spoke on behalf of his party. Similarly, there was no offensive position taken by any party or leader in any of the visual propaganda materials. On the other hand, only CHP has adopted attacks on the records of their opponents; Baykal declares other parties' failures as "inevitable" since they do not subscribe to leftist ideology.

In terms of emphasizing candidate characteristics in the visual propaganda we have to put RP to one side; RP promotes its mayors who have been quite successful in their relatively short period in office and not any one of their candidates. The remaining parties have promoted their leaders in their visual propaganda with varying emphases on different characteristics. Honesty and integrity have only been used by CHP while no party has referred to toughness or strength. On the other hand, rate of use of aggressiveness is four in nine. Table 10.3 outlines candidate characteristics according to parties.

Table 10.3 - Parties and Candidate Characteristics

Characteristics		Occurrence%	DYP	ANAP	RP	CHP
Total (for parties)			6	1	2	1
Honesty/ Integrity	1	11.1	0	0	0	1
Toughness/ Strength	0	00.0	0	0	0	0
Warmth/ Compassion	6	66.7	5	0	0	1
Competency	6	66.7	4	1	0	1
Performance/ Success	6	66.7	5	0	0	1
Aggressiveness	4	44.4	4	0	0	0
Activeness	6	66.7	5	0	0	1
Qualifications	6	66.7	5	0	0	1

All types of camera angles were employed in the nine visual propaganda materials prepared by the political parties, although some preferences are visible. ANAP favored a low camera angle which helps Yýlmaz exhibit an imposing posture. Baykal was shot straight-on, while previous leaders were shot with a slightly high camera angle (camera at normal eye level while subject is sitting) presenting a more sincere and warm relation with the viewers. Erbakan was shot with a high camera angle whereas all camera angles (in great variety) were used in DYP's visual propaganda. CHP and RP (in the single scene with Erbakan) have preferred medium shots (waist up) in contrast to DYP and ANAP who have employed all possible camera shots (tight, medium and long).

ELECTORAL SUCCESS

The general elections of 1995 ended in radical changes in the composition of the parliament; RP and DSP have increased their share of seats remarkably. Through these elections RP, for the first time in its history, became the top party in the parliament, while DSP has taken over the leadership of the left from CHP.

In order to compare the results of 1995 elections with those of the previous general elections, we have to compare their ratio of seats rather than pure numbers, because the total number of seats in the parliament were increased from 450 to 550 shortly before the elections and candidates of the Great Unity Party (BBP) competed in the elections within the lists of ANAP but returned to their original party (7 of them) after being elected. Thus comparisons of chairs and their ratios before and after the elections have been made after deducting this figure and are given in the Table 10.4.

Table 10.4 - Parties, their Seats and Seats Percentage

	Before The Election		After The Election	
Parties	Seat(450)	(%)	Seat(550)	(%)
DYP	163	36.2	135	24.54
ANAP	109	24.2	125	22.7
CHP	42	09.3	49	08.9
RP	38	08.4	158	28.7
DSP	20	04.4	76	13.4

It can easily be seen from the table that in terms of ratio of representation in the parliament, DYP suffered the greatest loss in 1995 elections, although ANAP and CHP also ended with losses. RP is the doubtless winner with a remarkable increase from 8% to nearly 29% (3.41X) and DSP is the runner up with an equally significant increase from 4% to 13% (3.05X).

As stated earlier, with the changes made in the General Election Law by the DYP and CHP shortly before the elections, the longest duration of propaganda on television was gifted to DYP, the major partner of the coalition, the second longest duration being given to CHP, the minor partner, and the third to ANAP, the major opposition. RP and DSP had no extra bonuses. At the same time, none of the major national television channels, nor daily newspapers with greater numbers of readers supported RP or DSP during the campaign period. Furthermore, many of those channels and newspapers were overtly against RP; attacking RP was the common attitude of all other parties too. All arrows were aimed toward RP (Türköne, 1996).

Why, then, did RP come out as the top party from the elections despite such harsh, and at times merciless, opposition? Two reasons might be suggested. First, negative public opinion developed against those parties who had been in power in previous years without significant achievements. Second, a similar negative public opinion seemed to develop against media in general. The negative attacks of sources (other parties and media) that were already being observed negatively by people turned into a positive effect; in short, two negatives made a positive.

Summary and Conclusion

Six out of nine visual propaganda materials of 1995 general elections (those of DYP and ANAP) seemed to be professional in their approach, both in terms of production techniques and the handling of issues. Each one of DYP's five visual propaganda materials handled a different topic; the material was both professional and highly persuasive in terms of selection of topics and their sequencing as well as their production. RP chose to promote the achievements of their mayors instead of their leader or any other candidate, yet they were not very successful in establishing clearly the links between municipal achievements and the general parliamentary elections. CHP chosen a classical approach in its efforts to increase its share of votes while also conveying some ideological messages in the meantime.

DYP's professionally prepared visual propaganda, however, did not help this party in its loss of seats in the parliament, despite occupying a longer duration on the television screen than other parties. DSP, on the other hand, did not lose anything due to not having any visual propaganda on television, nor did RP suffer because of its unprofessional material; both parties came out with considerable gains (in votes as well as in chairs) from the elections.

This research does not shed sufficient and convincing light on the role of visual propaganda on voter behavior in Turkish elections. Without audience reaction data it is impossible to determine the effect of the party visual propaganda. Much more research needs to be done on Turkey, as its electoral process remains challenging for scholars of democracy.

REFERENCES

Bostancý, N. (1996). RP'yi Anlamak. *Türkiye Günlü'ü* [Understanding the RP. *Daily of Turkey*] *38*, 67 -70.

Can, B.(1993). *Ikna Edici Ileti'imde Duygu ve Mantýk Kullanýmý* [*Using emotion and reasoning in persuasive communication*]. Izmir, Turkey.

Can, B.(1994). Siyasi Parti Liderlerinin Propagandalarýnda Seçmenlerini Ýkna Ýçin Kullandýklarý Materyal Organizasyonlarý [Party Leaders' Organization of Materials in their propaganda for Persuasion of Voters]. *Dü'ünceler* [*Opinions*], *7*, 49-60.

Çarkoglu, A. (1997). The Turkish general election of 24 December 1995. *Electoral Studies, 16 (1),* 86-95.

Ergüder, Ü. (1980). *Türkiye'de De'i'en Seçmen Davraný'ý Örüntüleri, Türkiye'de Siyaset [Changing Patterns of Electoral Behaviour in Turkey. Politics in Turkey].* Istanbul, Turkey: Der yayýnlarý.

Evren, K.(1990). *Kenan Evren'in Anýlarý, [Kenan Evren's Memories].* Istanbul, Turkey: Milliyet Yayýnlarý.

Holtz-Bacha, C., & Kaid, L.L. (1995). Television spots in German national elections:Content and effects. In L.L. Kaid & C. Holtz-Bacha (Eds.), *Political advertising in Western democracies* (pp. 61-88). Thousand Oaks, CA: Sage.

Johnston, A. (1991). Political broadcasts: An analysis of form, content, and style in presidential communication. In L.L. Kaid, J. Gerstlé, & K.R. Sanders (Eds.), *Mediated politics in two cultures: Presidential campaigning in the United States and France* (pp.59-72). New York: Praeger.

Joslyn, R. (1980). The content of political spot ads. *Journalism Quarterly, 57,* 92-98.

Kaid, L. L., & Holtz-Bacha, C. (Eds.). (1995). *Political advertising in Western democracies.* Thousand Oaks, CA: Sage Publications.

Kaid, L.L., & Johnston, A.(1991). Negative versus positive television advertising in U.S. presidential campaigns, 1960 - 1988. *Journal of Communication, 41,* 53-64.

North, R.C., Holsti, O., Zaninovich, M.G., & Zinnes, D.A. (1963). *Content analysis: A handbook with applications for the study of international crisis.* Evanson, IL: Northwestern University Press.

Resmi Gazete. (1995). (Official Gazette). 10.27.1995. Law No:298, item 52, p. 3644.

Rosenberg, S.W., & McCafferty, P.(1987). The image and the vote. *Public Opinion Quarterly, 51,* 31- 47.

Shields, A.S., & MacDowell, K.A. (1987). "Appropriate" emotion in politics: Judgments of a televised debate. *Journal of Communication, 37,* 78-89.

Trent, J., & Friedenberg, R.V. (1991). *Political campaign communication: Principles and practices* (2nd ed.). New York: Praeger.

Türköne, M. (1996). Ucuz Seçim, *Türkiye Günlü'ü* [Cheap Election, *Daily of Turkey*], pp. 38. 39-46.

NOTES

1. The most distinguished characteristic of MSP is that its founders and the majority of its followers are religious people who are more considerate about their belief system and worship. This has caused many people to label this party and its successor Welfare Party (RP) as "Islamist." This may not be a fair interpretation since the party does not suggest an Islamic constitution and the party rules and regulations do not contain such statements.

2. The term "Visual Propaganda" has been used in "Seçimlerin Temel Hükümleri ve Seçmen Kütükleri Hakkýnda Kanun" [Act on the Basic Provisions of Elections and Elector Logs]. For this reason we are using the same term.

Chapter 11

PARTY-CENTERED CAMPAIGNING AND THE RISE OF THE POLITICAL ADVERTISING SPOT IN GREECE[1]

Athanassios N. Samaras

The modern Greek state, while geographically in the East, is differentiated from the other neighboring countries in terms of a long tradition of democratic practice as well as participation in the European Union and NATO. On the other hand, it is differentiated from its West European partners in terms of the heritage of Orthodox Christianity and Ottoman Rule; the country did not fully share with the other Western European countries the experience of the transition from authoritarianism to democracy in terms of polity, and from feudalism to capitalism, in terms of social and economic structure (Clogg, 1992; Papacosma, 1983).

Diamantouros (1983) argues that the experience of half a millennium of Turkish occupation educated Greeks in "an instrumental attitude towards the law, one which placed a premium on manipulation and evasion," a reliance on the family and interpersonal relations as well as "a profound distrust of all concentration of power outside one's own hands, and of simultaneous pursuits of power at all cost" (p. 46). This, combined with the intense competition for limited resources and the centrality of the state in supporting clientelistic networks, explains the ferocity of the political struggle. Winning elections in Greece is more important than in other countries (Legg & Roberts, 1997, p. 131) and, once captured, the state has to be maintained at all costs (Diamantouros, 1983). The struggle to gain and maintain political power has been so sharp that, on a number of occasions in this century, Greek factions have deliberately sabotaged liberal parliamentary institutions (Papacosma, 1983).

After many years of alternating power between factions, in 1961 Georgios Papandreou consolidated the amalgam of parties formulating the center into a single party, the Enosis Kentrou (EK--Centre Union). The EK won the 1963 elections with a small majority and the 1964 elections with a landslide majority. The EK government colluded with the monarchy, but a military coup in April of 1967 created new instability (Clogg, 1987, 1992; Legg & Roberts, 1997). After a failed attempt to overthrow the military regime, the king fled the country, and the monarchy was abolished in 1973 (Dimitras, 1987). However, in 1981 the government returned to a more stable situation with the ascendance of PASOK (Panhellenic Socialistic Movement), inaugurated by Andreas Papandreou (son of Georgios). Loulis (1995) explains the change in 1981 as a return to centrist ideas: "the dominance of PASOK in the 1981 elections did not take place in an ideological vacuum but mirrored the dominance of centre-left ideas in the whole spectrum of politics, economy and foreign policy" (p. 57) after the junta.

In the period 1985-1989, PASOK's credibility was undermined primarily by the austere economic programme of 1985-1987 that followed campaign promises for "even better days" and various scandals involving Papandreou's involvement in extra-marital affairs and his health problems.[2] After a series of elections alternating power with other parties, PASOK, whose leader had only narrowly been acquitted of charges for his scandals, won the 1993 elections. After the death of Andreas Papandreou, Kostas Simitis was elected head of PASOK and subsequently won the 1996 elections.

This outline of the political context can be concluded with the following observations:

1. In Greece the actual terms Right, Center, and Left have designated three historical political families rather than abstract belief systems (Mavrogordatos, 1984). Despite the continuing threefold division, actual competition for government is effectively restricted to two contenders (Right-Centre) with the exclusion of the Left.[3]

2. Traditionally in Greek politics, the leader has been more stable and the party more transient in the formulation and signification of the political blocks. However, it is important that, while both ND (Nea Democratia) and PASOK have originally been signified and contained by the personality of their founder, in both cases they have outlived them. The critical event in each case was the replacement of the founder by a democratically elected leader within the context of the same party. Thus the *party label becomes a permanent system of signification* in Greek politics, parallel and more stable than the personality contest between party leaders.[4]

3. The leadership and its control of the party are not structurally guaranteed. Dispute and dissent are easier aroused and expressed under the new leadership. This creates a political context that supports the rise of intraparty conflict in the mass media.

This dominance of the parties within the Greek political system has important implications for the media. For one thing, control of the government relates directly to the media apparatus. For broadcasting this is self-evident; since before deregulation, broadcast media were an integral part of the state apparatus. For the print press, there is a second level of clientelistic relationships being developed with the state as the patron and the press as the client which guarantees a press/party system parallelism. Control of the media apparatus affects the intensity of political preferences through the content of the media representations of politics. The most important of these is the interparty conflict/interpretative framework which perpetuates the relevance of the party system in political and social life and organizes conflict and disagreement in society across party lines. This framework has the capacity to polarize the audience/electorate and to guarantee high intensity of political preferences.

To bring the analysis in line with the present time, it is clear that currently the system is in crisis. The intensity of political preferences has been falling, and in 1996 this finally affected the electoral results. Three reasons contribute to this: (1) the economy can no longer carry the cost of clientelistic relationships, (2) broadcasting deregulation increased the autonomy of the mass media in relation to the party system, and (3) a range of historical factors like the fall of the USSR and the legitimation crisis of the Greek political communication system have disaffected the polarity of the system.

MEDIA AND CAMPAIGN REGULATIONS

Broadcasting Deregulation and the Rise of the Polispot

Radio and television in Greece both began during periods of authoritarian rule. Regular radio broadcasts started in 1936 under the Metaxas dictatorship. Television also came to Greece extremely late, in 1966, and its advent coincided with the military dictatorship (Katsoudas, 1987; Zaharopoulos & Paraschos, 1993). Until the deregulation of 1987-1989 the Greek broadcasting structure evolved in an incremental manner, operating as the long propaganda hand of the government of the day.

Broadcasting deregulation in Greece resulted from the abuse of the state broadcasting monopoly by PASOK, rather than from any technological, ideological, or economic conditions. To broaden the base of available information, municipalities began to operate their own radio and television stations without specific legal rights beginning in the late 1980s. A large number of television stations took advantage of the confusion, occupied frequencies, and started broadcasting without authorization.

While the evolution of the Greek broadcasting system prior to 1987 had been incremental, its restructure due to the broadcasting deregulation has not been rational either. The new broadcasting structure has not been the product of an informed public debate and planning but of direct action aimed to break the state's monopoly of the broadcasting media. After monopolistic control had been lost the Greek state's role was reactionary, usually regulating after the fact and with a (so far) limited capacity to apply the regulation. Broadcasting deregulation resulted in the marginalization of the state system (ERT). This has been a rapid process evident in both the advertising revenue and audience share, resulting in the rapid decline of the financial position of ERT (Samaras, 1990; Papathanassopoulos, 1993). Demonopolization resulted also in the incapacitation of ERT as a propaganda arm of the state, and thus, the parties have lost direct control over broadcasting and their gatekeeping role in the political communication system. The representation of parties and politics through broadcasting is not now structurally guaranteed but negotiated.

Candidate-controlled time on Greek television traditionally took the form of Party Election Broadcasts (PEBs), allocated by an interparty committee during the campaign period and broadcast by the state stations. The composition of the interparty committee reproduced the balance of power in parliament as did the allocation of PEBs. The fall of the audience share of state channels after broadcasting deregulation undermined the importance of this persuasive format, leading to the emergence of paid campaign spots, or polispots. Polispots appeared for the first time on the private stations during the 1990 national elections. In essence the functional displacement of state television by private channels corresponded to the displacements of the PEB by the polispot. This displacement of persuasive formats is enhanced by the fact that while the state broadcasters (ERT) carry polispots, private stations do not carry PEBs.

During the 1996 elections a regulatory framework was in place. According to Decree 52135/12.9.1996 of the Ministry of the Interior and Public Administration, ERT as well as the private broadcasters, were obliged to give five minutes to each party for the presentation of their programs. Thus, while the polispot was not prohibited, the PEB was imposed on private, as well as public, stations. However, private broadcasters were able to satisfy this requirement by organizing programs where representatives of more than one party participate. During the 1996 elections, by law,[5] the total amount of polispot advertising per candidate per television station was set at one minute and on radio stations at three minutes, for the whole duration of the campaign. This, in effect, prohibited the employment of polispots by individual candidates.

However, as the regulatory framework for private broadcasters has evolved, that situation has changed. During the 1989-1990 election, polispots, like all the other aspects of private stations, were totally unregulated. During the 1993 election private stations remained off limits from the regulatory authorities. The National Broadcasting Council was restricted to regulating campaigning in the marginalized state broadcast channel, while it could only issue indictments to the private stations.

REGULATION OF POLISPOTS AND CAMPAIGN FINANCE

The high cost of campaign advertising has led to concern about the financial interests involved. Law 2429/96 which is the major piece of legislature dealing with such issues aims to increase the openness and accountability between politicians and their sponsors and to decrease the dominance of the latter.[6] The parties are provided with an annual percentage of 1.2% over the budget and 0.5% for every election while the annual total cannot exceed 1.7% despite the number of the elections that take place in a year. Parties have to annually publish their balances, and there is a maximum allowed expenditure for candidate MPs which is in proportion to the size of their constituency.

While political advertising is not prohibited, its use for individual MPs is limited by the allowed expenditures. Even in the biggest constituency, Athens B (suburbs) the total amount of allowed expenditure is merely adequate for the broadcasting of 18 repetitions of a 20 second spot. Furthermore, Decree 52135/12.9.1996 limits the number of broadcasts to one per channel for each candidate MP. The decrease of the number of allowed repetitions increased the production cost of spots to the extent that no polispots for individual MPs appeared in 1996.

Media Logic, Polispots, and the Representation of Politics

While traditional PEBs and polispots share the common element of party or candidate control, a set of interlocking factors differentiate the two: money, duration, and framing. The difference between polispots and PEBs is also characterized according to the degree of journalistic mediation and according to the degree of money involved (paid versus free media). There is also a clear interplay with the notions of media and party logic. The PEB is time allocated for free by the medium to the political structure. Its duration and timing are decisions imposed upon the media structure by the political system. Thus, the PEB is considered part of the party logic. Polispots, on the other hand, are time bought by the party/candidate from the channel; it is political communication subjected to the media logic.

In the United States, the polispot's duration has followed a trend from lengthier to shorter, from fifteen and thirty minute long formats to the 30 and 15 seconds spots (Diamond & Bates, 1988; Luntz, 1988). Kaid and Holtz-Bacha (1995) identify a reverse election between candidate communication and the commercialization of the format at an international level: "having to pay for advertising time leads to shorter spots and this might be seen as an indication of commercialization in the sense of adopting the format of political advertising" (p. 17).

An examination of the costs of political advertising in recent Greek elections helps to point up how high the cost of such campaigning can be. Table 11.1 provides data on expenditures by medium for 1993, 1994, and 1996. In 1996, candidates and parties spent over 5 billion drachmas for television, far outdistancing any other medium.

Table 11.1 - Expenditures for Political Advertising in Greece

	1993**	1994**	1996**
TELEVISION	7,471,358	2,077,541	5,275,291
MAGAZINES	33,418	44,234	23,534
NEWSPAPERS	633,320	395,266	748,690
RADIO	953,650	240,106	828,244
TOTAL	9,091,746	2,757,147	6,875,759

* In thousand drachmas. Data from Media Service SA.
** Data are available per year rather than per electoral campaign.

A few other observations about the trends in political advertising expenditures in Greece are worth noting. First, the governing party always has the highest level of political advertising. PASOK, while in government, outspent its main rival (ND) by 2 to 1 in both the Europarliament elections of 1994 and the general elections of 1996. On both

occasions PASOK won, while ND scored lower in votes than in the 1993 general
elections. Second, in the
in the Europarliamentary elections, where no actual power was involved the expenditure
was minimal. The polispot is a very expensive "toy" for those who do not aspire to
power. The two larger parties combined percentage moved from 87% in 1993 to 93% in
1996. This highlights the role of the polispot as a tool to perpetuate the dominance of
bipolarism and set the issues of access and levelling of the particular media terrain for the
minor parties. Third, the reluctance of the Communist party (KKE) to use political
advertising is also noticeable. Finally, political advertising is predominantly party
sponsored. Of the 15 billion drachmas spent during the time covered here, only half a
billion (4%) was paid by individual candidates during the general and the municipality
campaigns.

It is interesting that money spent on constructing the image of politicians may result
in a negative overall image of the political system. The high cost of political advertising
increases the cost of the campaign and thus makes the siren songs of the "vested
interests" more appealing to the ears of candidates and parties. This notion has penetrated
both audience's perceptions and politician's self-images. During an opinion poll that
appeared in 1994, 41% believed that politicians are financed by entrepreneurs, while the
percentage for the parties was even higher (50%). The vast majority believed that the
manner in which politics is financed creates obligations for both politicians (77%) and
parties (78%); while 81% answered positively to the question: "has there been in the last
years any decision made by politicians or parties that have been affected, directly or
indirectly, by their obligations to their financiers?" The high cost of advertising has often
been identified as the main cause of these negative perceptions of politics.

ATTRIBUTES OF GREEK POLISPOTS

The following analysis addresses the characteristics of Greek polispots and provides
a contextual interpretation of their role in the Greek system. West (1993) argues that
polispots cannot be explored in isolation from leadership behavior, the flow of
information, and the narratives of political campaigns.

One of the main dichotomies that organizes the analysis of spots is the distinction
that Shyles (1984) drew between image and issue. He defined images as character
attributes of candidates and issues as current topics and civic concerns linked to national
interest. Employment of issues is related to the agenda setting and priming function of the
spot (Ansolabehere & Iyengar, 1995) as well as the aim of the candidate to acquire
control (Dionisopoulos, 1986; Stewart, Smith, & Denton, 1989) of the spots; while image
is related more to the personalization of politics and parties and the televisual
representation of political activity.

The alleged preoccupation of the polispot with "image" is the focal point of many
critics who argue that it falls short of the requirements that democracy sets for political
information. Very often, in this form of criticism, references to the format (polispot) are a

synecdoche of the medium (television) and/or the mode of production (media logic). In a "low culture," iconolatric, and profit-oriented medium, the polispot is the most episodic political communication format. No wonder that for the normative democratic theory zealots the polispot is not a deliberation, but a heresy.

The Greek polispot is an instrument of image-making as well as of party dominance. The "videostyle" approach (Kaid & Davidson, 1986) combined with the dissociation of "image" from graphical representation (Shyles, 1984) suggests the incorporation of visual, verbal, nonverbal, and television production techniques in the analysis of projected images in the spots. Comparing the 1993 to the 1994 campaign, it is interesting to note that in terms of *format* there is a decrease in opposition-focused spots from 71% in 1993 to 32% in 1996 while introspective spots have respectively increased from 18% to 32% (a tendency that corresponds to the overall fall of negativity from the one campaign to the other). Also, due to the party-centeredness of the spots, formats focusing on a candidate such as the "staged press conference," the "question and answer confrontation," and the "documentary" almost never appear in Greek spots. In the Europarliament elections, PASOK employed predominantly a testimonial mode of the *vox populi* variety (71%) and videoclips (28%) while ND employed issue dramatization (67%) and introspection (33%).

Production Characteristics of Polispots

From the 1993 to the 1996 campaign there was an increase of the candidate-centered production techniques like *cinema verite* (from 4% to 22%) and the candidate head-on (from 0 to 12%). This increase was due to the emergence of new leadership in ND and PASOK in 1996 which (a) needed to be presented and (b) were not as loaded with negative connotations as the previous leadership and could therefore be employed as instruments for persuasion.[7] Such appearances have not been common. The Greek spots have been very intensely packaged around the sponsoring party and the icon of the opponent leadership. On the occasions that candidates appeared in a spot of their own party, they tend to maintain eye contact with the audience, to be mostly attentive/serious, formally dressed and to exhibit limited body movement.[8] On the rare occasions when the candidate was actually heard speaking in a spot for his own party he was fluent, with a moderate rate of speech and pitch variety. These were clear indications of the professionalization of the appearance of Greek politicians. Finally, in the majority of the cases the polispots were obviously *staged,* rather than appearing natural. In actuality, Greek spots, being intensely packaged and structured around the party, made few pretenses of genuineness.

A new presentation device employed by PASOK in 1996 was the use of the Internet screen and the presentation of the printed statements, visuals, and graphics as part of this screen. This obviously aimed to convey the image of modernity, give credibility to the spot by linking television with an information-intense medium, and allow the party to use thematic framing in the spot without using talking heads. Similarly ND used thematic framing without talking heads by presenting the specific policy proposals as superimposed letters over a bluish background. This persistence in avoiding talking heads in thematic format is evidence of both the intensity of packaging (professionalization) and the party-centric structure of the spots.

Music is also an element of the image-building process in polispots. It is used to express moods and create connotations that facilitate the audience's interpretation or a dramatic presentation. Patricia Cambridge(1995) in her research on the music in U.S. spots from 1968-1988 found an increase in the use of music by all candidates over the years, a relation between music and visual style, and a dominance of classical music, medium tempo, and major mode in polispot music. This evidence positively relates the use of music to the intensity of packaging of the spot and suggests that music is used as a background element that reinforces the message. In Greece, in both in the 1993 and 1996 elections, text dominated music in 90% of the spots which featured music. While only 3 out of 125 spots were videoclips (music only), 16 do not include any music at all. In the Europarliamentary elections, on the other hand, ND's spots revealed a balance between text and music while in PASOK's spots text dominated in 71% of the spots. A striking characteristic of Greek spots is the absence of music with strong connotations; music is used as a complementary rather than a dominant tool of persuasion. The music employed is predominantly instrumental and only in the case of ND is it marching.

The party symbol exists in all the party sponsored spots. This level of reference to the party symbols is important because they are elements of continuity as opposed to the leader who is a transient sign in the identification process of the follower with the party (Diamantopoulos, 1993). Thus, the high level of party symbols in the polispot, in a way, compensates for the intense personification in the representations of the party in the newscasts.

Symbols other than the party were more visible in 1993 (49%) than in 1996 (33%). To a large extent, the visibility of the other symbols is related to their integration into the logo of the party to construct the logo for the particular campaign. ND's logo in 1993, for example, was its party symbol superimposed over a Greek flag while in 1994 it was the EU flag with the Vergina Star in the center. PASOK in 1996 often supplemented the party symbol with a map of Greece. As a visual representation of the slogan: "Greece is non-negotiable." This icon makes direct references to PASOK's administration's stated intention not to negotiate the Turkish claims over Greek small islands and territorial waters in Egeo and at the same time is an implicit refutation of criticism for showing compliance during the Imia crisis. It is an heuristic similar to the combination of flag, party logo, and marching music employed by ND in the 1993 campaign.

Candidate versus Party Focus in Greek Polispots

In candidate-sponsored polispots the party logo appears in 75% of the spots which is twice as many cases as the icon of party leadership (33%). This is an indication that the synecdochal function of party leadership in 1993 had been relatively limited, mainly due to the negative connotations attached. Still however, in 1993, the candidate had a much better chance of appearing in a candidate MP sponsored spot than in one produced by the central party.

One difference between the U. S. and Greek spots is the eclipse, in the latter, of references to the candidate's family. Popkin (1997) argues that the American audience, by possessing only limited interest in politics and knowledge of policy issues, employs heuristics for decision making, such as the character and family of the candidate. Polispots are adaptive and offer precisely the kind of information that is appropriate for certain heuristics. Thus, the candidate constructs his credibility by appearing with his family. In Greece the party label maintains its connotative power to the extent that the need for employing such heuristic clues like family and personal life is minimized. The candidate, by standing as a synecdoche for his party, thus draws credibility from the party label rather than from his personal life. In the Greek polispots the candidate operates not as a person of his own sake but as a personification of the party.

Similarly in Greek spots there are no references to the legislative record of the candidate. In Greece the legislative process, by being organized at the party level, makes such references obsolete. In the U.S., on the other hand, there is no effective party discipline in the legislative process and thus the legislative record of each candidate provides heuristic clues about their partisanship, information used to evaluate consistency, and to channel funds and support from the PACs.

Issues in Polispots

There seems to be an equal distribution between spots emphasizing image and those emphasizing issue: 49% emphasized images, and 51% focused on issues in 1993; the corresponding percentages were 58% image and 42% issue in 1996. However, in 1994, there was a dominance of 85% for issue appeals, but image spots made up 83% of the spots in 1993 candidate spots. Appearances, however, are deceiving since issue references are often mere references to candidate issue concerns combined with emotional appeals aimed to construct a party image. This becomes evident by examining the specificity of the issue references. From the 138 party-sponsored spots, 25% did not incorporate any issue reference, 58% referred to candidate issue concerns, and 5% to a vague policy preference, while only 12% incorporated more specific policy references.

The high degree of policy specificity in a spot may be an autonomous factor that maximizes source credibility. In the U.S. "the experience of the 1992 campaign suggests that whenever a candidate makes a clear and confident offer, such as 'Read my plan' or 'Call my 800 number,' it is an important cue for voters. A candidate who is willing to have his or her program examined, and thus expose himself before the electorate, is giving people a chance to see his flaws" (Popkin, 1997, p. 172). Specificity, however, equals credibility for another reason: it cuts through the ambiguity that is inherent in valence politics and is often perceived by the electorate as covering or lying. While specific references (verbal and visual) to what the governing party has done builds credibility retrospectively, specific policy proposals perform the same function through future references. Thus, the former strategy suits the government while the latter the opposition. A number of such spots presenting very specific measures appeared in 1996 ND's campaign.

Finally in terms of *issues addressed,* the economy seems to be the dominant issue in all the elections. In 1996 national issues and foreign policy were also important aspects. Overall the agenda of issues was affected by campaign circumstances and not by an issue-ownership pattern that would enhance the ideological aspect of the intraparty conflict framework. This should be considered evidence of the extent that valence politics have homogenized political discourse in Greece.

Persuasion Appeals in Spots

In terms of *mode of persuasion,* emotional appeals were present in 93% of all party-sponsored spots in Greece, logical appeals were emphasized in 35% and source credibility in 36%. There was an increase in spots with source credibility appeals from 27% in 1993 to 40% in 1996, mainly due to the rise of the new leadership. Persuasive emotional appeals dominate in 64% of the spots, logical appeals in 22%, with source credibility in just 13% of the spots. As has been mentioned before, emotionalism is positively correlated with duration and the intensity of the packaging of the format. The use of persuasive appeals corresponds to the focus of the spot in the sense that image spots are predominantly emotional, while predominantly logical appeals appear more often than is expected in issue spots.

In terms of *campaign strategies,* Trent and Friedenberg's categorization of incumbent and challenger strategies does not derive from theory but is grounded in the experience of electioneering in the U.S. Previous research has shown a certain degree of consistency in different elections and most importantly in different countries (Kaid & Holtz-Bacha, 1995), and this suggests its potential applicability to the Greek situation. To test this, the party's use of strategies was analyzed vis-a-vis electoral position. Chi square analyses found that the incumbent consistently emphasized accomplishments, projected optimism for the future, and stressed the competence of the government office which, by taking the offensive position on the issues, borrowed a challenger technique. The other incumbent techniques were very rarely employed: the use of symbolic trappings to transmit the importance of the office and the relation of incumbency to legitimacy was employed on three spots each, appearing to represent the philosophical centre of the party not at all, and the "charisma and the office" strategy six times. Challengers, on the other hand, consistently called for changes and attacked the opponent's record.

Positive versus Negative Messages

According to their focus, polispot messages may consist of four general types: (1) Positive messages about themselves, (b) negative messages about their opponents, (c) comparisons of the candidates, and (d) responses to charges by opponents (Salmore & Salmore, 1985). Since comparisons and refutation are composed of candidate/positive and/or opponent/negative statements, the categorization can be summed up in a negative-positive[9] dichotomy. Kern (1989) suggests a sub-categorization of negative spots according to the intensity of the attack into soft-sell and hard-sell negative advertising.

To what extent does the positive/negative dichotomy correlate with other attributes of the polispot? An attribute embedded within the definition of the dichotomy is the focus of the spot on the candidate or the opponent. Trend and Friedenberg (1983) suggest that negativity correlates to electoral position, with challengers more likely to use negative advertising than incumbents. This was verified by Kaid and Davidson's content analysis of U. S. Senatorial races (Kaid & Davidson, 1986). While in a more conclusive analysis of polispots of U.S. presidential campaigns from 1960 to 1988, Kaid and Johnston (1991) found that the effects of electoral position on negativity was not statistically significant. According to the same study negative ads were characterized by more frequent appeals to voters' fears, the relatively rare inclusion of the candidate, and the employment of certain types of special effects, particularly computer graphics, slow motion and the juxtaposition of stills.

Structural differentiation between the Greek and the U.S. political systems raises questions about the extent to which such conclusions are transferable from the one country to another. Polispot negativity is organized at the candidate-level in the U.S. and at the party level in Greece. The difference is that intraparty conflict is expressed through polispots in the U.S. while such an incidence has not yet been noted in Greece. Another point of difference is the intensity of political preferences between the two countries which affects selective perception and the filtering of the ad content by the audience and thus determines the effect of the negativity. Ansolabehere and Iyengar (1995) found two effects of negative spots: demobilization and polarization. Demobilization (lowered voting turnout) for the independents and the apoliticals and polarization for the party-oriented. It is the proportion of the two categories that determines the overall societal effect of negative advertising.

In the analysis of negativity in Greek spots it is important to differentiate between the situations where the negativity is produced as part of bipartisanship and is thus a direct demonstration of the interparty conflict frame and situations where negativity is incorporated into the image-making process of the party. Into the first case fall the polispots of PASOK and ND during the 1993 and 1996 general elections. Into the second case fall the spots of the Europarliament campaign as well as the spots of minor parties in 1996. The construction of negativity in bipolarism employs attacks on the opponent as a person, attacks on the performance in past positions, attacks on the partisanship as well as negative association and namecalling. These aspects are intimately related to the binary nature of the opposition and are not shared by minor parties.

There are certain commonalties in the expression of negativity which become evident in considering the stylistics of the attacks. In the vast majority of cases, the attack is conducted by an anonymous announcer. This is the case in 95% of the spots in 1993, 100% in 1994, and 88% in 1996. Greek polispots seem to incorporate the American dictum that the candidate should avoid presenting attacks himself in order to minimize backlash. Given the party-centered nature of the Greek polispots, the anonymous announcer operates as the party voice and this suggests that the conflict is not between persons but between political blocks, between "us" and "them." Also, attack strategies with the potential to undermine the interparty conflict frame are very rarely used: only 5% of the negative spots used statements of a member of the opponent party to attack his party leadership and in only one spot were voters' statements used to attack the opponent. Another similarity is the widespread use of negative association in the attack.

A major difference between campaigns is related to the levels of negativity. The 1993 campaign seems to be the most negative of all with 65% being opponent focused, 20% balanced, and only 14% candidate focused. In 1996 candidate focused spots rose to 55%, opponent focused fell to 29% while balanced spots fell to 15%. These results verify Trend and Friedenberg's observation in the sense that in both the national elections of 1993 and 1996 the incumbent (PASOK and ND respectively) had higher levels of negative/opponent focused spots. In 1993 ND had high percentages of opponent focused spots for an incumbent because it was trailing considerably in the polls and attempted to scare the voters from voting PASOK.

A reason for the difference between 1993 and 1996 was the change of leadership in ND and PASOK. In 1993 the old leadership of the two parties, Mitsotakis and Papandreou respectively, had an ongoing 30 year old conflict between themselves, both were clearly defined and heavily loaded with negative connotations for the supporters of the opponent party. In 1996 new leadership had emerged in both parties. The "new blood" had both less negative connotations to exploit and a vested interest in perpetuating the image of "modernity" by decreasing the levels and intensity of negativity. Both the focus on the opposition and the appearance of negativity decreased from 1993 to 1996. The use of name calling declined from 69% within the attack-containing spots of PASOK and 64% in ND's spots in 1993 to 47% for PASOK and 19% for ND in 1996.

Fear appeals, another negative strategy, followed the same trend, decreasing from 85% of ND spots in 1993 to 16% in 1996 while PASOK's fell from 17% to 0. The reason for the heavy employment of fear appeals in 1993 was that ND lagged considerably in the polls. In 1993 ND referred to what PASOK was going to do based upon the experience of PASOK's administration from 1981-9. PASOK was focusing on what ND had done in the previous four years. PASOK was leading considerably in the polls so the use of a fear appeal on what ND was going to do once elected would legitimize the electability claims of ND. ND, on the other hand, utilized a fear appeal since PASOK was *ante portas*. In 1993 ND used largely rhetorical questions (80%) and capitalized on strong pre-existing negative connotations in order to further delegitimize PASOK and construct a fear appeal. The spots did not always need to be very specific.[10] PASOK fought back with extensive name-calling.

Another characteristic difference between 1993 and 1996 was the increase of negative references to the partisanship of the opponent. Such references rose from none in 1993 to 32% of the attack-containing spots of PASOK in 1996; the corresponding percentages for ND rose from 6% to 44%. This is a counter-conditioning strategy that both parties employed in order to transfer negative connotations from the old to the new leadership of the opponent party and enhance the polarization of the electorate. This is a method of strengthening partisanship through opposition (activation of the interparty conflict framework) and a lever for the consequent perpetuation of bipolarism.

In terms of the focus of the attack, in 1993, 65% of PASOK's spots containing an attack were predominantly against the party while 35% were against another politician (Mitsotakis); 56% of ND's negative spots focused on Papandreou, and 6% explicitly on PASOK while another 39% used the power of connotation to attack. In 1996, 94% of ND's attack-containing spots focused the attack against another politician while a mere 6% focused on the party. PASOK focused 32% of the attack-containing spots on Evert and 63% on ND. PASOK's focus on the opponent party should be considered a tool for limiting the potential of Samaras to absorb voters floating from ND to PASOK by counter-conditioning him with the negative connotations of the Mitsotakis administration. This was achieved visually by a form of intertextuality which incorporated icons of Samaras walking with the other member of the Mitsotakis prospective administrations from ND's 1990 polispot and verbally by the all-inclusive phrase: "and they are all responsible." In 1993 ND's focus on the opponent leadership was an attempt to activate the anti-right syndromes and polarize the electorate. Also, in 1993, they aimed to mitigate the anti-Papandreou syndrome of the electorate by projecting the experience of the 1981-1989 administration into the future by the means of fear appeals. In 1996 attacks on the opponent leadership aimed to undermine the personal popularity of Simitis which had the capacity to pull PASOK into an electoral win.

The overall increase of the proportion of attack spots focusing on the opponent leadership from 1993 to 1996 does not undermine the party-centered characteristics of the campaign because, due to the nature of the political system, there is a very strong synecdochical relation between the head of the party and the party itself. Even when the attack focuses very closely on the attributes of the opponent's character, his/her dominant role in the party structure and the power of oppositional decoding guarantees the synecdochical relation of the person with the party. Moreover, attacks on the opponent in person tend to be dovetailed with positive statements about the parties. Thus, an antithesis is constructed between the opponent leader and the sponsoring party. Swanson and Mancini (1996) claim that personalization undermines political parties because it engenders support for an appealing leader, not for the ideas and programs of the party as an institution. However, personalization poses a problem for the parties only when it takes place at the level of the individual candidates rather than at party leadership. Otherwise, the leadership personifies the party and thus extends the interparty conflict frame to those who are incapable of absorbing policy considerations. The dovetailing of the opponent leader with the sponsoring party, while it is counter to the requirements of liberal democracy, does not necessarily undermine the interparty conflict framework

The Party in Greek Polispots

Wattenberg argues that in the USA "television coverage of politics virtually ignores parties, as acquaintance with personalities is much easier to convey through the visual media than knowledge about abstractions such as political parties" (Wattenberg, 1996, p. 91). Subsequent research proves that the candidate- centered character of the campaign has had reverse effects on the partisanship of the polispot. Boiney and Paletz (1991, p. 13) argue that advertisers seem to feel partisanship is a cue relied upon less and less by voters. Kaid provides quantitative evidence for this trend: the party dominated 9% of all presidential spots in 1988 (Kaid & Holtz-Bacha, 1995) and 6% in 1996 (Kaid, 1998). British elections have proven that parliamentary systems can focus more on partisanship than is true in the U.S. situation (Johnson & Elebash, 1986; Kaid & Tedesco, 1993; O'Neil & Mills, 1986). However, in a larger context Kaid's international research challenges the notion of correspondence in the party versus candidate dichotomy between organizational structure and the content of the campaign by finding low results of party references in spots produced by party-centered systems and attributing causality for this to the communication format rather than to the political system. She argues that television has de-emphasized parties in many democratic systems (Kaid, 1997; Kaid & Holtz-Bacha, 1995), with the only exception being the UK where the contest seemed to be more sharply fought between two party philosophies (Kaid, 1997).

In the case of the Greek spots, the effects of partitocracy become obvious firstly through the use of party slogans and symbols. The party slogan appeared in 86% of the 138 party sponsored spots analyzed in this study, while the party symbol is the most often employed one. It exists in 100% of the party-sponsored spots and 75% of the candidate-sponsored spots. The fall from 100% to 75% is an indication of the effects of campaign structure on polispot content while the overall high level of the visual party reference is an effect of the partisan character of the political system on the spots.

To further examine the partisanship of the spots a continuum of mutually exclusive codes organized according to the lines of partisanship was constructed. The spots were differentiated according to: (a) emphasis on the party, (b) emphasis on the partisanship of the candidate, and (c) emphasis on the candidate. What is measured in this categorization is the focus of the projection of "us" in the spot. The predominance of the party is overwhelming in party-sponsored spots: 98% of 1993 spots, 100% of the Europarliamentary spots, and 87% of 1996 spots. Higher levels of spots emphasizing the partisanship of the candidate (3%) or the candidate himself (11%) appeared in 1996 as a result of the appearance of new party leadership. The nature of the structure in the candidate-sponsored spots reverses the results: 92% focused on the candidate while only one (8%) focused on the partisanship of the candidate. The mutual exclusivity of the codes focuses on the dominance rather than the mere presence of an attribute of the spot. In the case of candidate-sponsored polispots this obscures the effects that the partisan nature of the system on the spots. There is only one spot where the candidate built his credibility on his own position and past experience without incorporating any reference to the candidate's party. In all other cases party affiliation, even though not the most dominant attribute of the spot, was an essential aspect of the construction of the ethos of the candidate. For example, Korahais constructs his partisanship through a sense of belonging to the party. His introductory statement is: "I am Korahais of Nea Democratia." He constructs his image positively by associating himself with some of the positions of ND and negatively reproducing in the spot the dominant antithesis between ND and PASOK. Similarly, Sivenas constructs credibility and personal reliability through his loyalty to the party: "Vote for Nea Democratia, vote for Panos Sivenas, loyal and firm to the party." In Spanos' spot a visual construction of partisanship takes place by superimposing his image over a party rally with people waving flags.

Despite the intense competition the candidate MPs do not attempt to create a unique selling proposition by relating themselves with different social strata, vested interests (other than locality) or policy preferences, but attempt to associate themselves with positive connotations of wider appeal. While the former would have a destructive effect upon the party, the latter is constructive. Thus, although the emphasis of these spots is mainly on the candidate, the image is constructed predominantly either through partisanship or by means that do not undermine partisanship.

CONCLUSION

Prior to 1989, state broadcasting operated as a gatekeeper prohibiting the commodification of televisual political communication. The polispot is not merely a synecdoche of broadcasting deregulation, but is an expression of the media logic at the level of candidate-controlled communication. The functional displacement of channels results in the functional displacement of persuasion formats. The polispot by substituting for the PEB affects the representation of politics. As Kaid and Holtz-Bacha (1995) mention, commodification results in shrinking the duration of candidate-controlled communication. As this research shows, message length is intimately related to the degree of specificity, the nature of the persuasive appeal, and the overspill of negativity but not with negativity itself. Shorter duration correlates to low degrees of specificity of issue references, the dominance of pathos over logos, lower levels of negativity overspill, and more intense packaging.

The analysis of spots has shown that the Greek polispot is an instrument of image-making and partisanship. Its content is organized around party lines. The leadership appears predominantly in the opponents' spots and in these cases it dovetails with statements on the sponsoring party. Party leadership in Greek polispots has a strong synecdochical role by standing for the party. More importantly, negativity in the Greek spots is centralized and channelled towards the head of the party and the party label. There is no projection of intraparty conflict in Greek candidate-centered communication. Negativity in the Greek spots is organized optimally for the parties in the sense that it perpetuates the interparty conflict frame which is the hermeneutic pillar of partitocracy.

REFERENCES

Ansolabehere, S., & Iyengar, S. (1995). *Going negative: How political advertisements shrink and polarize the electorate.* New York: The Free Press.

Boiney, J., & Paletz, D. L. (1991). In search of the model model: Political science versus political advertising perspectives on voter decision making. In F. Biocca (Ed.), *Television and political advertising,* Vol. 1 (pp. 3-26). Hillsdale, NJ: Lawrence Erlbaum Associates.

Cambridge, P.O. (1995). *Music in political advertising: An analysis of the use of music in presidential campaign spots, 1968-1988.* Paper submitted to the Association for Education in Journalism and Mass Communication Convention.

Clogg, R. (1987). *Parties and elections in Greece: The search for legitimacy.* London: C. Hurst & Company.

Clogg, R. (1992). *A concise history of Greece.* Cambridge: Cambridge University Press.

Clogg, R. (1993). Introduction: The PASOK Phenomenon. In R. Clogg (Ed.), *Greece, 1981-89: The populist decade* (pp.VIII-XIV). London: The Macmillan Press.

Diamantouros, N. P. (1983). Greek political cultural tradition: Historical origins, evolution, current trends. In R. Clogg (Ed.), *Greece in the 1980s* (pp.43-69). London: Macmillan.

Diamantopoulos, T. (1993). *(The party phenomenon).* Athens.

Diamond, E., & Bates, S. (1988). *The spot: The rise of political advertising on television,* Cambridge, MA: The MIT Press.

Dimitras, P.E. (1987). Changes in public attitudes. In K. Featherstone & D. K. Katsoudas (Eds.), *Political change in Greece, before and after the colonels* (pp. 64-84). London: Croom Helm.

Dionisopoulos, G. (1986). Corporate advocacy advertising as political communication. In L. L. Kaid, D. Nimmo, & K. R. Sanders (Eds.), *New perspectives on political advertising* (pp. 82-106). Carbondale, IL: Southern Illinois University Press.

Johnson, K. S., & Elebash, C. (1986). The contagion from the right: The Americanization of British political advertising. In L. L. Kaid, D. Nimmo, & K. R. Sanders (Eds.), *New perspectives on political advertising* (pp. 293-323). Carbondale, IL: Southern Illinois University Press.

Kaid, L.L. (1997). *Political television advertising: A comparative perspective of styles and effects.* Paper presented at the International Conference on Images of Politics, Amsterdam, Netherlands.

Kaid, L. L. (1998). Videostyle and the effects of the 1996 presidential campaign advertising. In R.E.Denton, (Ed.), *The 1996 presidential campaign: A communication perspective* (pp. 143-159). Westport, CT: Praeger.

Kaid, L. L., & Davidson, D.K. (1986). Elements of videostyle. In L. L. Kaid, D. Nimmo, & K. R. Sanders (Eds.), *New perspectives on political advertising* (pp. 184-209). Carbondale, IL: Southern Illinois University Press.

Kaid, L. L., & Holtz-Bacha, C. (Eds.). (1995). *Political advertising in Western democracies.* Thousand Oaks, CA: Sage Publications.

Kaid, L.L, & Tedesco, J. (1993). A comparison of political television advertising from 1992 British and American campaigns, *Informatologia, 25 (1-2)*, 1-12.

Katsoudas, D.K. (1987). The constitutional framework. In K. Featherstone & D. K. Katsoudas (Eds.), *Political change in Greece, before and after the colonels* (pp. 14-33). London: Croom Helm.

Kern, M. (1989). *30-Seconds politics; Political advertising in the eighties*. New York: Praeger.

Legg, J. R., & Roberts, J. M. (1997). *Modern Greece: A civilization in on the periphery*. Boulder, CO: Westview Press.

Loulis, Y. (1995). (*The crisis of politics in Greece: Elections--public opinion--political developments*). Athens.

Luntz, F.I. (1988). *Candidates, consultants and campaigns*. New York:

Mavrogordatos, G.Th. (1984). The Greek party system: A case of "limited but polarized pluralism"? *West European Politics, 7*, 156-169.

Ministry of the Interior and Public Administration, 4/9/1996, Decree 51529.

Ministry of the Interior and Public Administration, 12/9/1996, Decree 52135.

O' Neil, H., & Mills, S. (1986). Political advertising in Australia. In L. L. Kaid, D. Nimmo, & K. R. Sanders (Eds.), *New perspectives on political advertising* (pp. 314-337). Carbondale, IL: Southern Illinois University Press.

Papacosma, V. (1983). The historical context. In R. Clogg (Ed.), *Greece in the 1980s* (pp. 304-42). London: Macmillan.

Papathanassopoulos, S. (1993). (*Liberalizing broadcasting*). Athens.

Pfau, M., & Kenski, H.C. (1988). *Attack politics: Strategy and defense*. New York: Praeger.

Popkin, S.L. (1997). Voter learning in the 1992 presidential campaign. In S. Iyengar & R. Reeves (Eds.), *Do the media govern? Politicians, voters, and reporters in America* (pp. 171-180). Thousand Oaks, CA: Sage Publications.

Salmore, S.A., & Salmore, B.G. (1985). *Candidates, parties and campaigns: Electoral politics in America*. Washington, D.C.: Congressional Quarterly Press.

Samaras A. N. (1990). *Central broadcasting organisations in defence: The European paradigm and the Greek case*. City University: Unpublished Master's Thesis.

Shyles, L. (1984). Defining images of presidential candidates from televised political spot advertisements. *Political Behavior, 6*, 171-181.

Stewart, C.J., Smith, C.A., & Denton, R.E. (1989). *Persuasion and social movements*. Illinois: Waveland Press, Inc.

Swanson, D.L., & Mancini, P. (1996). *Politics, media and modern democracy*. Westport, CT: Praeger.

Trent, J.S., & Friedenberg, R.V. (1983). *Political campaign communication*. New York: Praeger.

Wattenberg, M. P. (1996). *The decline of American political parties 1952-1994*. Cambridge, MA: Harvard University Press.

West, M. D. (1993). *Air wars: Television advertising in election campaigns, 1952-1992*. Washington, D.C.: Congressional Quarterly Inc.

Zaharopoulos, T., & Paraschos, M.E. (1993). *Mass media in Greece: Power, politics and privatization.* Westport, CT: Praeger.

NOTES

1. The author acknowledge the help of Lynda Lee Kaid, Tony Oustabassidis, David Hitchin, and Konstantinos Papavasillopoulos.

2. Loulis (1995) provides evidence through opinion polls of the contribution of these factors to the fall of PASOK in the eyes of the voters.

3. Definition and wording comes from Mavrogordatos (1984). Further support for this thesis is provided by the analysis of electoral results and of surveys (Dimitras, 1987; Loulis, 1995).

4. Legg et al. (1997) claim that "political parties in Greece, if identified by name alone, have a relatively short life. Party labels in some elections seem to have no connection with party labels used in prior elections ... This lack of name continuity, however, did not mean an absence of a continuous political tendency." While this statement may be accurate of the past it is not descriptive of the present of the Greek party system. PASOK and ND have been the standard-bearers of their respective political block for over twenty years and have remained so even after multiple changes of leadership. This proves that the party title rather than the leader of the block is emerging as the more permanent signifier system in Greek politics.

5. Law 2429/96 and Ministry of the Interior and Public Administration, 4/9/96, Decree 51529.

6. This is obvious from the full title of the law: "Financing of Political Parties, Publicity and Control of the Finance of Political Parties and Candidate MPs. Statements of the Financial Position of Politicians, Public Servants and Owners of Mass Media and other Directives."

7. PASOK constructed the presidentiality of Simitis with a spot showing him in a succession of photos shaking hands with world leaders while in another he appeared at the Sounion Temple. ND, on the other hand, used Evert to create a plain folks image. Evert was shown interacting with common people in the road or talking with people in a square or a small village.

8. A notable exception is the spots of Politiki Anixi, a personality based party, where an image of its leader, close up, smiling and casually dressed, appears almost integrated into the logo of the party. This image demonstrates both the leadership-centered character of

the party and its intention to use a youthful and friendly image in order to appeal to apoliticals. Another exception is the candidate-sponsored spots in 1993, where the dominant candidate expressions were equally split between smiling and attentive.

9. Positive messages are designed to promote the positive attributes of a candidate's character, position and performance in public office. Attack messages are negative in focus and designed to call attention to an opponent's weaknesses (Pfau & Kenski, 1988). The dichotomy is built according to the concepts of opponent focus, negative and attack on the one hand, and candidate-focused and positive on the other. Certain politicians and consultants who want to have both their cake and eat it, attempt to differentiate between negative and attack spot, so as to attack without been blamed for negativity. Similarly in Greece, a neologism has emerged, that of "black advertising" which is a synthesis of black propaganda and negative advertising and aims to transport connotations of falsehood and manipulation from the concept of propaganda to that of negative advertising. These phenomena, although interesting for propaganda analysis, do not affect the operation of this categorization.

10. For example, "Will people finally enjoy the fruits of their sacrifices or are we gonna start from scratch again?", "Will the fight for a strong economy and a strong Greece be completed, or are we gonna go back to the old- fashioned recipes of the past?", "Are we going to maintain our leading role in the Balkans or are we gonna get involved in unpredictable adventures?" The answer to all these questions is always the same: "Greeks will give us the answer on October the 10th. Because Greece does not go back only forward together with Nea Dimokratia" (Samaras, 1995).

Chapter 12

THE ROLE OF MEDIA IN THE
ELECTIONS IN THE CZECH REPUBLIC

Elizabeth Hughes

Permanently of greater importance than what someone really said, is what they talked about on television or on the radio, or what newspapers wrote about it. (President Václav Havel, *And You*, 4997/96 ISSN)

The media assumes a significant role in the Czech Republic as throughout Central and Eastern Europe. Not only does communication hold the key to affecting change, but in examining the interplay of media and the government, one can better judge the level of democratization present in a society. The metamorphosis from a state-owned media to a public/private competitive environment is core to considerations of democratization.

THE POLITICAL STRUCTURE

An understanding of the governmental system in place in the Czech Republic provides important background. In December, 1992, the Czech National Council adopted a constitution which established a parliamentary democracy in the country. Consisting of two chambers (the Chamber of Deputies and the Senate), the Parliament numbers 200 deputies and 81 senators elected by direct universal free suffrage. Deputies serve four-year terms elected by proportional allocation with a minimum 5% of the overall vote. In terms of the other chamber, senators are elected for six-year terms by majority vote in two rounds; senators can choose to renew their terms every two years. Ultimately, the Chamber of Deputies is the more powerful of the two chambers since it has authority over the Senate regarding the procedure of adopting legislation (Article 47 of the Constitution).

The Prime Minister, Deputy Prime Minister, and Ministers comprise the executive branch. While the President of the Republic appoints other members of the Government, the Prime Minister appoints the President. The executive branch has the right to initiate legislation and can voice an opinion on any proposed legislation. At the same time, the government is accountable to the Chamber of Deputies both in terms of fulfilling the state budget and in cases where its decisions come under question. While the President of the Czech Republic has the right to dissolve this chamber if the government secures a motion of confidence, the president would rarely exercise this option.

The democratic system of checks and balances between the branches of government witnessed a major test in the spring of 1997. On May 28, 1997, the government initiated austerity measures which prompted many attacks. In order to gain credibility for their approach, they voted unanimously for a vote of confidence by the Chamber of Deputies. The government needed at least 101 votes of the 200-member Chamber.

Even though the coalition of the Civic Democratic Party (ODS), Christian Democratic Union--Czechoslovak People's Party (KDU-CSL), and Civic Democratic Alliance (ODA) controlled 100 of the 200 seats, the vote was by no means assured. As a result, a tense situation arose when the main opposition party, the Social Democrats (CSSD), announced it would vote against the government as Jirí Pehe (1997) described for Radio Free Europe: "Suddenly, the vote assumed new importance as the ruling coalition entered into intense negotiation with individual members. Finally, Independent deputy and chairman of the Budget Committee, Jozef Wagner, took the decisive vote *for* the government after securing some assurances from the ruling coalition." This situation set the stage for dramatic events that gave the media an important role.

MEDIA STRUCTURE AND INDEPENDENCE

Just after November, 1989, the media began to act independently from any governmental limitations. State television and radio broadcasters no longer accepted their director generals' regulations, and as evidence, the number of dailies and weeklies appearing at the newsstand increased rapidly. According to Professor Milan Smíd of Charles University, "no bureaucrat or state official had the courage to stop them by referring to still-valid Communist law" (Smíd, 1996, p. 125). Thus, media freedom existed immediately after 1989 in an "unofficial" capacity.

Officially, after the first free general elections in June, 1990, the federal government presented a program in July with reference to a media policy. The newly-established government affirmed their willingness to create a private broadcasting sector while making references at the same time to the Czechoslovak Television (CST) and Czechoslovak Radio (CR) as "state media."

In several Central European countries, the relationship between the media and the government remains a close one. Slavo Splichal (1994) describes the danger of drawing assumptions about this relationship in his study of media in Central and Eastern Europe after the fall of communism. New broadcasting laws and demonopolization do not necessarily translate into "differentiation of the media and democratization of the communication sphere" (p. 159).

The former Czechoslovakia took the necessary steps towards becoming the first former East bloc nation to adopt and implement a new broadcasting law in October, 1991. This first piece of legislation was very basic in scope, and in fact, according to Smíd (1996), there had already been double-digit amendments to the Broadcasting Law in 1995. In terms of printed media, the Press Law (the Act on the Periodical Press and Other Information Media) passed in 1966 was modified slightly in 1990 by apparently dropping the reference to journalists' duty to support the Communist Party. No significantly altered Press Law had appeared as of the end of 1997.

Even with the broadcasting law in place, then, to what extent is the television sector founded on democratic principles? Television broadcasting has a tradition of 45 years in the Czech Republic. While viewers had limited options in the past, a dual system offering both public and private channels with a wider selection of programs began in 1993. Gradually, more and more private operators are buying the rights to new frequencies, but this evolution is slow in coming.

In view of the Czech Republic's status as a potential member of the European Union, the European Commission published a document, *Agenda 2000*, outlining necessary steps for the country (Agenda 2000, 1997). The audiovisual sector foresees a dual system based on democratic principles as a component of becoming an eventual member of the European Union (Law 468/1991). At the time of this report in 1997, Czech legislation in the audiovisual sector had not yet met the demands of the European Commission. Two of those areas which do not meet the EU requirements include the level of independence afforded to producers and publicity spots (p. 52).

The political parties had decided in January, 1993, to allocate a channel to the Czech company CET 21, and the first private television station, TV NOVA, obtained its channel in February, 1994. At the time of this report, four terrestrial national channels exist in the Czech Republic, namely CT1, CT2, TV NOVA and Premiéra/Prima. While TV NOVA has traditionally dominated as the most widely-viewed channel with around a 70% market share, CT2 and Premiéra/Prima channels have begun to grow their market share.

Czech Television operates two complementary channels--ÈT1, the country's public service channel and ÈT2, a program service developed in a European context. The overlap of government and media occurs in several different councils which supervise the public station. Elected by the Parliament, each council consists of nine members who serve for five years and in turn appoint a director general. In the television arena, the Council of Czech Television assumes this role and appoints the general director of Czech Television. In February, 1998, the Council voted on a new leader of CT which will affect the path the public station takes. Jakub Puchalský, a 29 year old former employee of the BBC, was elected General Director over Ivo Mathé, a veteran of Czech Television.

As Chairman of this council, Jan Jirák led the vote for the general director. The Czech Broadcasting Council was looking for a someone who would lead Czech Television in a completely different direction (Jirák, 1998). With his BBC experience, Puchalský was recognized as the candidate with training in an independent broadcasting environment. This appointment will have a profound influence on the future of Czech television. In fact, as described by Jirák, CT was already inspired by BBC in its own Code of Ethics, or Code of Practice.

TV NOVA, Primiéra/Prima TV, and Regional Television

In 1996-97, Central European Media Enterprises Ltd. (CME), a Bermuda-based company, increased its ownership of the channel to 93.2 percent. Thus, while the company CET21 remains the license holder, CME is virtually the exclusive owner of TV NOVA. Private media look to the law on radio and television broadcasting councils for its licensing procedures and conditions. According to some working in the Czech media sector, like Peter Dudek (1998) of Radio Free Europe, TV NOVA presented a proposal "of gold," including promises of a certain number of cultural offerings and more. They presented this proposal to the Parliament followed by heavy lobbying. He admits that TV NOVA has proven to be commercially successful, but the television station created a loophole for themselves in order to gain more programming freedom. In any case, the typical Czech citizen now has a choice between public and private television offerings.

Regarding regulations that the private media must respect, political advertising is not allowed. Even the public television station cannot show political advertising 48 hours before elections. In the past, the Broadcasting Council had at its disposal an administrative measure allowing it, in theory, to direct the owner's investment in the Czech audio-visual sector. As of 1995, the Czech Parliament passed Act No. 301/1995 which prohibits this influence, thus leaving CME to invest according to its own will. The TV NOVA programming strategy thus reflects more of the expressed interests of their viewers in nationally-produced programs.

Owned in part by the state, the Investment and Post Bank owns the majority stock (76%) of Primiéra/Prima TV. The bank is to be fully privatized in the near future, and with the Bank's top management under charges for embezzlement, the time is ripe for a foreign owner to assume the reins. Japan's NOMURA, the Dutch ING BANK and ABN-AMRO have expressed interest and are reported to have the best chance at eventually acquiring the channel.

TV Prima has focused their programming according to the interests of the Czech middle class (i.e., domestic issues, indigenous entertainment and Czech personalities). Although this channel is officially separate from Czech TV and TV NOVA, the independence of this television channel is disputed by some. TV Prima remains a "sister" organization of TV NOVA meaning that the latter has influence over the former. According to Peter Dudek (1998) of Radio Free Europe, the controlling owners of TV NOVA have overlapping control over TV Prima.

According to the Czech Broadcasting Council's report, 6 regional and 49 locally-licensed TV broadcasters exist in the Czech Republic. Nine of these licensed stations broadcast as a part of Prima TV, while others decided to join the project Galaxy (Galaxy TV) which began in December, 1996. Competition may arise in the future as Galaxy TV and Prima TV vie for the only remaining unoccupied frequency for terrestrial broadcasting (7th channel). The Broadcasting Council will decide the outcome of this competition.

Broadcasting Council Chairman Jirák remains optimistic that regional and local media will contribute toward a wider spectrum of programming. As predicted by Kroupa and Smíd (1996), competition will also continue between Czech Television and TV NOVA as domestic production increases and Czech audiences continue to opt for domestic programming. It will depend on TV revenues and the ability of TV companies to invest independently and wisely in the programming and ads in line with the interests of its Czech audience.

The Press

The role of the press is evolving in the Czech Republic, and with it, the extent to which political advertising is used. With the exception of certain magazines (*Respekt* and *Reflex*) and daily newspapers (*Mlada Fronta Dnes, Hospodarske Noviny, Lidove Noviny*), the press has inherited a bad image.

According to Cedomir Nestorovic (1995) in his *Le Marketing en Europe*, press or publicity has acquired a reputation of unreliability since in prior regimes politicians had used this technique to promote a certain ideology. The Czech people understood what was conveyed through the media with a suspect eye as a learned pattern of behavior under the Communist regime.

At the time of this report, highly-circulated printed media sources in the Czech Republic are generally independent. Although some may have party affiliations, they do not serve as the outlets of the party line, but this is not to say that some journalists are not on the payroll of particular parties. The picture of media in the Czech Republic is, however, evolving as evidenced by the Center for Independent Journalism. At a conference in March, 1998, sponsored by the Center in Prague, journalists discussed the changes since 1989. The media "has learned its lessons," in the words of Milada Cholujová (1998) from the Center for Independent Journalism. Journalists are beginning to admit that they were selectively covering stories in order to support the new government and prevent the Communists from taking power again.

At the same time, the function of advertising has a different tradition in Central Europe than is the case further west. Publicity served as a means of conveying information and propaganda in Central Europe, while further west, publicity served as an instrument to promote sales. Milan Slezák (1998) of *Týden*, a weekly news magazine in Prague, refers to the "deeply-rooted" aversion for every massive advertising campaign in the Czech Republic. This is important to recognize when examining the role of political advertising in the Czech elections.

THE 1996 PARLIAMENTARY ELECTIONS

Evaluated by the European Commission as "libres et sincères," the 1996 parliamentary elections witnessed the victory of the center right coalition. In the last days before the election, polls indicated that two parties were running neck and neck--Prime Minister Vaclav Klaus's Civic Democratic Party (ODS) and Milos Zeman's Czech Social Democratic Party (CSSD). The ODS has been in power since July 1992. Under Prime Minister Klaus, the party promoted a conservative approach to the economy. While most voted for this fiscally conservative, market-oriented approach (30%), other parties attracted a significant voting percentage as well. Led by Zeman, the CSSD portrayed itself in the same light as the Western European version of a social democratic party and won 26% of the vote (Central Electoral Commission, 1996). Thus, the CSSD attracted many voters because of its platform promoting the state's role in assuring its citizens education, health benefits and pensions.

According to Joe Schneider (1996) from Radio Free Europe/Radio Liberty, the director of the polling firm STEM, Jan Hartl describes the Czech people as having an "intense interest in politics" (p. 1). Voters seemed to have been divided on two major issues and cast the ballot according to the party's position on these issues. Those who considered the Czech Republic's economic growth and competitiveness of more importance chose ODS, while those who evaluated the country's social safety net as more important opted for CSSD.

Led by Miroslav Grebenicek, the Communist Party of Bohemia and Moravia (KSCM) placed third in the election by gaining 10% of the vote. Ironically, 50 years after the Communist coup, some Czech citizens chose to vote for the successor of the former ruling party of Czechoslovakia. As the Czech population began to feel the affects of the difficult economic reforms taking place, older Czech voters looked to this party to save their pensions and protect their livelihoods.

The Christian Democratic Union--Czechoslovak People's Party (KDU-CSL) grabbed 8% of the vote following the lead of Deputy Prime Minister and Agriculture Minister Josef Lux. Typically strong in southern Moravia, this coalition party advocated a tougher policy toward crime and appealed to a large number of Catholic voters. Recognized as the party of the extreme right, the Assembly of the Republic-Czechoslovak Republican Party (SPR-RSC) took its direction from Miroslav Sladek. Their platform attracted the anti-German, anti-Romani vote and fueled the support of a typically young, uneducated male representation of Czech voters (8%). Finally, led by Deputy Prime Minister Jan Kalvoda, the Civic Democratic Alliance (ODA) won thirteen seats by attracting 6% of the vote. Trade and Industry Minister Vladimír Dlouhy actively promoted the ODA, and its typical voter profile was the young professional looking for an alternative to the ODS.

The Role of the Media

The quality of political advertising used during the 1996 parliamentary elections was not only sub-standard but according to many, "laughable." Peter Dudek (1998) from Radio Free Europe attributes this not only to uninteresting slogans and ads but also to the fact that advertisements would appear for a set amount of time between TV programs. Consequently, viewers knew in advance to avoid watching the television at a certain moment during the day, as opposed to those aired in the U.S. when ads are interspersed within the day's programming.

As Milan Slezák (1998) from *Tyden* describes, election parties have found that direct contact with the electorate is more effective in addition to the indirect means of television or the press. He bases these findings on pre-election polls. Given the former quality of political advertising, the voter will most likely respond less favorably to the potential strategy of TV spots. The 1992 elections go far to prove this hypothesis. As a result of the Czech Social Democratic team and Zeman and Zemak's countrywide strategic campaign tour, they accumulated more votes than expected. In the 1996 elections, Mr. Sladek, often likened to Le Pen in France, received around 6% of the vote by travelling to speak with voters directly instead of launching any significant media campaign.

In 1996, Czech Television showed news and current affairs over 50% of the air time as measured by ÈT--Analysis of Programme and Audience. At the same time, advertisements consumed only .2% of CT's air time. In terms of political advertising, public media are restricted in several ways. Political parties are allowed free advertising time, but they are limited to fourteen hours in total during the two weeks before the elections. As a result, CT fixes one hour of television spots a day. According to Chairman Jirák (1998), the penetration has been extremely low since television viewers knew in advance that for an entire hour, they would see nothing but television spots. At the same time, the potential of using Czech Television to reach a distinct Czech voting public exists. Since the public television station performs various sociological surveys based on a pre-established criteria including age, sex, level of education, domicile and economic activity, they have a very clear profile of their viewers. According to their survey of 750 respondents, more men than women watch television, and more rural than urban dwellers tune into their programs.

It is also interesting to note the varying profiles of those who chose channel ÈT1 with predominantly domestic programming or ÈT2 with a European-wide offering. According to CT, ÈT1 attracted older, less-educated, female audiences, while ÈT2 typically drew university-educated men who were also actively involved in the economy.

In addition to CT's in-house research, MEDIAN and Gfk Prague conduct MEDIA PROJECT, a multi-media research of television, radio and press ratings. Research is based on approximately 15,000 interviews a year as supervised by the Association of Communication and Media Organizations (ACMO). Research of this kind is acquiring more and more sophisticated tools. For example, AGB Media Facts Ltd. and ACMO have agreed to the use of the peoplemeter method of measuring TV ratings electronically as of June 1, 1997. These tools may serve to target a distinct voting sector in the future.

EVOLUTION OF MEDIA LEGISLATION

Elections in 1997 slowed any significant activity addressing media legislation in 1996. In the fall of 1996, the Cabinet was restructured resulting in significant changes for the country. Three ministries (Privatization, Economics, and Economic Competition) were abolished, while one new ministry, namely the Regional Development and Housing Ministry, was created.

According to Kroupa and Smíd's (1997) *Study on the Development of the Audiovisual Landscape in the Czech Republic 1996-1997*, the new government addressed media policy within the span of one short section which referred only to the free access to information, mass media plurality and the protection of intellectual property. In any case, the issue of a state media policy was finally made clear after a very long period of confusion. Since November 1, 1996, the Ministry of Culture has had jurisdiction over media policy. As a result, the audiovisual department of the Ministry of Culture became part of the media department under Jiri Mejstrik, former General Director of Prima TV. Mejstrik left his post as of June 1, 1997, to assume a leading role in the private sector. At the time of this report, the media department was in the midst of preparing a draft press law introducing the right of reply equally to the press and to electronic media.

THE PARLIAMENTARY ELECTIONS OF JUNE 1998

The call for a vote of confidence mirrored several developments throughout 1997. In fact, in January, polls reflected that 87% of Czechs trusted the President, while only 50% trusted the government. According to the Institute for Public Opinion Research (IVVM), one-third (34%) of those Czechs polled believed in the Chamber of Deputies. Obviously, the national mindset had changed since the beginning of the year. Throughout the political and economic challenges of 1997, the popularity of CSSD had grown to about 27-30% of the vote by the end of the year. On the other side, the country witnessed a fall in the popularity of ODS which stood at 17-20% at the end of 1997.

In January, 1998, Milos Zeman was re-elected as party chairman for CSSD. At the same time, the ODS elected Michael Zantovsky as their chairman after a scandal with former chairman Jan Kalvoda left his position open. The strategic alliance of Kdu-CSL and the ODA had consistently stood as one against ODS, but the alliance was beginning to crumble. Zantovsky contributed to the weakened state of the wall by throwing verbal stones at the KDU-CSL ministers. While he criticized their work, he specifically targeted Defense Minister Miloslav Vyborny for the "very bad state" of the army hurting the possibility of the Czech Republic with NATO. KDU-CSL chairman Josef Lux, in turn, attacked Prime Minister Klaus. Lux accused the premier of holding back information from the International Monetary Fund (IMF) on the state of the Czech economy and suggested Klaus end his term. Although the parties worked together to address problems resulting from the floods in the summer 1997, strife arose again in September.

Funding scandals rocked the Czech political scene in the spring of 1998. While elections were slated for June, both the right and left wing governments suffered from rumors of dubious political funding practices. Foreign Minister and ODS deputy chairman Zieleniec resigned signifying the beginning of the end for the Klaus government. Zieleniec had claimed that questions existed about ODS' financing and with reason.

According to the daily *Mlada fronta Dnes*, companies had been depositing large sums of money into an ODS Swiss bank account (CTK Press Review, January 31). These companies had each won large privatization contracts. It is difficult to determine whether the media prompted these questions as part of a political strategy of attacking ODS, but the *Mlada fronta Dnes* is recognized as one of the most objective, least-biased papers. Peter Dudek (1998), Radio Free Europe, confirmed this position saying that most people already questioned the funding practices used by parties in the Czech Republic.

In an interview in the daily tabloid *Blesk*, Tomas Chudlarsky characterizes these problematic cases of sponsorship as a "consequence of imperfect legislation and the growing up of the business area into the power area." He further qualified the situation commenting, "No wonder after morals have been pushed aside over the past years. Now the dirt is surfacing and we, once a miraculous child of the post-communist Europe, have developed into an almost deterring example" (CTK Press Review, January 31).

In February, 1998, the major political parties jointly agreed that there would be no TV or radio advertisements during the pre-election campaign. The reasoning was twofold. First, the expense is formidable. Not only are political advertisements expensive for the parties but also for the taxpayers since each party receives a partial subsidy from the state. Secondly, in the midst of dubious finance campaign scandals, neither party wants to be faced with additional reasons for the press to delve further into their ledgers. According to Jaroslav Veis (1998), Advisor to the Chairman of the Senate, TV and radio spots simply "did not work," and in fact, "some media even publicly announced they would not run it."

Thus, at the time of this report, political advertising did not play a significant role in the June, 1998, elections. Instead, political debates among parties were scheduled. Apparently, Sunday noon debates and evening discussions constituted the most accepted format in the Czech Republic in anticipation of the 1998 elections. In the mind of Jaroslav Veis (1998), established parliamentary parties would benefit more from this format than newly emerging parties. At the same time, he questioned whether public television is prepared to handle the complications inherent in hosting a series of debates.

If the 1996 parliamentary elections are any indication of what will occur in the 1998 elections, parties may decide at the last minute to pursue media strategies in any case. Political parties had initiated similar proposals prohibiting political advertisements, and in the end, they chose to air several television spots anyway.

CONCLUSION

While the use of the media and press in the elections is limited at this stage given the history of sub-standard television spots and the negative reception of the Czech voting public, this situation will most likely evolve. Private ownership of television channels will necessarily promote change to meet the interests of their viewers. As borders continue to open, and the viewing public is exposed to the political campaign strategies used further west, they may opt for this type of coverage.

Of course, one could dispute whether or not this necessarily constitutes "progress." In an interview with the Czech daily newspaper, *Mladna Fronta Dnes*, President Vaclav Havel admitted that political campaigning "could be a lot worse. And it tends to be a lot worse, even in some far more mature democracies." Czech politicians are reacting to their public's preferences in choosing to adopt the debate format instead of launching a series of political spots.

How many television viewers would opt for debates of substantial content over some of the television spots shown today in more mature democracies? Will the Czech public continue to view advertising, including political advertising, with a suspect eye? Will the political parties decide to invest appropriate funding to improve the quality of political ads, and how will legislation governing political advertising change? The answer to these questions will contribute to the evolving role of the press and media in the political picture of the Czech Republic. As this emerging democracy matures, the countries of Central and Eastern Europe will most likely adopt some of the techniques used further west; however, those more mature democracies could also learn some important lessons from their counterparts to the East.

REFERENCES

Agenda 2000 (1997). Avis de la Commission sur la demande d'adhésion de la République *Tchèque à l'Union européenne,* Bulletin de l'Union européenne, Commission européenne, Supplément 14/97.

Central Electoral Commission (1996). *An overview of the model of elections into the House of Deputies of the Parliament of the Czech Republic on May 31st and June 1st, 1996*; and *Brief review on method of election to the Senate of the Czech Republic's Parliament from November 15 to November 16, 1996.* Prague: CSU (Ceský Statistický Úrad).

Cholujová, Milada (1998). Personal Interview. Prague, March 3, 1998.

CTK (1998, January 23). Press review. CTK Czech News Agency. Praha.

Dudek, P. (1998). Personal Interview. Prague, March 3, 1998.

Jirák, J. (1996). Media '95. *Media '95: Experience and expectations-- Five years after* Prague: Karolinum Charles University Press.

Jirák, J. (1998). Personal Interview. Charles University, Prague, March 4, 1998.

Köpplova, B., & Jirák, J. (1996). Changes in the structure of Czech mass media. In *Media '95: Experience and expectations--Five years after*. Prague: Karolinum Charles University Press.

Kroupa, V., & Smíd, M. (1996). The limitations of a free market: Czech Republic. In *The development of the audiovisual landscape in Central Europe since 1989*. Bedfordshire, UK: John Libbey Media.

Kroupa, V., & Smíd, M. (1997). *Study on the Development of the Audiovisual Landscape in the Czech Republic*. Unpublished manuscript. Prague.

Nestorovic, C. (1995). *Le Marketing en Europe Centrale* [Marketing in Central Europe]. Paris: Librairie Vuibert.

Pehe, J. (1997, June 9). Czech: Parliament readies for vote of confidence tomorrow. *Radio Free Europe/Radio Liberty, Inc.*

Schneider, J. (1996), June 3). Czech coalition struggles to stay on track. *Radio Free Europe/Radio Liberty, Inc.*

Slezák, M. (1998). Personal Interview. Prague. March 3, 1998.

Smíd, M. (1996). Media policy--Does it exist in Central East Europe. In *The development of the audiovisual landscape in Central Europe since 1989*. Bedfordshire, UK: John Libbey Media.

Splichal, S. (1994). *Media beyond socialism: Theory and practice in East-Central Europe*. Boulder, CO: Westview Press.

Veis, J. (1998). Personal Interview. Prague, March 15, 1998.

Chapter 13

COMPARING AND CONTRASTING THE STYLES AND EFFECTS OF POLITICAL ADVERTISING IN EUROPEAN DEMOCRACIES

Lynda Lee Kaid

As other chapters in this book have made clear, political candidates and parties in most of the newly evolving democratic systems in East and Central Europe have embraced some form of political television advertising as a way of generating electoral support. The role that this form of political programming takes varies from country to country. In some cases these differences are a result of fundamental differences in the legislative constraints placed on the parties and on the media. For instance, as Chapter 2 pointed out earlier and as the chapters on individual countries illustrate, some countries allow candidates and parties to buy time for political advertising and some countries prohibit such advertising, allowing only "free time" broadcasts on public stations.

These differences in political and media system variables often prompt researchers to throw up their hands in despair, lamenting that the differences are so great that no meaningful comparison is possible. The research reported here rejects that premise and attempts to provide a comparison across countries of the styles and effects of modern political television broadcasts.

RESEARCH ON CONTENT AND EFFECTS

Most research on political television advertising has been conducted in the United States, where television spots are the dominant form of communication between candidates and voters (Kaid, 1981, 1996). Among Western democracies, there is no question when it comes to political television advertising that the United States has done it first, most, and, arguably, best. Perhaps the most distinguishing aspect of the American system is its commercial nature; because television stations are primarily private entities selling advertising time, American candidates at every level of elective office are free to buy almost unlimited amounts of advertising time on television. Also distinctive to the American system is the almost unregulated nature of the message content; candidates and parties can say or do almost anything in political spots because the value placed on free speech rights in the United States insists that political speech be unfettered (Kaid, 1991). While other democracies have often been accused of "Americanization" of their political television offerings, some limitations on the adoption of American practices have been imposed by media, political, and cultural system differences. Probably the most noticeable difference is in the quantity of spot advertising allowed, since most other countries allow no or limited purchase of time, providing instead free time on public channels to candidates and parties (Kaid & Holtz-Bacha, 1995). While in many countries this free-time system may allot commonly 3 or 5 or 10 spots per candidate in an election campaign, the two major party U.S. presidential candidates in 1996 purchased time in the general election campaign for over 100 spots, costing nearly $200 million (Devlin, 1997).

Because of the pervasiveness of the political television spot in American campaigns, there has been much more research on the content and effects of political commercials in the United States than in other democratic systems. However, the past two decades have seen an increased interest in research on the political broadcasts in other countries. Most of the research across all democracies falls into two categories, content/style research and effects research.

Content and Style

Although some researchers have provided historical, critical, or descriptive overviews (Devlin, 1997; Diamond & Bates, 1984; Jamieson, 1992) of political spot content in American campaigns, few scholars have offered comprehensive or systematic descriptions. Joslyn's (1980) seminal work on spot content, although limited by a small convenience sample, established that the dominant content of American political spots has been issue content. The issue content was not particularly specific or policy-oriented, but it made up the major content of the spots analyzed. Other researchers have confirmed this emphasis on issue information in television spots at all campaign levels in the United States (Kaid, 1998, 1994; Kaid & Davidson, 1986; Kaid & Johnston, 1991; Kern, 1989; Shyles, 1983, 1984). Some of this work has been done in the broader context of describing the concept of "videostyle," the verbal, nonverbal, and production characteristics that define how a candidate presents himself/herself to voters through political spot advertising (Kaid, 1998, 1994; Kaid & Davidson, 1986; Kaid, Tedesco, Chanslor, & Roper, 1993; Kaid, Tedesco, Chanslor, & Roper, 1994; Wadsworth & Kaid, 1987).

Research on the content and style of political party/candidate broadcasts in other countries has been much less comprehensive or systematic. A few studies have compared content in British spots and have found a similar dominance of issue content in British

PEB's (Johnson & Elebash, 1986; Kaid & Holtz-Bacha, 1995; Kaid & Tedesco, 1993). Similar findings validate the importance of issue content in political broadcasts in France (Johnston, 1991). In Germany, however, the 1990 campaign spots showed a strong emphasis on candidates and image content (Holtz-Bacha & Kaid, 1993; Holtz-Bacha, Kaid, & Johnston, 1994).

Effects of Political Television Advertising

Most research on effects has also focused on the United States. Early researchers verified that political spots do, in fact, have cognitive, affective, and behavioral effects on voters (Kaid, 1981). Atkin and his colleagues determined that political spots could overcome selective exposure, thus guaranteeing that nonsupporters, as well as supporters, were exposed to a candidate's message (Atkin, Bowen, Nayman, & Sheinkopf, 1973).

Both survey research and experimental studies in the United States have yielded strong support for the effectiveness of political spots. One of the earliest effects verified by researchers was the ability of ads to communicate issue information to voters. Patterson and McClure (1976) used survey research to show that voters learned substantially more issue content from spots than from television news in the 1972 presidential campaign. Researchers in experimental studies have also demonstrated that spots can have strong effects on a candidate's image (Basil, Schooler, & Reeves, 1991; Cundy, 1986; Kaid, 1994; Kaid, 1997; Kaid & Chanslor, 1995; Kaid, Leland, & Whitney, 1992; Kaid & Sanders, 1978) and on vote intent (Basil, Schooler, & Reeves, 1991; Kaid & Sanders, 1978).

Other democracies have not often measured precisely the effects of political spots on voters. As with other aspects of political television and the possible "Americanization" of their systems, most countries have preferred to assume that party broadcasts were not very important to voters. However, research on early PEB's in Britain suggested that they did affect voter knowledge levels (Blumler & McQuail, 1968) and may have had some effects on undecided or low-interest voters. Research on the 1988 French presidential election did indicate that exposure to party broadcasts affected images of French presidential candidates Chirac and Mitterrand ((Kaid, 1991). Kaid and Holtz-Bacha have measured experimentally the reactions to German chancellor candidates after viewing election spots during the 1990 and 1994 national elections (Holtz-Bacha & Kaid, 1996; Kaid & Holtz-Bacha, 1993).

With this background in mind, the research presented here seeks to compare some of these findings on the style and effects of political television ads to several of the evolving democracies discussed in this volume and to provide some comparison of these findings with research from more established democracies such as the United States and Britain. The questions asked are simple ones: Are there similarities or differences in ad styles across countries? What effects can be identified from exposure to these television ads?

MEASURING THE STYLE AND EFFECTS OF ADS

Style comparisons are best addressed by content analysis methods. Here, content analysis is applied to a broad spectrum of spots across a number of countries and years. Effects questions were addressed with experimental techniques, measuring the effects of exposure to the television spots during election campaigns over the past ten years in several countries.

Content Analysis

The content analytic procedures were applied to a sample of spots from seven countries: the United States (1996 presidential election), Russia (1996 presidential campaign), Germany (1994 national election), Turkey (1995 parliamentary election), Britain (1992 and 1997 general election spots for the Labour and Conservative Parties only), Poland (1995 presidential election), and Greece (1996 national election).[1] The number of spots from each country varied; the samples were composed as follows:

United States--109 spots (43 Dole and 66 Clinton)
Germany--52 spots from all parties allocated TV time
Britain--16 broadcasts from Labour and Conservative
 (4 each for each election in 1992 and 1997)
Poland--81 spots from all parties allocated TV time
Turkey--9 spots for four major parties
Greece--76 spots from all parties
Russia--36 spots from eight presidential candidates

The categories developed for the content analysis followed the procedures set forth in prior studies of "Videostyle" (Kaid & Johnston, 1991; Kaid, Tedesco, Chanslor, & Roper, 1993; Kaid, Tedesco, Chanslor, & Roper, 1994; Wadsworth & Kaid, 1987). Verbal content categories included image versus issue content of the ads, types of appeals used in ads (emotional, logical, ethical), negative versus positive focus of the ad, and specific candidate qualities stressed in the spot. Nonverbal categories focused on setting of the ad, speaker in the ad, and presence of other nonverbal cues such as music. The television production technique categories encompassed production styles of the spots (cinema verité, slides, head-on, etc.). Not all categories are reported here. The content analysis was done by trained student coders; in the case of foreign ads by native speakers of the language. Intercoder reliabilities were calculated using the formula suggested by Holsti (North, et al., 1963) and averaged +.86 across all categories for all samples.

Experimental Studies

Date for the experimental studies also come from several countries.[2] In each country the subjects were drawn from adult community groups and from university students[3] at various locations within the country: (1) The U. S. sample consisted of 525 students from 19 different universities[4] throughout the country who viewed the spots on October 30/31 prior to the November 5, 1996, presidential election. (2) The German data are from 1994 (201 students from two locations in Western Germany and two locations in the East German states who participated in the experimental sessions on October 6-14) German national elections held in October of 1994. (3) In Britain, 106 students from three locations (Cambridge, Leicester, and Glasgow) were subjects between April 25-30, just prior to the May 1, 1997, parliamentary elections. (4) The experiments in Poland took place on November 10-18 prior to the November 19, 1995 Polish presidential election; the subjects were 203 students from three universities (University of Lódz, Catholic University in Lublin, and M.Curie-Slodowska University in Lublin). (5) In Romania, the data come from the 1996 presidential election which took place in December, 1996; subjects were a mixed group of 125 students and older adults recruited from the community. The Romanian data were gathered in two locations (in Bucharest and in Sibiu) on November 6-9, 1996, prior to the national election on November 17.

In each case the data were gathered using a before-after experimental test design. Respondents were given pretest instruments to measure their attitudes toward candidates/parties, they were shown samples of spots from the campaign, and then a posttest instrument was administered to measure attitudes and effects after exposure to the spots. The questionnaires used in the pretest and posttest experiments for all studies were virtually identical and were translated from the original English version into German, Romanian, and Polish by native speakers. A major component of the questionnaires was a semantic differential scale designed to measure candidate image (Kaid, 1995). This scale consisted of 12 bi-polar adjectives[5] and achieved acceptable reliability coefficients, even when transferred across languages.[6]

COMPARING STYLES AND EFFECTS

Comparison of Styles of Spots

Across the seven countries analyzed here, the most common element of the spots is that the majority of ads concentrate on issues, rather than images of candidates or parties.[7] As Table 13.1 indicates, issues are the dominant content of spots in the United States (83%), Russia (58%), in Germany (69%), in Poland (56%), and in Britain (88%). The exceptions are Greece (42%) and Turkey (67%), two countries that would not ordinarily like to be thought of as on the same side.

Table 13.1 - Content and Appeals of Political TV Broadcasts

	U.S.	Greece	Germany	Russia	Britain	Turkey	Poland
	1996	1996	1994	1996	1992 & 1997	1995	1995
n =	109	76	52	36	16	9	81
Emphasis of the Ad							
Issues	83%	42%	69%	58%	63%	33%	56%
Image	17%	58%	12%	42%	37%	67%	30%
Combination	0	0	19%	0	0	0	14%
Focus of Ad							
Positive	33%	71%	NA	72%	69%	89%	93%
Negative	67%	29%	NA	28%	31%	11%	7%
Dominant Type of Appeal							
Logical	35%	22%	23%	39%	56%	33%	21%
Emotional	40%	64%	33%	47%	25%	55%	67%
Source Credibility	25%	13%	4%	14%	19%	11%	12%
Combination	0	0	40%	0	0	0	0
Political Party							
Emphasized in Ad	6%	87%	44%	8%	50%	NA	4%

This is not to say that Greek and Turkish parties did not mention issues in their spots. However, the issues mentioned were often vague and non-specific, mentioned more to serve as a backdrop to the enhancement of the party's image than to advance a particular policy. A few differences are apparent when examining the specific party/candidate emphasis within each individual country. For instance, in the 1997 British election, the Conservatives placed far more emphasis on issues in their spots, while the Labour Party concentrated on the image of their popular young leader Tony Blair.

Table 13.1 also shows that another commonality across countries is the positive focus of the ads. The United States is the outlier here, of course. In the 1996 election, as in the 1992 one, the U.S. spots were predominately negative (67%). The percentage was even higher for Bill Clinton since over 70% of his spots were negative ones. In the other six countries the dominant focus of the ads was positive, ranging from 93% of the ads in Poland to 71% and 72% in Greece and Russia, respectively. In Germany the coding for spot focus was not comparable, since there the coding did not dichotomize between positive and negative, as a dominant ad emphasis, but rather reported whether or not an attack was made in the ad, not whether the ad was overall negative or positive. On this measure, about 2/3 of the German spots included some type of negative attack, whether or not the spot itself was predominantly positive or negative. Using that measure (whether an attack was made in the spot, even if negativity was not the major focus of the spot) would also increase the negative focus for several other countries. For instance, although most Greek spots were positive, 55% of them contained a negative attack on the other party or their candidate. The same was true in Turkey where over half the spots contained some type of attack.

There has been discussion that the use of television in campaigns has de-emphasized political parties in many democracies. Table 13.1 indicates that this is certainly true in political spots in some countries studied here. The number of spots whose content focused primarily on the political party in each country was generally quite small in the United States (6%), Russia (8%), and Poland (4%). However, in Britain, where the contest seems to be more sharply fought as a battle between two party philosophies, half of the spots focused on the party itself. In 1997 this took on particular meaning in Britain as Labour Party spots sought to reinforce for voters the notion that the party was offering a "New Labour" Party. In Greece the party emphasis is traditionally great, indicating as Samaras points out in Chapter 11, that the party is still the dominant force in Greek politics. This trend may provide some evidence that spots are contributing to a declining emphasis on parties in other democratic systems, however, resulting in a more personalized campaign system.

Spots were also categorized according to whether the dominant type of appeal or proof offered in the ad was logical, emotional, or ethical, corresponding to Aristotle's original distinctions between logos, pathos, and ethos. Here, too, there is great consistency among countries. Whether the democracy is old or new, well-developed or emerging, emotional proof is the dominant form of persuasion used by parties in their television messages. The British spots were the most likely to use logical proof, relying on this form of persuasion in 56% of the ads. Other countries found emotional proof to be more attractive. Emotional proof was dominant in the Greek spots (64%), Turkish spots

(55%), Polish spots (67%), and Russian ads (47%). However, the German and American spots showed more balance among the three types of proof. British spots also used some emotional proof (25%), a good example being the famous "Jennifer's Ear" spot used by the Labour Party in 1992. Spots in the United States were high in emotional appeals, partly because of a tendency to use fear appeals in negative spots, a tactic that was prevalent in a great many Clinton spots that attempted to cast Bob Dole as an old, somewhat sinister figure.

Nonverbal and Production Aspects of Spots

One of the most interesting nonverbal aspects of spots is the subtlety conveyed by whether or not the candidate himself/herself is the speaker in the spot. As Table 13.2 shows, in none of the democracies analyzed here were the party leaders or major candidates likely to be the dominant speakers in their spots. American and German broadcasts trail all others in this regard with the party spokesperson being the main speaker only 6% and 8% of the time, respectively. In the 1996 U.S. ads, for instance, Bill Clinton almost never spoke or appeared in his ads, let alone was the main spokesperson. Since 70% of Clinton's ads were negative ads, it is not surprising that he left the speaking to anonymous announcers. Surprisingly, Russia, with 39% of the spots featuring the major party leader, and Poland (with 31%) lead all other countries on this category of comparison. Perhaps this was due to the strong personalities at work here, Yeltsin and Zhirinovsky in Russia and Walesa and Kwasnieski in Poland. These two elections were also characterized by the fact that they were presidential contests, not just parliamentary battles. However, while this might be expected to increase the presence of the party's standard-bearer, this does not hold true for the United States.

The setting of a spot is also an important nonverbal indicator. Formality is a major distinction in settings, and in this sense there are major differences among the seven countries compared. Russian settings in 1996 were very formal (44%), as were over half the American settings (56%). The Polish (19%), British (19%), and Turkey (33%) spots use formal settings much less frequently. The tendency toward informal settings (44%) in the British examples are partly a result of the style of the 1997 British ads. In particular, the Labour Party relied a great deal on "dramatizations" in their spots or in the cinema verité style used to chronicle Tony Blair's ideas in the 1997 ten-minute PEB often referred to as "Blair, the Movie."

Table 13.2 - Nonverbal and Television Production Aspects of TV Broadcasts across Countries

	U.S.	Greece	Germany	Russia	Britain	Turkey	Poland
	1996	1996	1994	1996	1992 & 1997	1995	1995
n =	109	76	52	36	16	9	81
Setting							
Formal	56%	NA	34%	44%	19%	33%	19%
Informal	13%	NA	8%	8%	44%	22%	25%
Combination	15%	NA	10%	6%	38%	44%	56%
Not applicable	17%	NA	48%	41%	0	0	0
Candidate Is Dominant Speaker							
	6%	NA	8%	39%	25%	11%	31%
Production Technique							
Cinema verite	23%	22%	NA	19%	50%	04%	
Slides w/ print, movement, voice-over	6%	0	NA	0	0	0	2%
Head-On	5%	12%	11%	25%	12%	22%	16%
Animation & special prod.	9%	0	8%	31%	0	22%	0
Combination	49%	66%	NA	33%	38%	44%	78%

NA=data not available

These differences in style also relate to the classification of spots according to production techniques. With so few spots relying on the candidate as the dominant speaker in the spot, it is not surprising that very few spots use the traditional candidate statement or "head-on" production technique. Table 13.2 displays the various production techniques. In most countries (a different system of coding this category was used in Germany), the production techniques are marked by the combination of various types of production. This multiplicity of production techniques, over the straight candidate statement style, is a mark of the growing sophistication in technology available in all countries and considered by some to be a mark of Americanization. Even less developed democracies like Poland found such production techniques desirable as a way to hold viewer attention. The "head-on" technique was not important in any country. Although the total category of "head-on" production was only 12% in Britain, the notable examples of this were the direct candidate statements on European Union issues by John Major in the 1997 campaign. In Germany, the majority of the spots using this technique were those from the smaller parties (not the CDU/CSU or SPD Parties) whose production budgets often did not allow for more varied and sophisticated production techniques. The highest percentage of head-on techniques was in Russia (25%) which is probably also related to the fact that Russian spots have the highest percentage of appearance of their party leaders in their spots.

Another point of interest related to production techniques has been the increasing use of special effects video techniques in spots. The use of special sounds and music is one aspect of this trend. In some countries, for instance, music was used in 100% of all political advertising productions (Britain). One spot in the 1997 British Labour Party's arsenal relied solely on pictures, music, and words printed on the screen; there were no verbal or spoken messages in the entire spot, which attacked and ridiculed the Conservative Party. The United States led in the use of combinations of special effects techniques, with frequent use of computer graphics, superimpositions, slow and stop motion techniques. British ads also capitalized on such techniques, using slow motion, montages, superimpositions, and computer graphics in several broadcasts. The Russian and Turkish spots were also notable for their use of such techniques.

Effects of Exposure to Political Spots Across Countries

Effects data from experimental studies were available for five countries (1996 U.S., 1997 Britain, 1995 Poland, 1996 Romania, and 1994 Germany) in which similar experiments were conducted. The comparisons here are based on the extent to which exposure to a sample of spots from the campaign affect the ratings of each candidate or major party leader.

In comparing the pretest and posttest image scores for each leader in each country, the 12 items (7 point scale) on the semantic differential were summed. These mean scores are compared before and after viewing the ads in each country in Table 13.3. These data demonstrate that political advertising exposure can significantly affect a leader's image rating. In almost every country, this is true for one and sometimes both of the candidates/leaders. However, sometimes the direction of the change is positive, and sometimes it is negative. In the United States, in 1996 Clinton's ratings increased significantly after viewing, while Dole's image score decreased. The tendency for the spots to result in significantly higher evaluations of the candidate or party leader was also true for Scharping in Germany in 1994, for Blair in Britain in 1997, Constantinescu in Romania in 1996, and Walesa in Poland in 1995. In addition to the case of Dole in the U.S. in 1996, a negative change after exposure was present for Iliescu in Romania in 1996. After watching their television portrayals, respondents rated them lower than before.

Table 13.3 - Effects of Political Broadcasts on Candidate Images across Countries

(Summary mean of 12-item semantic differential scale, measured from 1-7)

	Pretest	Posttest
United States 1996 (n=525)		
Clinton	4.51	4.59*
Dole	4.48	4.34*
Germany 1994 (n=202)		
Kohl	4.03	3.99
Scharping	4.31	4.44*
Britain 1997 (n=106)		
Blair	4.30	4.43*
Major	4.07	4.15
Romania 1996 (n=125)		
Iliescu	4.44	4.37*
Constantinescu	4.93	5.01*
Poland (n=203)		
Kwasniewski	4.74	4.85
Walesa	3.76	3.98*

* t-test between pretest and posttest score is significant at $p < .05$.

There are also remarkable similarities to the absolute ratings and scores of the leaders among the countries. With a maximum possible score of 7, all of the scores cluster between 3 and 5. Clinton and Constantinescu both have scores well above the midpoint. In Poland Walesa was experiencing low ratings, probably because of economic reforms and political disillusionment.

Gender Differences in Reactions to Spots across Countries

The 1996 presidential election in the United States gave new impetus to the discussion of a gender gap in reactions to political candidates, with the results of the election indicating a clear difference between the preferences of male and female voters. The data from the most recent experimental studies were analyzed by comparing male and female reactions to the candidates in the various countries before and after viewing the political spots. Table 13.4 summarizes these results, showing that the differences are most pronounced in the United States and in Germany. In line with other election observations, women in the United States rated Clinton (4.40) significantly higher than did men (4.19) in the pretest before seeing the television broadcasts. Women also rated Dole (4.21) significantly lower than men (4.41). Viewing the broadcasts affected female voters in a predictable way; there was a significant increase in their evaluations of Clinton and a significant decrease in their evaluations of Dole. While male evaluations of Clinton did not change much from pretest to posttest, the spot exposure did result in men evaluating Dole significantly less positively. Clinton's extremely negative spots clearly had the desired effect on Dole, even among those male voters who had viewed him more positively than Clinton initially.

Table 13.4 - Images of Candidates By Gender after Viewing Political Spots
(Summary mean of 12-item semantic differential scale, measured from 1-7)

	Male		Female	
	Pretest	Posttest	Pretest	Posttest
United States 1996				
Clinton	4.19[2]	4.22[2]	4.40[2]	4.45[1,2]
Dole	4.41[2]	4.31[1,2]	4.21[1,2]	4.08[1,2]
Britain 1997				
Major	4.36[2]	4.33[2]	3.92[2]	3.78[2]
Blair	4.28	4.31[2]	4.34	4.59[1,2]
Germany 1994				
Kohl	3.97	3.87[1]	4.08	4.13
Scharping	4.37	4.47[1]	4.24	4.42[1]
Poland 1995				
Walesa	3.87	3.99	3.70	3.95[1]
Kwasniewski	4.66	4.76[2]	4.86	5.00[1,2]
Romania 1996				
Iliescu	4.43	4.31[1]	4.44	4.40[1]
Constantinescu	4.92	4.95	4.94	5.03[1]

[1] t-test difference between pretest and posttest within the gender is significant at $p < .05$.
[2] t-test difference between gender (i.e., males versus females) but in same time period (i.e., pretest or posttest) is significant at $p < .05$.

The results for Britain and Germany demonstrate some similar patterns. Table 13.4 shows that in Britain John Major was much more highly regarded in the pretest by men than by women, although there was no significant difference by gender in pretest evaluations of Tony Blair. After viewing, males did not show significantly different evaluations of either candidate, but women evaluated Blair higher and Major lower after viewing. In Germany, differences between the two candidates are as pronounced as between Clinton and Dole in the U.S. Women as well as men viewed challenger Scharping even more positively after having watched the spots, but the results were different for the incumbent chancellor. There were no significant differences between male and female pretest ratings of Helmut Kohl. After viewing, however, male ratings of Kohl declined significantly.

Female voters in Poland also demonstrated some differences from their male counterparts. Both genders were initially more positive about Kwasniewski than about incumbent Lech Walesa. However, only women were affected by the exposure to the political television programs, raising the evaluations of both candidates. Women, who were less positive about Walesa than men in the pre-test, ended the viewing sessions with their ratings of Walesa at a similar point to that of males. However, women ended the viewing sessions with significantly higher ratings of Kwasniewski than did males.

It is interesting to observe that the television spots were so successful for Walesa, although he still ended the experimental sessions and the election with lower ratings than his challenger, Kwasniewski. In press coverage of the campaign, Walesa was often cited as the less telegenic of the two candidates. Some observers called Kwasniewski "a television producer's dream: composed, affable, and unflappable....good looking and a smooth talker, ... one of those candidates who looks even better and performs better on television than in person" (Perlex, 1995, p. A8). However, the controlled and pre-planned environment of the political broadcasts may have shown Walesa to his best advantage, allowing him to enhance his image, at least for female voters.

The data from Romania do not show similar patterns. Table 13.4 indicates that there were few gender differences in reactions to Ion Iliescu and Emil Constantinescu in Romania.

CONCLUSION

Despite differences in media and political system variables, these comparisons across several democratic systems of the advertising styles and effects of exposure show some striking similarities across cultures, even when the countries in emerging democracies like Poland and Romania are compared to more mature democracies like the United States and Britain. Summary findings indicate:

1. Most countries concentrate the content of their ads on issues.
2. The political broadcasts across countries are overwhelmingly positive, not negative in their focus. The United States is the notable exception.

3. Despite the emphasis on issues and positivity, most leaders and parties rely on emotional, rather than logical proof, to make their points. Britain is an exception.

4. Candidates and leaders across all countries are rarely the main speakers in their own or their party's broadcasts, relying instead of anonymous announcers to make their pitch.

5. Most parties and leaders have de-emphasized the political party in their ads. Greece is the most dramatic exception.

6. While earlier research (Kaid & Holtz-Bacha, 1995) found substantial differences in production styles, there is an increasing similarity in these across countries as well.

7. No matter the country, the political system, or the media constraints, political broadcast exposure can have a significant effect on candidate images, sometimes positive and sometimes negative.

8. There appear to be gender differences in several countries, and there is some indication that female voters are more likely to be affected by exposure to political spots; and, when they are, the spots are more likely to result in higher positive evaluations for the candidates than is true for male voters.

The research reported here is admittedly limited by many factors. The content analysis results are obviously affected by the fact that the spots formats and lengths are not the same in each country. The experimental results also have limitations. While the research is strengthened by its uniformity of method and measuring instruments across countries, the differences in the political and media systems, the cultural differences, and the varying maturity of the democratic traditions may influence the findings. Use of student subjects also raises additional concerns. However, the patterns of style and effects identified here suggest that additional research is certainly warranted.

One area that might be pursued is further determination of the effects of advertising exposure. Experimental and survey work could help isolate more detailed effects. For instance, the experimental work completed in Germany, France, and the United States has indicated that in France and the United States viewers are much more likely to recall *image* characteristics of candidates than *issue* stances after viewing ads (Kaid, 1991). Further research might attempt to tie exposure to voting patterns, as well.

Replication of the results in other countries might be helpful in determining the effect of political and cultural system variables on similarities and differences. The comparison of Britain and the U.S. to emerging democracies such as Poland and Romania, relatively new and less mature democracies, can help to isolate other variables that might affect the outcome of exposure to the political broadcasts. What these results clearly point up is the fact that, both in terms of style and in terms of effects, political broadcasts have remarkable similarities across cultures.

These similarities in styles and effects of advertising messages might also provide some clues about the increase in political cynicism that is a growing feature of democratic systems. In the United States there is some evidence that exposure to political advertising may be increasing levels of political cynicism (Kaid, McKinney, & Tedesco, 1999), and in some cases exposure to negative advertising appears to decrease turnout

(Ansolabehere & Iyengar, 1995). The content and effects of political broadcasts in other democracies studies here may also be a factor in the increased government distrust and the decline in voter turnout levels experienced in these systems.

REFERENCES

Ansolabehere, S., & Iyengar, S. (1995). *Going negative: How political advertisements shrink and polarize the electorate.* New York: The Free Press.

Atkin, C., Bowen, L., Nayman, O.B., & Sheinkopf, K. G. (1973). Quality versus quantity in televised political ads. *Public Opinion Quarterly, 40,* 209-224.

Basil, M., Schooler, C., & Reeves, B. (1991). Positive and negative political advertising: Effectiveness of ads and perceptions of candidates. In F. Biocaa (Ed.), *Television and political advertising,* Vol. 1 (pp. 245-262). Hillsdale, NJ: Lawrence Erlbaum Associates.

Blumler, J.G., & McQuail, D. (1969). *Television in politics.* London: Faber and Faber.

Cundy, D. T. (1986). Political commercials and candidate image: The effect can be substantial. In L. L. Kaid, D. Nimmo, & K. R. Sanders (Eds.), *New perspectives on political advertising* (pp. 210-234). Carbondale, IL: Southern Illinois University Press.

Devlin, L. P. (1997). Contrasts in Presidential campaign spots of 1996. *American Behavioral Scientist, 40,* 1058-1084.

Diamond, E., & Bates, S. (1984). *The spot: The rise of political advertising on television.* Cambridge, MA: MIT Press.

Garramone, G.M. (1984). Voter responses to negative political ads. *Journalism Quarterly, 61,* 250-259.

Garramone, G.M. (1985). Effects of negative political advertising: The roles of sponsor and rebuttal. *Journal of Broadcasting and Electronic Media, 29,* 147-159.

Garramone, G.M., & Smith, S.J. (1984). Reactions to political advertising: Clarifying sponsor effects. *Journalism Quarterly, 61,* 771-775.

Gurevitch, M., & Blumler, J. G. (1990). Comparative research: The extending frontier. In D. Swanson & D. Nimmo (Eds.), *New directions in political communication: A sourcebook* (pp. 305-325). Newbury Park, CA: Sage.

Holtz-Bacha, C., & Kaid, L. L. (Eds.). (1993). *Die Massenmedien im Wahlkampf.* Opladen: Westdeutscher Verlag.

Holtz-Bacha, C., & Kaid, L. L. (Eds.). (1996). *Wahlen und Wahlkampf in den Medien: Untersuchungen aus dem Wahljahr 1994.* Opladen, Germany: Westdeutscher Verlag.

Holtz-Bacha, C., Kaid, L.L., & Johnston, A. (1994). Political television advertising in Western democracies: A comparison of campaign broadcasts in the U.S., Germany, and France. *Political Communication, 11,* 67-80.

Jamieson, K.H. (1992). *Packaging the presidency: A history and criticism of presidential advertising,* 2nd ed. New York: Oxford University Press.

Johnson, K. S., & Elebash, C. (1986). The contagion from the right: The Americanization of British political advertising. In L. L. Kaid, D. Nimmo, K. R. Sanders (Eds.), *New perspectives on political advertising* (pp. 293-313). Carbondale, IL: Southern Illinois University Press.

Johnston, A. (1991). Political broadcasts: An analysis of form, content, and style in presidential communications. In L. L. Kaid, J. Gerstlé, & K.R. Sanders (Eds.), *Mediated politics in two cultures: Presidential campaigning in the United States and France* (pp. 59-72). New York: Praeger.

Joslyn, R.A. (1980). The content of political spot ads. *Journalism Quarterly, 57*, 92-98.

Kaid, L.L. (1981). Political advertising. In D.D. Nimmo & K.R. Sanders (Eds.), *Handbook of political communication* (pp. 249-271). Beverly Hills, CA: Sage.

Kaid, L. L. (1991). The effects of television broadcasts on perceptions of political candidates in the United States and France. In L. L. Kaid, J. Gerstlé, & K.R. Sanders (Eds.), *Mediated politics in two cultures: Presidential campaigning in the United States and France* (pp. 247-260). New York: Praeger.

Kaid, L. L. (1994). Political advertising in the 1992 campaign. In R. E. Denton (Ed.), *The 1992 presidential campaign: A communication perspective* (pp. 111-127). Westport, CT: Praeger.

Kaid, L. L. (1995). Measuring candidate images with semantic differentials. In K. Hacker (Ed.), *Candidate images in presidential election campaigns* (pp. 131-134). New York: Praeger.

Kaid, L. L. (1996, October). *The effects of advertising in election campaigns.* Paper presented at the International Colloquium on Effects of Election Campaigns, University of Montreal, Montreal, Canada.

Kaid, L. L. (1997). Effects of the television spots on images of Dole and Clinton. *American Behavioral Scientist, 40*, 1085-1094.

Kaid, L. L. (1998). Videostyle and the effects of the 1996 Presidential campaign advertising. In R. E. Denton (Ed.), *The 1996 presidential campaign: A communication perspective* (pp. 143-159). Westport, CT: Praeger.

Kaid, L.L., & Boydston, J. (1987). An experimental study of the effectiveness of negative political advertisements. *Communication Quarterly, 35*, 193-201.

Kaid, L. L., & Chanslor, M. (1995). Changing candidate images: The effects of television advertising. In K. Hacker (Ed.), *Candidate images in presidential election campaigns* (pp. 83-97). New York: Praeger.

Kaid, L.L., & Davidson, J. (1986). Elements of videostyle: Candidate presentation through television advertising. In L.L. Kaid, D. Nimmo, & K.R. Sanders (Eds.), *New perspectives on political advertising* (pp. 184-209). Carbondale, IL: Southern Illinois University Press.

Kaid, L. L., & Holtz-Bacha, C. (1993). Audience reactions to televised political programs: An experimental study of the 1990 German national election. *European Journal of Communication, 8*, 77-99.

Kaid, L. L., & Holtz-Bacha, C. (Eds.). (1995). *Political advertising in Western democracies.* Thousand Oaks, CA: Sage.

Kaid, L. L., & Johnston, A. (1991). Negative versus positive advertising in U. S. presidential campaigns, 1960-1988. *Journal of Communication, 41*, 53-64.

Kaid, L. L., Leland, C., & Whitney, S. (1992). The impact of televised political ads: Evoking viewer responses in the 1988 presidential campaign. *Southern Communication Journal, 57*, 285-295.

Kaid, L. L., McKinney, M.S., & Tedesco, J.C. (1999). *Civic dialogue in the 1996 presidential campaign: Candidate, media, and public voices.* Cresskill, NJ: Hampton Press.

Kaid, L. L., & Sanders, K. R. (1978). Political television commercials: An experimental study of type and length. *Communication Research, 5*, 57-70.

Kaid, L. L., & Tedesco, J. (1993). A comparison of political television advertising from the 1992 British and American campaigns. *Informatologia, 25*, 1-12.

Kaid, L.L., Tedesco, J., Chanslor, M., & Roper, C. (1993). Clinton's videostyle: A study of the verbal, nonverbal, and video production techniques in campaign advertising. *Journal of Communication Studies, 12 (1)*, 11-20.

Kaid, L. L., Tedesco, J., Chanslor, M., & Roper, C. (1994 April). *Videostyle in the 1992 campaign: Presidential presentation through televised political spots.* Paper presented at the Midwest Political Science Association Convention, Chicago.

Kern, M. (1989). *30-Second politics: Political advertising in the Eighties.* New York: Praeger.

North, R. C., Holsti, O., Zaninovich, M. G., & Zinnes, D. A. (1963). *Content analysis: A handbook with applications for the study of international crisis.* Evanston, IL: Northwestern University Press.

Patterson, T. E., & McClure, R.D. (1976). *The unseeing eye.* New York: G. P. Putnam, 1976.

Shyles, L.C. (1983). Defining the issues of a presidential election from televised political spot advertisements. *Journal of Broadcasting, 27*, 333-343.

Shyles, L.C. (1984). Defining "images" of presidential candidates from televised political spot advertisements. *Political Behavior, 6*, 171-181.

Wadsworth, A.J., & Kaid, L.L. (1987, May). *Incumbent and challenger styles in presidential advertising.* Paper presented at the International Communication Association Convention, Chicago, IL.

NOTES

1. The spot sample for the U. S. spots was provided by the Political Commercial Archive at the University of Oklahoma. The author wishes to express appreciation to Holli Semetko for assistance in obtaining the British 1992 ads and John Tedesco for his assistance in the content analysis process; Sarah Oates (Glasgow) and Stephan Henneberg (Cambridge) for assistance in obtaining copies of the 1997 British election PEB's; Andrzej Falkowski and Wojciech Cwalina for the content analysis of the Polish spots; Christina Holtz-Bacha for assistance with the German spots; Sarah Oates and Yuri

Maleshev for assistance with the Russian spots; Baki Can for his work on the Turkish spots; and Athanassios Samaras for work on the Greek spots.

2. The author would like to thank the following individuals for their help in data collection and analysis for this project: John Tedesco and Yang Lin (University of Oklahoma Political Communication Center); Christina Holtz-Bacha, Andreas Weiß, and Pascal Meiser (Johannes Gutenberg University, Mainz, Germany); Lori McKinnon and Dorina Miron (University of Alabama); Andrzej Falkowski and Wojciech Cwalina (Lublin University, Poland); Hans-Jörg Stiehler (University of Leipzig); Wolfgang Donsbach (Technische Universität Dresden); Robin Hodess, Stephan Henneberg, and Nicholas O'Shaughnessy (Cambridge University); Ralph Negrine (Leicester); Sarah Oates (Glasgow University); and Gillian McCormack (New Caledonian University in Scotland).

3. Because of differing subject availability, not all subjects were chosen in the same way (i.e., in some locations subjects were chosen randomly from student subject pools and in others students were used as part of intact general communication, mass communication, psychology, and political science classes). In other cases adult groups were recruited from the community to participate in the study.

4. The nineteen universities were located in the following regions: East and Southeast (Maryland, Pennsylvania, Florida, Alabama, South Carolina); Midwest (Illinois-2 locations, Indiana, Ohio, Minnesota, Arkansas, Iowa, Missouri); Southwest (Oklahoma-2 locations, Texas); West (California-2 locations, Oregon).

5. The bipolar adjective pairs making up the semantic differential are: qualified-unqualified, sophisticated-unsophisticated, honest-dishonest, believable-unbelievable, successful-unsuccessful, attractive-unattractive, friendly-unfriendly, sincere-insincere, calm-excitable, aggressive-unaggressive, strong-weak, active-inactive.

6. Cronbach's alpha levels for the 12 item semantic differential scale on pre-test/post-test measures ranged from lows of .49/.59 for pretest/posttest scales for Kohl in Germany in 1990 to highs of .96 for Bush in 1992.

7. The definition of issue and image used here is the same as that used in many other studies (Kaid & Johnston, 1991; Kaid & Sanders, 1978). Issue ads concentrate on a candidate or party concern for or position on policy or public concerns, such as foreign policy, taxes, etc. Image ads, on the other hand, display a candidate's personal qualities or qualifications, such as honesty, compassion, etc.

ABOUT THE AUTHORS

BAKI CAN is currently an Associate Professor at the University of Ege in Izmir, Turkey, where he specializes in the study of political propaganda. He has written on voter persuasion for specialized publications in Turkey, and he has also served as a consultant for mayoral candidates and current members of the Turkish Parliament.

MIKE CHANSLOR is Archive and Research Specialist for the Political Communication Center at the University of Oklahoma. He taught communication and television production for several years at Truman State University in Missouri. His research specialties include political and mass media, and his research has been published in *The Journal of Broadcasting and Electronic Media*, as well as in a number of books in the political communication area.

WOJCIECH CWALINA is Assistant Professor in the Department of Experimental Psychology at the Catholic University of Lublin. His research specialties include political marketing psychology, organizational and management psychology, and analysis of media coverage. Among his publications are numerous articles in psychological journals and chapters in books about political marketing and mass communication. He works as a marketing specialist and campaign advisor for the Solidarity Election Action in Lower Silesia Division. He is also a lecturer in the psychology of marketing and consumer behavior in the Postgraduate Course of Marketing Psychology at the Adam Mickiewicz University in Poznan and a lecturer in political marketing psychology in the School of Social Psychology at the Polish Academy of Science's Institute of Psychology.

ANDRZEJ FALKOWSKI is Professor of Experimental Psychology, Catholic University of Lublin, where his research specialty is cognitive psychology, including consumer behavior, marketing, and political advertising. He is a Fulbright Scholar (University of Michigan). Mentioned in the *Who's Who in the World* and in *Men of Achievement* (14th. ed.), his publications include numerous articles in consumer behavior and cognitive psychology journals, as well as books, including *Psychological Judgment and the Process of Perception* (Amsterdam, 1992) and *A Similarity Relation in Cognitive Processes: An Ecological and Information Processing Approach* (Delft, 1995). He is advisory editor of the *Handbook of Political Marketing* (Sage, 1999).

CHRISTINA HOLTZ-BACHA is a professor at Johannes Gutenberg University in Mainz, Germany. She is the editor or author of many books and articles on political communication, media structure, and gender-related topics in communication. She is the editor of a book series on Women and the Mass Media and co-edits the German journal *Publizistik*.

ELIZABETH HUGHES is communication consultant with Lucent Technologies and currently works in Moscow. She previously served as the European Program Coordinator in Brussels for Emerson College.

CLIFFORD A. JONES is a visiting professor in the College of Law at the University of Oklahoma where he teaches courses in European Community Law, federal courts, and international law. His research specialties include media concentration law, campaign finance reform, and international competition law. In addition to publications in journals and as book chapters, he recently authored *Private Enforcement of Antitrust Law in the EU, UK and USA* (Oxford University Press, 1999).

LYNDA LEE KAID is Professor of Communication and George Lynn Cross Research Professor at the University of Oklahoma where she also serves as the Director of the Political Communication Center and supervises the Political Commercial Archive. Her research specialties include political advertising and news coverage of political events. A Fulbright Scholar, she has also done work on political television in several Western European countries. She is the author/editor of 14 books, including *The Electronic Election, New Perspectives on Political Advertising, Mediated Politics in Two Cultures, Political Advertising in Western Democracies*, and *Political Campaign Communication: A Bibliography and Guide to the Literature*. She has also written over 100 journal articles and book chapters and numerous convention papers on various aspects of political communication. She has received over $1 million in external grant funds for her research efforts, including support from the U. S. Department of Commerce, the U.S. Department of Education, the National Endowment for the Humanities, and the National Science Foundation. Kaid is a former president of the Political Communication Division of the International Communication Association and has served in leadership roles in the National Communication Association and the American Political Science Association.

LORI MELTON MCKINNON is an assistant professor of advertising and public relations at the University of Alabama where her research interests focus on the content and effects of mass-mediated political communication. In addition to authoring several chapters in books, she has published her research in *Journalism and Mass Communication Quarterly, Journal of Broadcasting and Electronic Media*, the *Harvard*

International Journal of Press/Politics, Argumentation and Advocacy, and *The Electronic Journal of Communication*.

VALENTINA MARINESCU is a researcher and teaching assistant in the School of Sociology at the Romanian Academy in Bucharest, Romania. She specializes in the study of political sociology and has presented papers on new media systems in Romania at several conferences, including the 1994 conference on Women and Politics in Bulgaria. She has authored/co-authored numerous reports on research projects related to media, political, and social trends in Romania, including a new book on the 1996 Romanian presidential election.

DORINA MIRON is a research assistant in the Department of Political Science at the University of Oklahoma. She completed a Ph.D. in communication in 1999 at the University of Alabama. In Romania she worked as an editor for print media outlets and as a producer for Radio Romania. She has authored a number of research reports on media in Romania and recently co-authored a book on the 1996 Romanian presidential election.

MISHA NEDELJKOVICH is an Associate Professor of Journalism and Mass Communication at the University of Oklahoma. In addition to his professional broadcasting experience in the former Yugoslavia and in Japan, he received a Fulbright grant to study film at UCLA. He has presented numerous papers at national and international conferences on film, television and politics, and new media technologies.

SARAH OATES is a Research Associate in the Politics Department at the University of Glasgow. She has been working on the Russian elections for the several years and has authored many articles and convention papers on television in Russian campaign.

LILIA RAYCHEVA is a Professor in the School of Journalism and Mass Communication at the St. Kliment Okhridsky Sofia University in Bulgaria. A Fulbright Scholar, she has also done post-doctoral work at New York University in film and television. She has received numerous grants and awards from organizations such as Bulgarian National Television, the Union of Bulgarian Journalists, the Open Society Fund, the American Council of Learned Societies (ACLS), and Cox Center in Georgia. She has authored and/or edited 7 books, including *One Minute Is Too Much* (Regalia-6 Publishing House, Sofia, 1995), *The Creative Process in Television* (Sofia University Publishing House, Sofia, 1991), and the *Dictionary of Television Journalism* (Science and Art Publishing House, Sofia, 1979). Dr. Raycheva has also authored more than 40 professional papers and journal articles.

JOLÁN ROKA is Senior Research Professor at the Löránd Eötvös University in Budapest. She specializes in the study of Hungarian media and has presented papers on the role of voter manipulation in media at many conferences, including the 1994 British Film Institute conference in London, "Turbulent Europe: Conflict, Identity, and Culture."

BOHDAN ROZNOWSKI is an Assistant Professor in the Department of Industrial Psychology at Lublin; he has written over 20 papers on social perceptions, attitudes, advertising, and cross-cultural issues in numerous journals and currently serves as vice-president of the Central European Center for Behavioral Economics.

ATHANASSIOS SAMARAS holds a doctoral degree from the Graduate Center in Culture and Communication at Sussex University. He has produced promotional documentaries and CD-ROMs and organized a political communication data bank sponsored by the telematic programme of the European Union. Currently, he is doing his military service in the Greek army.

JOHN C. TEDESCO is an Assistant Professor in the Department of Communication Studies at Virginia Tech University. He served as Archive and Research Specialist (1998-99) with the Political Communication Center. His research specialties include political advertising, campaign communication, news coverage of political events, and political public relations. Dr. Tedesco's articles appear in the *Harvard International Journal of Press/Politics*, *Journal of Broadcasting and Electronic Media*, *Argumentation and Advocacy*, *Journal of Communication Studies*, and the *Handbook of Public Relations*, and he has written chapters for numerous communication books.

INDEX

D

E